The Psychiatrist and the Dying Patient

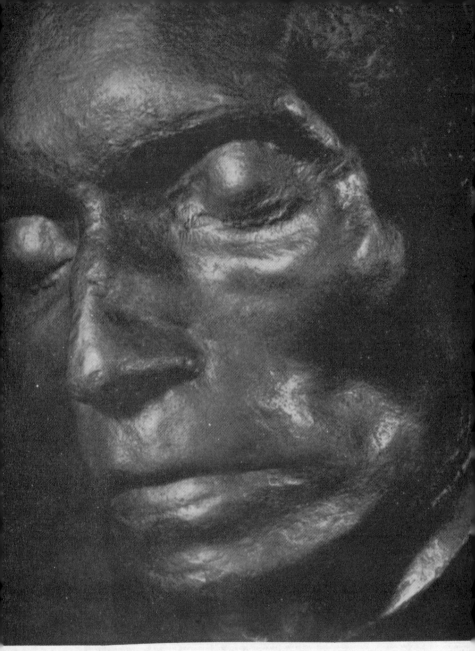

DEATH MASK OF BEETHOVEN

THE PSYCHIATRIST
AND THE
DYING PATIENT

K. R. Eissler, M.D.

INTERNATIONAL UNIVERSITIES PRESS, INC.

NEW YORK

To

R.

CONTENTS

List of Illustrations ix

Acknowledgments xi

Preface xiii

Part One—Introductory Essays   1

    I. The Three Thanatologies of the 1920's   3

   II. Upon Aspects of the History of Freud's Thanatology 10

  III. Further Remarks on "The Theme of the Three Caskets" 16

  IV. Freud's Thanatology 30

   V. Selective Problems Inherent in Freud's Thanatology 35

  VI. Obstacles to Evolving a Thanatology 39

 VII. Individualism and Attitudes toward Death . . . 51

VIII. Remarks on the Place of Death in the Human Species 59

  IX. Death and the Pleasure Principle 71

   X. Death and Ego Formation 81

  XI. Remarks upon the Feeling of Identity and Mutation of the World 87

XII. Remarks upon the Death Mask of Beethoven.   95

XIII. Death and Self-Preservation.............. 100

XIV. Remarks upon Death as a Psychologically
     Determined Event 104

XV. Death and the Masses................... 108

XVI. On a Possible Effect of Modern Medicine
     upon Artistic Creation.................. 113

XVII. Problems of Euthanasia................. 116

Part Two—**Three Case Histories**   123

Introduction 125

Case One 128

Case Two ....,.... 154

Case Three 198

Part Three—**Concluding Remarks**   243

Appendix 313

Bibliography 319

Index 330

List of Illustrations

DEATH MASK OF BEETHOVEN   *Frontispiece*

Original by Joseph Danhauser, in Wiener Städtisches Rathausmuseum
Cast by Willy Kauer, Vienna
Photograph, Trude Fleischmann, New York

INFANTE PHILIPP PROSPER, by *Velazquez*   *Facing page* 304
Section of Portrait
Original in Kunsthistorisches Museum, Vienna
Photograph, Kunsthistorisches Museum, Vienna

CAPTURE AND BLINDING OF SAMSON BY THE PHILISTINES,
by *Rembrandt*   *Facing page* 305

Original in Städelsches Kunstinstitut, Frankfurt
am Main
Photograph, Städelsches Kunstinstitut, Frankfurt
am Main

ACKNOWLEDGMENTS

Acknowledgment is due to Willy Kauer, Vienna, for permission to reproduce his cast of Beethoven's death mask, and to Trude Fleischmann for permission to reproduce her photograph of the cast; to the Kunsthistorische Museum, Vienna, for permission to reproduce part of Velazquez's portrait of the "Infante Philipp Prosper"; to the Städelsches Kunstinstitut, Frankfurt-am-Main, for permission to reproduce Rembrandt's "Capture and Blinding of Samson by the Philistines"; to Dr. Eleanor Nicholes for her outstanding editorial work; to Drs. Paul Kramer, Arnold Rubinstein, and Joseph P. Weinmann for reading the manuscript and for their valuable suggestions. Not the least portion of my thanks goes to Dr. A. S. Kagan, the publisher, and to Miss Lottie M. Maury for her patience and constructive help.

PREFACE

This study of the relationship between the psychiatrist and the dying patient falls into three parts: a series of essays, in which I try to discuss some problems of death under a variety of psychological aspects; three case reports, in which I try to discuss mainly some technical problems of the psychiatric treatment of patients who are approaching death; and, finally, concluding remarks which aim at the psychological foundation of an *orthothanasia,* that is, a right, true, or proper manner of dying.

In view of the scant knowledge which has been gathered regarding a psychology of death—a *thanatology,* in *sensu strictiori*—I have felt free to follow in an impressionistic manner a series of ideas and opinions which cannot be called strictly scientific. The reading of these introductory essays is not indispensable for an understanding of the clinical histories, however, and the reader who wishes may begin this account with the case histories.

PART ONE

Introductory Essays

I

THE THREE THANATOLOGIES OF THE 1920's

For centuries the prevailing idea of death in the Western world was that which had been expressed in antiquity in the image of the Parcae, particularly in Atropos, who carried the shears and presided over the moment of man's death. This image has been preserved to the present day in the metaphor "cutting the thread of life," or in the symbolic image of death carrying a scythe. In this conception death is the sudden stopping of action and continuity, a pin-point event at the end of life. This was the dominant concept in Occidental societies for over a thousand years during which there was an intensive preoccupation with death in all artistic and cultural pursuits.

Then in the third decade of the twentieth century three thinkers, a metaphysician, a biologist, and a psychologist— Heidegger, Ehrenberg, and Freud—made death the central concept in their respective ideologies. To each one, death appeared to be the precondition to life and the key to an understanding of life. These three ideologies might be viewed as the beginning of a new era of Occidental thinking upon death—or they might, on the other hand, represent its summation. But, however challenging it might be to attempt a historical outline of European thanatology as part of this introduction, demonstrating how these three thinkers fit into the total picture of the philosophy or psychology of death—which problems their new theories settled and which they introduced—I must abstain from such an endeavor. Suffice it to say that in the first decades of this century there was a turning away from the concept of death as a sudden, fortuitous event at the end of life.

An important figure in the transition was Georg Simmel, who had in 1910 already formulated some basic ideas (these were reformulated in 1918, the year of his death) which were to recur as characteristics of the various thanatologies evolved in the subsequent decade.

According to Simmel, death is to be reckoned with not only in the last hour of life; it is, rather, a formal quality of life itself, coloring all its contents. The urge for more life is simultaneously flight from death; life consumed in approaching death is spent in trying to escape it; without death, that is to say, life would be totally, essentially different, in a way not to be imagined. Simmel thought he could find the intricate intertwining of life and death in human action per se. As he pointed out in 1918, in man's knowledge *that* he will die—in contrast to his ignorance of *when* this will happen—is to be found a basic antinomy implicit in the structure of human action. This formulation reminds us of what Jaspers (1919) called the consciousness of the antinomic structure of the world.

The cornerstone of Heidegger's ontological analysis of existence (1927) is the presence of death in each moment of life prior to the actual occurrence of death, and this *"donnée* of death" is independent of any knowledge of death. Heidegger goes beyond biology or psychology: it is his position that whether death has been observed or is anticipated as a future event—whether it is, for any reason, a content of consciousness or not—existential analysis reveals that existence is *existence (or being) toward death (Sein zum Tode)*. An ontological analysis of existence must include the totality of existence *(Ganzheit des Daseins)*, which is characterized by the fact that part of it does not yet exist. This not-yet-existing portion of existence—the part still in arrears, so to speak—is essential if existence in its totality is to be analyzed. The part in arrears, however, also includes the end, and therefore the ontological analysis of existence must also include the end.

Yet ontological analysis reveals a variety of meanings which the concept of an end might have. The assignment of the proper meaning to what is called the end of life, or existence, is a fundamental question in ontological analysis. Following Heidegger, that part of a debt which is in arrears disappears when the rest of the debt is paid; that is to say, that which belongs together finally comes together when all parts belonging to the same type of existence finally meet. When a fruit ripens, a different type of not-yet-existing existence comes into being. This is not the addition of parts but an organic change of the fruit. Yet the ripe stage is not an end in the sense in which death is an end of an existence still in arrears. Death deprives existence of its specific potentialities, while ripeness accomplishes just these potentialities.

A pathway ends and by this ending has simply accomplished its function *qua* path. The last stroke of the brush finishes the painting, that is to say, gives it its total existence. Death does not fall into any such type of ending. Existence does not simply disappear, nor is it perfected, nor brought into a condition in which it becomes available or disposable. Here Heidegger draws a conclusion which is difficult to integrate but which is stringent in its logic. Just as existence, as long as it exists, is also that which is still in arrears (that is to say, it includes that which has not yet become), it is always also its own end, since the end is part of the existence still in arrears. This is illustrated by a beautiful passage from the fifteenth-century epic, *Der Ackermann aus Böhmen*. "As soon as a man comes to life, he is immediately old enough to die." Thus in the system

of Heidegger's ontology, dying does not mean that existence has reached an end; rather, death is a mode of being
upon which existence enters as soon as it has begun.

I do not wish to continue here with all the consequences
which derive from this step of ontological analysis. The
main point is that Heidegger does not analyze existence—
that is to say, life—by beginning with life and concluding
with the conditions of life which are reached when life
ends, but that his whole analysis of existence rests on the
retrograde projection of the end into the beginning. Thus
the analysis of existence is predicated, so to speak, on the
existence of death before the existence of life. Whether
one agrees with Heidegger or not, he must concede—and
perhaps admire—the merciless logic with which Heidegger
reversed the scales and sequences of customary thinking.

It is difficult to present the ontology of existentialism,
not to speak of integrating it; in contrast, it is comparatively easy to follow an exact scientist, even when he
reaches almost the same conclusions as Heidegger. I refer
to the biologist Rudolf Ehrenberg (1923), who states his
position at the very beginning of his textbook: "The basic
principle [Grundgesetz] which will have to carry all that
follows should be denoted as 'The law of the necessity of
death.'" Ehrenberg also reverses customary sequences in
substituting "without death no life" for the common-sense
statement "no life without death."

Ehrenberg sees the essence of all life processes in their
leading to structurization. In so far as structures are irreversible they decrease the life potential. Death occurs when
the degree of structurization or its quantity has reached a
limit which makes life processes impossible. This end result is only the consummation of effects which have taken
place innumerable times in the simple, atomistically conceived units of life processes. Death, therefore, is not a
preventable accident (Betriebsunfall), nor is it caused by

the incapacity of the organism to remove metabolic products; it is the condition which sets in when life has fulfilled its function of converting the unstructured into structure. Thus death is not a consequence introduced into life and enforced by some morphologic or physiologic properties of cells or organisms but is, rather, an expression of the essence (*Wesensausdruck*) of life. The isolated biological process is seen in the context of the supraordinated system of the person.

A detailed discussion of Ehrenberg's biological theories is not possible here, but I cannot forego mentioning briefly one aspect which is of utmost importance to a psychiatry which would devote itself to the study of individuality. In Ehrenberg's theoretical framework man's age is not measured by his distance from his birth but by that from his death. The question, then, would not be how long *has* he lived but how long *can* he live. The felicity of this approach is striking. Man is not, or at least should not be, interested in how much of his life has passed but only in how much he still has to live. Translated into terms of human biography this means: How much structurization is this person still capable of? For the tendency of life on the psychological level is the same as on the organic, namely, to form structure.

This view of the total organism is also valid for the single cell. The age of the single cell is not measured in terms of the number of past cell divisions but by the extent to which it has become the carrier of the total destiny of the organism of which it is a part. The incessantly dividing cell is bare of a destiny (*schicksalslos*), but the cell which increasingly loses its capacity of growth by having grown within an organism has become a participant in the history of the growing individual organism. These thoughts are of utmost importance in view of the relation between growth and death which will be discussed at a later point.

The earliest of the three thanatologies which distinguished the third decade of the twentieth century was Freud's *Beyond the Pleasure Principle,* published in 1920. In this paper Freud introduced the final revision of his theory of instincts, the history of which comprises four well-circumscribed steps (Bibring, 1936), each integrating a vaster area of observable data. Among all Freud's papers this one is set within the widest frame, bringing organic evolution and even cosmic influences (Sterba, 1932) within the aspect of a psychobiological theory. I will refer chiefly to this paper when speaking of Freud's thanatology because here Freud presented the problem and the meaning of death in the most extreme—one feels inclined to say radical—form he was ever to find for it. Death in the form of a death instinct becomes a force which dominates life, and the goal of all life is discovered in death.

I would like at this point to make a brief remark about the relationship of the three thanatologies to each other. Without claiming for them any real historical connection, it can be said that Ehrenberg's biology could be viewed as a text written for the purpose of verifying—within the scope of biology—Freud's basic principle (Bernfeld and Feitelberg, 1930). There is only one point of difference regarding the place anabolism and catabolism hold in both theories. Whereas Freud (1923) regards them as the physiological equivalents of the life and death instincts, Ehrenberg regards them as processes of life, but he considers as dead the catabolic products which remain unchanged within the biological unit. It is beyond my knowledge to appraise the significance of this difference. However, I do not think that Freud's theory stands or falls with his evaluation of these two essential types of biological processes. Also with Heidegger's ontology: in so far as I could grasp its bearing upon the problem of death—any reader of his *Sein und Zeit* will confirm the difficulty of penetrating his metaphysical edifice (Wach, 1934)—it sounds much like a discourse written for the purpose of adjusting philosophy to Freud's conceptions. Since those essays are influenced predominantly by Freud's psychoanalytic psychology, I will make an attempt to trace the historical development of Freud's thanatology before presenting its main points.

II

UPON ASPECTS OF THE HISTORY OF FREUD'S THANATOLOGY

I have outlined some of the ideas pertinent to the great thanatologies which made their appearances in that fateful decade in which so much was prepared that would shortly thereafter cast its indelible spell upon the future of Europe. One might speculate to what extent this sudden cluster of thanatologies may have been related to the First World War and its subsequent destructive effect upon European economy and society. Looking back from the vantage point of three more decades of history, one wonders—if such connections are valid at all—whether it might not have been the presentiment of things to come which brought the concept of death to focal attention.

The holocaust of the First World War left specific traces in some thanatologies. Rosenzweig (1921) begins his book, *The Star of Redemption,* as follows:

From death, from the fear of death, all recognition of the universe starts. To throw off the fear of the earthbound, to deprive death of its poison sting, Hades of its pestilent breath, this philosophy presumes to do. Everything mortal lives in this fear of death; each new birth increases the anxiety by one more reason because it adds to that which is mortal. Incessantly the womb of the untiring earth gives birth to something new, and each is bondaged to death, each is awaiting with fear and trembling the day of its journey into the dark. [See also Appendix, i.]

THE HISTORY OF FREUD'S THANATOLOGY

There is historical evidence (Rosenzweig, 1953) that these lines had been written in the trenches of the First World War.

Similar questions of specific influence were raised regarding Freud's thanatology. Brun (1953), in his critical inquiry into Freud's theory of the death instinct, assumes some influence from the First World War and, in addition, asserts that the first signs of Freud's fatal disease caused his preoccupation with the problem of death. Although Pfister confirmed this suggestion, it is probably incorrect: Freud's first systematic contribution to thanatology was published in 1920, three years prior to the first of the many surgical interventions he had to undergo. The type of disease from which he suffered makes it practically impossible to assume that any of its symptoms would have been noticeable at that time. With most writers, as with Brun, Freud's interest in death, the incorporation of the death instinct into his theory of the instincts, is viewed like a foreign body in the development of his theories, or like an unexpected and therefore most surprising step for which a personal reason beyond the realm of scientific necessity must be made responsible. I think this is wrong. First, there are personal reasons which are responsible when a scientist does *not* evolve theories showing surprising and unexpected turns, and second, an exact and detailed study of Freud's work will, I believe, demonstrate that this last section of his theories was actually an organic extension of what he had created before. Perusal of Freud's writings proves that prior to 1920 he had taken cognizance of phenomena which did not find a corresponding place in his theoretical frame of reference, and that gradually these phenomena—quite possibly under the additional impact of subsequent observations and experiences—enforced a revision of his theories. One can observe that until 1920 explanation of and speculation about clinical data refer-

ring to death—in the most general meaning of the term—
were isolated from systematic elaboration upon analogous
data derived from still other sources.

Before 1920 the problem of death had appeared within
the clinical field, principally in the form of the child's
wishes for the deaths of beloved persons (Freud, 1900). In
this context the absence of the representation of death in
the unconscious was postulated and the proposition that
death equals absence upheld as being the only one valid
in the child's imagery regarding the subject matter. This
view was confirmed by nonanalytic investigators (Anthony,
1940). Furthermore, clinical problems of hostility, destructiveness, and cruelty were considered to be manifestations
of sadism, and all corresponding phenomena were attributed to that component of the sexual instincts. Although
this is a cursory description, it will suffice at this point.
Independent of these clinical inquiries there are other
thoughts on death in works and papers devoted to so-called
"applied" psychoanalysis.

A comparison of Freud's *Three Essays on the Theory of
Sexuality* with his book on *Wit and Its Relation to the
Unconscious,* both of which were published in 1905, will
demonstrate this. In the former, hostility is considered to
be almost entirely a manifestation of sadism. To be sure,
Freud speaks of an appropriative instinct (*Bemächtigungstrieb*), but the position of that instinct among the others
is left unclear; it appears in the discussion suddenly, more
or less like a foreign body.

In the latter book, however, when discussing the tendencies of jokes, Freud clearly distinguishes between sexuality
and hostility. Unless it is harmless, a joke shows either hostility (serving aggression, satire or defense) or obscenity
(serving denudation). Evidently both tendencies are unfriendly, but one serves a sexual goal and the other an
aggressive one. Perusal of the text will show, moreover,

that this division is not concerned with a matter of mere classification. Freud devotes considerable space to extensive remarks regarding the origin and vicissitudes of human hostility. Although frustration is described by Freud as the main source of enmity, he nevertheless writes also of the endowment children have in terms of strong dispositions toward hostility. Evidently the idea of innate or inborn hostility was present at that time, though it was mentioned only in passing. The mechanisms so well known to Freud from his clinical work, when he was studying the vicissitudes of the sexual drives, are mentioned also as defensive tools against hostility.

Thus he writes: "Since the time when we had to renounce the expression of hostility by means of actions . . . we have formed a new technique of invective similar to that regarding sexual aggression . . ." (my own translation). Among the many external reasons for hostility—which make strange reading amidst the din of the socioculturists' clamor that Freud overlooked the cultural factor—Freud also mentions the shortening of the human lifetime, as if he had harbored the hope that a lengthening of human life might decrease the intensity or the extent of hostility. However far Freud still might have been in 1905 from a precise formulation of his later theory of the death instinct, the outline can be discerned, though dimly.

As a next step in Freud's development toward a thanatology, I should perhaps take up his book *Totem and Taboo* (1912/13), in which he wrote so much about aggression and death. Aside from the difficulty of integrating the full meaning of this extraordinary work, which is still underestimated by most sociologists and historians, I am not certain that it introduced a new aspect relating to death. The importance which Freud attributed to ambivalence as a motor of societal development is, however, striking, and it would seem that the psychoanalytic theory of that time did not account sufficiently for the apparently inescapable excess of ambivalence throughout the development of mankind. It is noteworthy that ambivalence, which held the exclusive position of a psychopathological phenomenon, plays here a decisive and constructive role, inasmuch as without it—according to Freud's reconstruction—group life would have been tied forever to an archaic form. The function which in *Totem and Taboo* Freud attributed to ambivalence was later to be replaced by "the struggle between Eros and the death instinct" (Freud, 1930).

In 1913 Freud himself saw that his theory was incomplete since nothing was known of the origin of ambivalence. The alternatives at that time were to regard it either "as a fundamental phenomenon of our emotional life" or as a secondary acquisition stemming from the parent-child relation; that is to say, the alternatives were innateness or reaction. Although it seems that Freud felt more inclined toward the latter alternative when he wrote *Totem and Taboo,* it is evident that he foresaw even at that time the possibility of the solution which he was to introduce later. Be this as it may, a more profound understanding than I have at my command might reveal in *Totem and Taboo* a more significant approach toward Freud's final theoretical appraisal of the destructive instincts.

A poignant constellation is found when Freud's essay on "The Theme of the Three Caskets" (1913) is reread with an eye to his final thanatologic theories. In this paper Freud tries to interpret the unconscious meaning of a theme that has appeared almost universally in folklore and literary art, namely that of a man who has to choose among three women or their symbolic representations. The surprising result of his analysis was his perception that the third woman—who is regularly the one chosen—represents death. This result can truly be called surprising, because in examining Freud's position around 1913 one cannot find a justification for such a finding. And, one may ask, why should a poet mask this theme in such a way that extraordinary interpretative acumen is necessary in order to unravel it? Actually, no sufficient reason *can* be found in the theoretical edifice of the psychoanalysis of 1913 for an unconscious motive which would necessitate repression and symbolical presentation of this theme. Therefore Freud had to add an *ad hoc* theory in order to make his interpretation plausible. Freud maintained that insight into the necessity for death was transformed into the fantasy of free choice of the most lovable. This then would mean a reaction formation produced by the reversal into opposites of two elements in the proposition "I have to die," which would indicate a particularly strong revulsion of the ego. (It seems that the reversal of two elements into opposites is significant of defenses against the idea of death. All Souls' Day becomes Halloween by the reversal of sadness into merriment and the substitution of children for the deceased ones [Sterba, 1948].) I must repeat that to assert that an author like Shakespeare—who with relative frankness presented the oedipal complex and pregenitality —would resort to such profound substitutions in order to conceal the necessity of human death would have led to a contradiction with the psychoanalytic theory of 1913. Be this as it may, some additional remarks about the two principal sources, *The Merchant of Venice* and *King Lear*, from which Freud derived the interpretation become necessary here.

III

FURTHER REMARKS ON "THE THEME OF THE THREE CASKETS"

It may seem strange that Freud should establish an identity between two plays which appear so vastly different from each other. However, Goddard (1951) also sees in Shylock a forerunner of Lear. The manifest difference between both characters is greater than most twentieth-century readers can experience since Shylock unavoidably means to us a tragic character. Yet in Shakespeare's time the play, since it led to Shylock's conversion to Christianity, was a comedy with a desirable and most happy ending (an opinion which I maintain despite the claim of Shakespeare scholars to the contrary; see Sir Arthur Quiller-Couch, 1926). Nonetheless, there can be detected in the background of both plays a frame of reference which is identical, though it appears superficially to be concerned with opposites. As I would formulate it in general terms, the problem of the *Merchant* is that of arrested action whereas in *Lear* it is that of unbound action. These extremes appear with particular poignancy when the action of the two plays is viewed in the context of succeeding generations whose interests are at loggerheads.

In the *Merchant* Antonio is impeded by a depression, Portia by her father's last will, Jessica by her father's religion, Bassanio by his poverty, and Old Gobbo by physical handicap. Only Shylock seems to be free to act, except when he is restrained by orthodoxy, expressed in his state-

16

ment that he will buy, sell, talk and walk with the Gentiles, but not eat, drink, or pray with them (I, iii, 35).

In *Lear* the principal characters possess or acquire freedom of action with the onset of the play. In the possession of unrestrained power, the King distributes his realm voluntarily and spontaneously among his offspring, who thus receive without effort that for which the young must so often battle with the old. To a certain extent, if the *Merchant* is compared with *Lear*, it could be said that the fundamental situation of the former would lend itself to tragedy and that of the latter to comedy.

In the *Merchant* it is a trifle which sets arrested action in motion and causes a whirlwind bordering at times upon tragedy but always finding its way back into the comical, at least in the eyes of Shakespeare and his contemporaries. Bassanio borrows money, thus entangling Antonio with Shylock, who sups with Gentiles, thus giving Jessica the opportunity to elope. Bassanio gains Portia, making it possible for Antonio to be saved and Shylock to suffer his fate.

In *Lear* the direction of the plot is reversed. Despite full freedom of action all intentions come to naught. Lear loses the well-deserved pleasures of old age; both Goneril and Regan lose lover, kingdom, and life; Edmund loses life, honor, and mistresses; Cordelia, seemingly unambivalent and loyal to the call of heart and duty, causes her father's death and the destruction of a kingdom.

All of them follow uncompromisingly and with unrestrained passion their demonic intents, and none of them can reach his goal. Not even poor Gloucester can achieve suicide, which might be called the last and inalienable right of man. (I delete the final resolution: the reunion of Lear and Cordelia and their dying together, the punishment of the culprits and the onset of a benign reign.) The singularly tragic effect of the play stems, I believe, from the enormous discrepancy between the extreme freedom of action (caused by the lack of internal restraint in most of the principal characters as well as by external conditions in their environment) and the utmost failure of effort. This idea can also be discovered in the *Merchant,* though for aesthetic reasons (this being a comedy), it is deeply hidden.

In this play, as I mentioned before, action is arrested at the outset for external reasons and also because the principal characters abide by certain principles. Shylock, for example, accepts orthodoxy as a binding frame of reference; Portia similarly accepts her father's last will. It is remarkable that although they are drawn as strong-principled personalities, almost all the characters in the *Merchant* betray their convictions at least once in the course of the play. Antonio is ready to "break a custom" (I, iii, 65) in order to raise the money; Shylock lends money without asking for interest and goes out to sup with Bassanio; Bassanio takes off Portia's ring and gives it to a seeming stranger. Even Portia seems to become disloyal to herself. The poet intimates in her instance a breach of principle, as Rank (1911) showed in the analysis of a slip she makes. (If the analytic investigation were extended, one could show that the betrayal of her conviction was even greater, although it was converted into a harmless slip for the aesthetic reasons of the comedy.) Some have suggested—and I feel inclined to agree—that the song preceding Bassanio's choice betrays the secret of the proper casket (Sir Arthur Quiller-Couch, 1926); others have objected to such a view (Parrot, 1949).

If we abstract from the plot that which was enforced by the character of the play as a comedy, we will find a result similar to that found in *Lear,* namely that action leads to naught. When Bassanio returns to Belmont without Portia's ring, she says she will deny herself to him forever until she sees the ring again. Since Bassanio has had to depart before the marriage was consummated, this means that despite his selection of the right casket he will not get any further than the previous suitors, whom Portia had ridiculed and gleefully dismissed. The comedy quickly abolishes this tragic potentiality, but this should not prevent acknowledgment of the hidden meaning, particularly when it is remembered that Bassanio gave the ring away at Antonio's request. This apparently was Antonio's revenge for all the sufferings he had to undergo in order to serve Bassanio's strivings for pleasure. (I do not pursue the homosexual implications.) The futility of action is openly demonstrated in Shylock. Bradley (1904) cannot believe in Shylock's acceptance of defeat; but we can as well refuse to believe this as to believe that a wife reconciles herself to a husband who gives away his ring the first time he leaves her. Shylock is not a tragic figure, but we can easily reconstruct what would happen if he were. Either he would achieve his vengeance and insist upon the pound of flesh, knowing that this would lead to his own execution, or he would commit suicide. In one passage he intimates that he prefers the death sentence to the conditions of his amnesty. Thus we find hidden behind the glittering surface of the comedy the same pessimistic outlook on human action so clearly presented in *Lear*.

In both plays there is a comical character for whom the iron laws subjecting the principal characters are not valid. Launcelot in the *Merchant* has preserved the freedom of action. In his humorous words can be seen the crux of the whole matter. His conscience tells him to stay with his master, but the fiend is at his elbow and tempts. He decides to follow temptation, thus demonstrating what is at the bottom of human inaction.

The analogous character in *King Lear* is the Fool. He is the only one who remains outside of the realm of action, only meditating and talking. When Bradley thinks that "the ignorance in which we are left as to the fate of the Fool" is caused by Shakespeare's shortening of the play, I feel inclined to disagree. The Fool has no fate and no destiny in the manner of Shakespearean characters. As a matter of fact, we do not know anything personal about him—whence he came or who he is. His vanishing into thin air conforms to his being beyond action—like the chorus in ancient tragedy.

Once Launcelot and the Fool are seen as homologous characters, in so far as both of them are demonstrating a principle which is in contrast to that of the main characters, many parallels will be noted in the plays. Launcelot deserts his master; the Fool is his master's most loyal servant. Launcelot helps his master's daughter desert her father; the Fool's great regret is Cordelia's disavowal. Lear represents the pinnacle of arbitrary and independent power; Shylock is an outcast, a victim of the whims of his scorners. Shylock—temporarily at least—acquires power of life and death over his main antagonist; Lear loses all power and becomes a wretched outcast. Portia, like Cordelia, is most obedient to her father's will; Jessica can be compared to the evil daughters. The parallel becomes more striking if we consider that in her relationship to Shylock, Portia is a fusion of two women. When she acts the role of the young doctor of Rome she sides first with Shylock, pretending concern that Shylock gets his rights. She even tempts him to insist on the letter of his pact and does not warn him of the consequences, as she should have done if the love of one's fellow men had been as strong in her as she would have it in Shylock. No sooner has she apparently passed judgment in his favor than she turns against him and becomes his destroyer. Her first function makes her not dissimilar to Cordelia, the second function to Regan or Goneril. Thus we notice that Shylock also is contending with three daughters, the two Portias and Jessica.

Consequently, by showing the identity of the three caskets in the *Merchant* with the three daughters in *Lear*, Freud pointed to an important identity in the fate of the two principal characters, seemingly so far apart. The poet seems to say: whether man is impotent and powerless or whether he is in possession of greatest power, he is brought to naught by female cunning or cruelty, as the case may be, a thought which would not need a guise in symbols or other substitutions. But the thought of man vainly struggling against women becomes offensive when we put "death" in place of "woman" and "longing" in place of "struggle against." Indeed, if Cordelia represents death, as Freud thought in 1913, then the conclusion is stringent that the central conflict of the tragedy goes on between man's unwillingness to die and his secret longing for death. By trusting Portia, Shylock expresses this connection almost without reserve.

How near his later theory was to the forefront of Freud's mind at that time can be seen particularly from one passage. Freud believes he perceives in the three women among whom a man has to choose the three ancient goddesses of destiny, the Parcae. In describing their functions Freud refers to basic psychoanalytic conceptions. The first of the Parcae, Clotho, represents "the fateful tendencies each one of us brings into the world" and the second, Lachesis, "that which is experienced" by us in the course of life. Constitution and accidental experience, however, are also the two sources upon which Freud built his theory of neurosis. Yet the third goddess, Atropos, representing the inevitable, that is to say Death, still stood apart from the main stream of psychoanalytic theory of that time.

If my interpretation of the two Shakespearean plays is correct, it would mean that Freud's interpretation of the three caskets and of Lear's three daughters did not refer to an isolated element but comprised the deepest meaning latent in both plays. The futility of human striving while rebelling against death, the secret ways in which man's demon drives him closer to death by those very actions with which he would postpone his own dreaded end—these elements would be comprehended in the theme to which, so I suppose, Freud reacted when analyzing the plays. The connection between man's destructiveness and the biological necessity of death, which later became so important a part of Freud's theory, is also foreshadowed in his essay by his remark that by repudiating Cordelia—that is to say, by not accepting death—Lear caused "his own and the general ruin."

Again, as in the book on jokes, we notice that in a non-clinical paper devoted to a theme of literature Freud made a forward step toward the formulation of a new theory. Yet the corresponding conclusions regarding clinical data lagged behind the insights he had gained from applied psychoanalysis.

Although my supposition will not heighten the clinician's trust in the theory of the death instinct (and even may be used as an argument against it, since no biologist would acknowledge Shakespeare's plays as a valid source of a biological theory), I believe that my suggestion—in case it should be verified—would only prove the independence of Freud's observation from those biases which scientists habitually form in accordance with their theories.

Muir (1952), in discussing psychoanalytic interpretations of Shakespeare, makes an astute remark (though one which is, despite its almost general validity, singularly inapplicable to Freud) : he warns against the unreserved acceptance of Freud's or Adler's or Jung's interpretations of Shakespeare because "they conform to the general theories of their authors." He correctly observes that in most cases the interpreter of literary characters draws out of them as much as he has first poured into them on the basis of his general psychological conceptions. I believe I have shown that Freud, at least in his interpretation of "The Theme of the Three Caskets," greatly transgressed the theoretical formulations which he had at his disposal *at that moment,* gaining new insight which apparently was not accessible to him within the confines of clinical observation.

Indeed, there was a valid reason for this—always supposing that the history of the theory of the death instinct is correctly seen by me. The genius may make visible an aspect of reality which is deeply buried and therefore barely accessible to direct observation; thus the analysis of the great literary creations may provide the stuff for a correct interpretation which could be easily missed were it not for the intuitive power of the artist who makes explicit that which usually remains submerged in the unconscious.

It is fitting to quote here a remark which Georg Simmel (1918) made about Shakespeare's characters, a remark which will explain the historical nexus between Shakespeare's heroes and Freud's thanatology.

> In Shakespeare's great tragic figures we sense almost from their first words the inevitability of their end. This is not seen, however, as an inability to untangle the threads of destiny, or as a threatening fate, but as a deep necessity; rather I would like to say, it is a property of their total inner life which is woven into the dramatic, finally lethal event and which evolves a form which can be comprehended by logic. . . . Death belongs to the *a priori* determinants of their lives. . . . In contrast, subordinate figures die in these tragedies as the external course of events brings it about; they are somehow killed without any consideration at all of the "when" and of the "whether-or-not." Only those others are allowed to die from within; the maturation of their destinies as an expression

of life is per se the maturation of their deaths. [See also Appendix, ii.]

I think Simmel is right in his characterization of this aspect of Shakespeare's tragic figures. It is an aspect which, despite its validity for human life in general, cannot be observed—or perhaps only rarely—in the clinical area, particularly of psychoanalysis. Those on whose foreheads the destiny of death is written do not go into analysis, and therefore it is quite conceivable that the inspiration for the theory of the death instinct came to Freud for the first time when he was submerged in the destiny of a Shylock or of a Lear. The next step, then, might have been a turn toward clinical reality in order to pursue there the clue which he got in Shakespeare's tragedies. It should be unnecessary to state that this development did not have to proceed upon conscious pathways.

The next step, however, did not lead Freud to a paper which could be called clinical in the narrower sense of the word. The problem of death was taken up again in connection with psychological observations made within a sociocultural area. I am referring to the essay "Thoughts for the Times on War and Death" (Freud, 1915a) which gave many a critic cause for seeing in Freud's theory of the death instinct a personal reaction (divorced from valid observation) to the horror of the First World War. Although I could not ascertain the exact time of Freud's writing this paper, I surmise that it must have been at the end of 1914 or at the beginning of 1915. It was published in the first issue of the fourth volume of *Imago* (1915) but this imprint is not as reliable as it might appear because the publication of printed matter was often delayed at that time due to the necessities of the war. However, it seems almost certain that the paper was not written after exhausting years of despair and horror, but was a rather quick response to the very evident fact—observable, of course, with the first serious war moves—that there is more aggression in man than one would have thought from his behavior in peacetime and that man's attitude toward death is usually the outcome of the mechanism of denial, so long as he does not face death as a reality which may befall him or his loved ones at any moment. If Freud's previous papers about death are considered, one must conclude that in writing his essay "On War and Death," ideas were formulated which had lain dormant for an undetermined length of time but which crystallized suddenly when reality struck the spark converting preconscious contents into conscious ones. The paper is put down with such firmness, without any sign of hesitations or groping, that one cannot assume the construction of an *ad hoc* theory for the explanation of a new and surprising observation. Moreover, what had been dimly viewed in the essay on the "Three Caskets" is formulated now more explicitly and elaborately, with the addition of new conclusions organically evolved from previous ones.

Even in organization, the paper bears the earmarks of the gradual evolvement of the ideas. Thus an essay upon the destructiveness of man (which was only lightly touched upon in the "Three Caskets") precedes the essay upon death, which had formed the subject matter of the previous paper. Nonetheless, the two essays are isolated, being put together only for the peripheral reason that they were written in a time of war. Five more years were to pass before the two seemingly disconnected themes were synthesized in one comprehensive theory. It is cogent to assume that the profound and meaningful connection between human destructiveness and the problem of death was latently present in 1915—beyond the connection which Freud made in the second part of the essay—but that the explicit presentation of that interconnection could not yet go beyond the external form of an additive apposition.

The idea which is indirectly expressed in the first part and which also demanded theoretical clarification with increasing urgency concerned the counterpart of the sexual drives which had been called by Freud the self-preservative or ego drives. It turned out that these drives aimed at destruction far beyond the necessities of self-preservation or of sexual gratifications. Their goals were apparently definitely beyond the scope of sadism or any other sexual factor. According to one remark, they seemed to Freud even older than the forces of love. At least in the second part of "Thoughts on War and Death" we find the statement, half questioning and half assertive: ". . . for love cannot be much younger than the lust to kill." Again it would be wrong to maintain that Freud was driven by the impressions of war and its excesses to make such an extreme statement. In a metapsychological discourse published in the same year, but probably written earlier than the essay on "War and Death," we find the statement: "The relation of hate to objects is older than that of love" (Freud, 1915b). But at this early period hate was defined in terms of the infant's repudiation of the world, its aversion to stimulation. In the essay on "War and Death" Freud goes an organic step beyond and raises the question of whether or not the active desire to destroy precedes love. He also raises the question of how man can overcome such archaic impulses at all in view of their intensity and their primordial nature. The answer is: these egotistical drives— as Freud called them often—are socialized by the admixture of erotic components. Thus the concepts of fusion and defusion of instincts, which will become so important later, are here introduced.

The advance made in this part of Freud's essay on "War and Death," beyond the paper on the theme of the "Three

Caskets," consists of the presentation of a new, well-defined and circumscribed area of psychopathology: not only do the unmastered sexual drives threaten the reality-adjusted interplay of the various ego functions but also their counterpart, the self-preservative (egotistic, ego-) drives, may lag behind in their development and remain in their crude, archaic form. Under circumstances favorable to the recrudescence of these archaic drives, man's behavior will be transformed in a way which is as profound and essential as that which occurs under the sway of a recrudescence of archaic sexual drives. However, the psychopathology of the two groups of instincts is different. The impact of culture may lead to the neuroses in the case of the sexual instincts, to malformations of character in the case of the egotistic ones. Furthermore, the latter instincts have the privilege of arising in their original form under proper provocation from without.

In the second part of the essay on "War and Death" Freud extends a thought, confined in "The Three Caskets" to a very special and limited area, into a comprehensive view: man's attitude toward death bears upon all of his actions. Freud distinguishes between the effect which the meaning of death has when it is experienced as an accident from the meaning it has when it is felt as a necessity. Yet even when man accepts the *accident* of death as unavoidable, his view is still based on an attempt to deny the full necessity of death terminating life.

According to Freud's view of 1915 there are three basic constellations in which man must come to grips with death: his own death, the death of beloved persons, and the death of enemies. The first is inacceptable to man's unconscious, the second is reacted upon with ambivalence, and the latter is wished for. The desire for the destruction of the enemy is the junction where the problem of death and the problem of hostility are forever joined. The unavoidably ambivalent reaction to the loss of a beloved person was (and probably is over and over again for each generation) the crucial situation under the impact of which the division of body and soul is established in our minds, the first step toward the denial of the reality of death, but also the archaic situation where psychology was born.

The absence of a representation of one's own death in the unconscious (a sign of greatest weakness or exquisite greatness—as the case may be—in the construction of the psychic apparatus) necessitates the conclusion that nothing instinctual inclines one toward the belief in his own death. This is an extremely important point made by Freud and one which has been, I believe, almost completely lost in the later arguments against Freud's theory of the death instinct.

A close approximation to the final formulation of the theory of the death instinct is encountered in the essay "On War and Death" of 1915, in which Freud describes a new pattern of the interconnection between love and hate. One such pattern had been stated earlier: the admixture of love with the egotistical drives socializes them. Freud made a further statement: by means of the twin opposites of love and hatred—almost always operating simultaneously toward the same object—love is kept ever vigilant and fresh, guarding itself against the hate that lurks behind it; thus the most intensive unfolding of love may occur as a reaction against the ever wakeful impulses of hate.

It is strange to think that this essay was called a pessimistic one. Actually it shows the way in which man can convert into harmony that which nature has embedded in his biological substratum as a seemingly unbridgeable contradiction. Nor is it pessimism when Freud appeals for a revision of the attitude of essential denial of death which modern man has evolved, concluding with the advice *Si vis vitam, para mortem.* It seems to me that Freud did not mean this as an apothegm but that under the guise of a maxim he expressed the idea of the inextricable inter- weaving of life and death. Yet this wealth of new ideas— derived from observation, concisely formulated, and ac- cessible to time-honored methods of validation—was some- how still not integrated into the general theoretical edifice of psychoanalysis.

IV

FREUD'S THANATOLOGY

A synthesis of the seemingly divergent was achieved by Freud in *Beyond the Pleasure Principle* (1920a), the first comprehensive treatise which can rightly be called the cornerstone of his thanatological system, despite subsequent revisions and additions (Freud, 1923, 1924b, 1932). In this treatise most of the threads which had previously been left at loose ends were woven into a well-founded biological theory. Later additions, plus the introduction of the structural aspect (Freud, 1923), transformed this biological foundation into a comprehensive theory of the human personality.

In Freud's theoretical system death found its focus in the concepts of the death instinct and the repetition compulsion (Bibring, 1943). Freud discovered an aspect of the drives which had not been integrated into psychoanalysis, namely the tendency of drives to reestablish a condition which had once been present, but the equilibrium of which had been disturbed. The function of the drives would then be to guarantee that any organismal deviations would not become permanent institutions, and that all life must return to its starting point. Nietzsche (1881/82) had expressed a similar thought in the following words:

Out of consciousness originate innumerable bad choices which cause the unnecessary and premature

ruin of animal and man. . . . If the preserving organization of the instincts were not so much more
powerful and if it did not serve as a regulator of the
whole, mankind would have to perish through its
distorted judgments, its indulgence in daydreams with
open eyes, its superficiality and credulity, briefly,
through its state of consciousness. [See also Appendix,
iii.]

Also, in describing the conservative aspect of the instincts, Nietzsche was preoccupied with the repetition compulsion since at the time he wrote the above quotation he
was working upon the essay, "The Eternal Coming Back"
(Die ewige Wiederkunft).

It is easy to see that the re-establishment after a disturbed condition is the principal aim of our drives. Hunger imposes upon us the necessity of eating which in turn
leads to the restoration of tissue metabolites which had
been lost previously by the activity of cells. Thus the
organism is protected against destruction. The automatic
and compelling effect of the drives contributes indis-
pensably to the preservation of life. Yet life itself is the
maximum deviation which can be imagined from a previous condition, if the principal tenet of modern biology
is accepted, namely that life developed from an inorganic
state. The problem which Freud faced was whether or not
there is a drive which also guarantees the return of an
organism to the primary inorganic state from which life
had taken its original start. Freud's answer was positive,
and he believed he had discovered that drive in the form of
the death instinct. Those drives which are so indispensable
to the preservation of life, which favor and protect life, are
never able to prevent the ultimate attainment of the quiet
work of the death instinct. A struggle goes on between the
instincts which serve the goal of preserving life and the
instincts which reduce life until it returns whence it

originally had come. However, I believe one could also view the panorama of instinctual processes as a secret co-operation between the two, as Freud has done at one point. Without the instincts of life, the death instincts would reach their goal in short-circuit-like manner. Life would cease as suddenly as a clock whose spring has broken. The instincts of death would—if that image is accepted—find their proper resistance in the instincts of life which would thus enable the instincts of death to take their full and unbending course.

Whereas Freud's previous theory of instincts had taken single functions as a starting point, this new theory was based on more comprehensive entities such as the ultimate function of cell groups. The interest of biologists had been aroused—before Freud—by the difference of destiny between the cells forming the soma and those forming the germ plasma. The former had to die whereas the latter harbored potential eternity. Freud used this biological aspect of the ultimate destinies of the two cell groups, believing that he recognized in them the activity of two distinct biological forces of instinctual quality, the instinct of death relentlessly leading the organism back into its original state and the instincts of love creating, over and over again, new life. Thus Freud saw in death one of the basic goals of the organism, one which was present with the beginning of life. By definition life contained its own ultimate abolishment, in a way which would be postulated by Heidegger a few years later.

Freud's theory unquestionably meant vast progress. It enlarged the extent of phenomena which had been covered by the aggregate of psychoanalytic theories and put man into a comprehensive context of the development of life. It was based on assumptions about the origin of life, assumptions confirmed and made plausible by later research (Oparin, 1936). But it seemed to suffer from a drawback.

The death instinct was a biological force working silently toward its goal, seemingly unobservable in its psychological manifestations. Was it therefore a construction superfluous in psychological research? By no means. Freud discovered its manifestations in an unforeseen area of greatest clinical importance, namely in those phenomena which are covered by the terms of aggression, hostility, or destructiveness.

Whereas earlier Freud had considered almost all manifestations of destructiveness and hostility as a form of sexuality (sadism), he now attributed these phenomena to the death instinct, which becomes visible in these shapes. According to this theory, the death instinct, working quietly to convert the organism into an inorganic state, can and must be diverted partially from its primary aim and directed toward the environment of the organism. But its aim of destroying life persists after this diversion, in which case it is not directed toward the destruction of the life of the organism which harbors it but toward the destruction of other organisms. It looks as if this instinct did not care what it destroys as long as it is given the opportunity of destroying (Freud, 1930). In this respect the death instinct does not behave differently from the instincts of love, which likewise do not care whether they are satisfied by direct contact with external objects or whether they take the organism itself as an object.

The richness of instinctual phenomena and their derivatives must, according to this last of Freud's theories, be viewed as the interplay of these two instinctual forces. Rarely, if ever, observable in their purity, in almost all instances their manifestations are fused in a varying proportion. The study of their fusion and defusion, of their co-operation, of their neutralization or of their—usually dramatic—conflicting courses is the most important part of a dynamic and genetic psychology of the instincts.

At this point, in order to avoid an impression which a

reader unfamiliar with psychoanalytic literature may gain
—I must add that Freud's theory of the death instinct has
been rejected by most of his followers. Brun (1953) has
followed up statistically the number of papers in favor of
and against this theory. The statistical result is most unfavorable to Freud. A book such as that by Nunberg
(1932), in which the development of the ego is consistently
viewed under the aspect of Freud's theory of the death
instinct, has remained a solitary feat.

Recently Szasz (1952) has tried to show in detail that the
theory lacks an adequate biological foundation. I shall not
pursue the many arguments which have been raised, but
only quote a poet. In a late poem, announcing to a beloved
woman the approach of his death, Rilke (1925) wrote:
"The ego founders upon the id" *(Das Ich versagt am Es)*.
In this one line Freud's theory was compounded and
synthesized. The preceding verses show that Rilke had
understood Freud well. He wrote of how he had been
reached by old demands from far distant generations, demands from which he had wrested so much, striving against
their resistance yet supported by their strength.

Thus Freud seems again to have been better understood
by the poets than by the physicians.

> Tell no one but the sages
> For the crowd sneers instantly:
> "I shall praise the living thing
> Which longs for death in flames."
>
> *Sagt es niemand, nur den Weisen,*
> *Weil die Menge gleich verhöhnet:*
> *Das Lebendige will ich preisen,*
> *Das nach Flammentod sich sehnet.*

[Goethe, on the 31st of July 1814; Selige Sehnsucht, in
Westöstlicher Diwan. Buch des Sängers.]

V

SELECTIVE PROBLEMS INHERENT IN FREUD'S THANATOLOGY

Freud's reclassification of the destructive phenomena and his elevation of them to a position independent of the sexual-erotic phenomena has been generally accepted, most analysts paying even more attention to the former than to their counterparts, the libidinal phenomena. But whereas Freud regarded and described the destructive phenomena as the unavoidable and necessary manifestations of the organism, as otherwise it would not continue to survive, most analysts have thought of the destructive elements as reactions to frustration. Their coming and passing would—according to this view—depend entirely on whether the organism encounters gratification in its milieu or whether frustration is imposed upon it. I believe that this argument can be easily repudiated; clinical observation makes it very certain that the occurrence and intensity of aggression cannot be correlated with environmental conditions (Freud, 1930). To be sure, frustration becomes one of the circumstances which stimulate the diversion of the death instinct from the organism toward the objects of the environment. It is well known that biologically enforced or biologically necessary processes can be enhanced or weakened by stimulation from without. They can even be reduced to a minimum, to the organism's detriment, or overstimulated, again to the detriment of the organism.

Of course, there is a host of problems attached to Freud's theory which he had not time to tackle. If the organism can rid itself of the dangerous death instinct by channeling it toward the environment in the form of hostility, one would expect a regularly beneficial effect from such a deflecting process. It is conceivable that in primordial times those individuals had the best chance of survival who achieved maximum diversion of destructive energy through these channels. In historical times the whole problem has changed, since individuals discharging aggression beyond the limits of law and custom endanger their own existences by provoking the intercession of the group. Furthermore, it seems—and this can be observed in the clinical study of the major psychoses—that too intensive a flow of aggression toward external reality has an injurious effect on ego functions. In other words, it seems that those functions by which the personality maintains contact—in the broadest meaning of the word—with reality are injured if they carry too much destructive energy (Heinz Hartmann, 1953). It seems as if the psychic apparatus per se were built in such a way as not to tolerate the discharge of too intensive destructive energies. However, the question still is moot whether this deleterious effect is caused by the superego alone or whether a personality unencumbered by a superego would be capable of discharging large quantities of destructive energies without danger to itself.

It is even more difficult to comprehend that the most decisive instinct should have a goal which is not represented in man's unconscious. I believe that Freud's theory of the death instinct does not militate against his earlier statement (Bernfeld and Feitelberg, 1930) that nothing instinctual in man inclines him to believe in his own death (Freud, 1915a). If this view is maintained (and I do not see how it could be otherwise), some far-reaching changes must be made in over-all concepts and definitions which have been used in the general psychoanalytic theory of instincts. However, this problem is peripheral.

Freud's view that aggression is part of man's inheritance rather than a reaction to frustration has been called pessimistic. It is not evident why his description of the tremendous obstacles which have to be overcome if man is to become civilized has been so evaluated. As far as can be seen from his writings, Freud did not seem to assume that aggression cannot be subjected to the process of civilization and thus be diverted from its original goal; he stated only that man's aggression is not a secondary formation due to environmental factors but a biological necessity which poses a particularly heavy task upon the civilizing process. Likewise, it is not clear why the concept of a death instinct has also been viewed as a pessimistic outlook upon life—as if Freud had destroyed the hope of eternal duration of individual life. As far as I know, individual organic death has been accepted as a necessity from the dawn of civilization. What Freud added was the theory that instinctual forces propel the individual toward that event. Also it seems as if some had interpreted Freud's theory as implying a particular wish or longing in man to die. To be sure, following Freud's publication certain phenomena were scrutinized with greater care and in greater detail, and the masochistic component or the tendency toward self-destruction was found to be much greater than had been thought initially (Menninger, 1938). This self-destructive tendency will occupy us later in a different context, but here I want to mention only that Freud's general theory does not include the assumption of self-destructive forces in man beyond those within the biological realm; that is to say, the theory of the death instinct per se does not require the assumption of an inescapable—conscious or unconscious— wish to die. It does, however, necessitate the assumption of a wish to kill. The internal biological forces are necessary and unavoidable, as are those which are diverted against external reality.

Whatever truth is contained in Freud's last conception of the instincts, it must be admitted that this theory is one of the most comprehensive mental edifices man ever has constructed. In the physical world the tendency toward re-establishment of former conditions, toward the elimination of a disequilibrium, can also be noticed. Thus Freud has provided a frame of reference which may lead to a consistent and uniform view of the total universe, fulfilling an age-old dream of mankind struggling to find order within the bewildering variety and seeming contradictoriness of phenomena.

VI

OBSTACLES TO EVOLVING A THANATOLOGY

Since Freud has made death a central concept of his psychological system one would have expected that psychoanalysts would devote more effort to the study of death itself. Strangely enough this has not happened. In general death is still viewed as a purely biological phenomenon unless it is consciously or unconsciously induced by man himself. But biological science has little to offer on the phenomenon of death. Times have not changed since Tolstoy, wishing to orient himself on this topic, found to his distress that scientists did not have much to say about death (Walker, 1942). Death is almost always viewed as a phenomenon of deficit caused by a dysfunction, although it is the necessary and logical conclusion of an episode. I would say that even the bare, and clinically the most conspicuous, facts have defied explanation. The pathologist is quick to explain death by referring to certain cell changes in one or several organs, yet in doing so he ignores the fact that in other instances life has been concluded only after disease has ravaged these organs to a far greater extent (Bloch, n. d.). Schorr (1931) objects strongly to considering the patient's basic sickness and its complication as the causes of death. "Much that passes at autopsies as cause of death has been present previously. . . . It is useless and inappropriate to look for any causes of death." He suggests a search for those conditions which are effective for each individual and also those which are irreconcilable with life during the last period of the struggle for existence. Fully agreeing with Schorr's objection to the last sickness as the cause of death, I nevertheless think that this author also is not free from the view of death as mere deficit. A predominantly biological, that is to say one-sided, conception of death has prevented an empirical study of the psychology of death.

Not only the exclusively biological attitude but external factors also are responsible for this lag in research upon death. The analyst and psychiatrist rarely have an opportunity to study the phenomena of death except when as psychiatrists in state hospitals they encounter large numbers of senile and arteriosclerotic patients. But quite aside from the conditions in state hospitals, which are unfavorable for penetrative psychological research, the senile and the arteriosclerotic patients are not adequate subjects for such an investigation. Their means of communication have been so deeply injured by disease and age that while we can study the pathology of certain ego functions, we cannot penetrate to the core of the problem pertaining to our subject matter.

The analyst encounters the problem of death mainly in the form of his patient's fear of death, of his patient's wishes for his own or someone else's death, of the patient's reactions to the actual death of a beloved or hated person, or of an actual threat of death to himself. The latter, in particular, could be an important source of information except that for evident reasons a psychoanalyst can only investigate situations in which death has been successfully warded off. The ideal investigatory situation would be that of Lazarus who returned to the world of the living, but the chronicler was apparently so fascinated by the fact of revival that he forgot to let us know what Lazarus experienced before, during, and after his death. Unfortunately, instances like those of Lazarus never occur in psycho-analytic practice. To a certain extent the opposite happens, however. When death incidentally threatens, the patient is taken to the hospital and the psychoanalytic exploration comes to a standstill. The analyst may have an opportunity of occasionally seeing this patient, thus getting glimpses of some of his internal processes, but any data so accumulated cannot compare with the wealth of material with which he is provided under less tragic circumstances. Moreover, the situation of death is so heavily burdened by emotions, prejudices, fears, traditional beliefs, and compassion, that a scientific inquiry in a clinical setting would be feasible only with subjects with whom the inquirer has been unacquainted. Moreover, if death is viewed as a meaningful process in which the preceding life finds its consummation and toward which all preceding life processes converge, then the terminal inquiry into the psychic process of dying subjects would not adduce the information requested unless by chance the data and results of a previous extensive psychoanalytic investigation conducted by another person were known. When Heidegger (1927) says, "a psychology of 'dying' throws light rather upon the 'life' of the 'dying' than upon the dying itself," he points to one of the pitfalls into which an empirical investigation into the psychology of death may stumble, although I do not think that he decribed here a necessary barrier to empirical research.

The knowledge that a person is in the state of dying or is approaching death makes him distinctive. As soon as we know that a person is in such a state, or in danger of such a state, our whole emotional orientation changes. This, however, seems not to be true for those who are constantly in contact with dying persons.

While I have had little opportunity to observe the response of persons who encounter the death of others as an almost daily routine, I could well imagine that the following type of response is not infrequent: I believe I have noticed in a few instances that dying may be conceived of as a malicious act performed for the sake of annoying others. One physician complained bitterly that most of his fatal patients died at night and that he had to get up to sign their death certificates. There was no doubt that he had the fantasy the patients could have died at a different time had they not meant to annoy him. The factor of time also plays a role for those who attend dying patients as a routine. One physician was particularly preoccupied with arranging circumstances in such a way as to have the patient die when his relatives were still in the hospital in order to get the permission for an autopsy immediately. That the time factor plays a prominent role when death becomes routine is, I believe, deeply rooted in the general psychology of death, but here it evidently serves defensive purposes. Recently in the United States an execution was ordered which was considered unjust by a significant percentage of the population; in order not to offend against the Holy Sabbath, great care was taken to have the execution a few hours earlier than customary. Thus occurred the macabre situation in which religious awe led to the shortening of the human life span instead of prolonging it. But here we have inadvertently introduced the connection between dying and killing.

Apparently modern man cannot integrate into his unconscious the idea of natural death; thus every instance of death carries the implication of force—that is to say, murder—an idea which language still expresses in the image of cancer as the greatest killer (Sterba, 1948). Also the type of person who becomes compulsively preoccupied with the time factor in death usually has to ward off deeply repressed but concomitantly intensive, murderous impulses.

The theme of doing harm to the dying person is wide-spread. The mere sight of the defenseless seems to stimulate impulses of aggression. Perhaps the onlooker cannot quite tolerate the idea of death by internal reasons, since they would also threaten his own existence; whereas death by human aggression may impress him as avoidable. Thus the fear of death would be a decisive factor in the impulse to kill.

There is also a psychosociological factor unfavorable to the scientific inquiry into death which must be mentioned, although I must apologize for the perfunctory manner in which I will treat this particular aspect. If we look at the emotional climate favorable to a scientific inquiry, we may easily discover that it concerns two opposites. The object of the inquiry may be of a nature which per se seemingly evokes only mild emotional responses in the inquirer—for example, the sun and the stars—or it may concern an object which per se arouses the inquirer's feelings quite strongly. In the latter instance, however, there must be the implication that the inquiry concerns preventable processes. Diseases fall within this category. Death is a process which arouses extremely intensive emotional processes; and, though liable to delay, death is known to be unavoidable. Thus all the problems which are associated with the postponement of death are regular objects of scientific inquiry while the phenomenon of death itself has been chiefly a matter of speculation. Therefore a vast amount of knowledge has accumulated regarding death induced by disease, implying situations of a preventable or potentially preventable nature, but there is little knowledge of death as an unavoidable, logical process which is the last and ultimate consummation of life.

It is difficult to decide whether the recognition of the inescapability of death or the futility of such recognition plays the greater role in man's reluctance to face squarely,

on the intellectual level, the issue of death. It is known
that in a previous phase of the cultural process, Occidental
thinking, feeling, creation, and speculation were imbued
by concentration upon this very issue. Long stretches in the
history of the Christian churches are filled with intensive
submersion into the idea of death. On the many reasons
for that preoccupation I want to quote here only Georg
Simmel's (1918) characterization of the Christian concept
of death, which he called the "colossal paradox," since it
viewed life *a priori* under the aspect of its own eternity.
Thus the Christian preoccupation with death contained in
itself a solace through denial that death ended life. With
the rise of science, the intensive preoccupation with death
has stopped. Where once death had been one of the factors
which had helped the churches to hold their sway over
the bodies and souls of Occidental man, today religion—
yes, even superstition—and preoccupation with death are
so closely associated in the minds of many that elaboration
upon the topic strikes most people as esoteric, tending to
arouse suspicion. Wach (1934) points out—quite rightly—
that philosophy, and also science, in its emancipation from
religion and the churches, had shown a reserve or even con-
straint in penetrating into the core of the essential problems of life and death.

   In some historical periods death is looked on as a termination which does not merit further speculation (Mauthner, 1922-1924). For medieval man it was the beginning, a
moment infinitely more important than the moment of
birth. Although preoccupation with death is often (and
sometimes quite rightly) connected with ignorance and
superstition, it is impressive to notice how frequently great
cultures crystallize around preoccupation with death. The
unquestionable weakening of Occidental man's impulse
toward the creation of culture, so that his impulse expends
itself now almost entirely in science, may have been caused

also by the deficit in meaning which the conception of death has suffered. One receives the impression that the intensity of service to the dead and the proneness for scientific discovery are in a reverse proportion; indeed, it seems as if something like the denial of death were a prerequisite of the expenditure of full effort on science. A comparison of civilizations such as the Chinese with the American may confirm this viewpoint. Present-day American culture is remarkable by the fact that a bereaved person does not make his state externally noticeable. Quite rightly previous cultures and some contemporary ones consider a state of bereavement one which should be brought to the attention of the group. A state of bereavement is one of a profound ego change. A significant part of the ego has—at least temporarily—been destroyed, but the process of mourning may eventually restore the ego to its previous state (Freud, 1917c). Mourning may easily be disturbed, and just as once upon a time the leper announced his coming by a bell, the external trappings of bereavement should announce a person whose state deserves tact and consideration to prevent temporary, or even permanent, damage. With the denial of the meaningfulness of death, of course, this danger had also to be denied, and modern man is expected to maintain the aggregate of his social functions undisturbed by the occasional accident of losing a beloved person, just as he is expected to depart from life without causing a disturbance (an act the provider may achieve with seeming ease by letting the insurance company continue where he has left off). Many other customs and peculiarities of American culture could be mentioned in order to illustrate the supreme effort to deny death, an attitude characteristic of present American civilization. Indeed, death is one of those unsavory facts which cannot be integrated into an essentially hedonistic civilization. I say "essentially hedonistic" because of the marked tendency to integrate the unpleasurable by declaring it to be pleasurable. The necessity and unavoidability of suffering and of pain are not fully accepted, and their unquestionable existence is conjured away by the bold assurance that the implications of the reality principle fall within the confines of the pleasure principle. But no writer has been ingenious enough to give his booklet the title "How to Enjoy Your Own Death and That of Your Beloved Ones." Since death, in our times, cannot by any fancy be converted into a pleasurable process, it must remain a foreign body, denied by silence rather than recognized as the possible Alpha and Omega of life itself.

Strongly as science is engaged in man's effort to reduce the evils that threaten life, and effectively as science has been in producing the tools thereof, the banishing of death from man's destiny would amount to a supreme catastrophe. It is a fascinating challenge to think through to its last and bitter consequences the idea of man's becoming immortal or, more precisely, his being unable to die. I believe it would lead to this paradox: that if mankind wanted to survive under such conditions, death would have to be rediscovered.

Not finding a channel of release within the organism, the death instinct would throw its full brunt against its surroundings and the vanished opportunity of killing would arouse sadism to an unheard-of magnitude. Those who doubt the innateness of the death instinct would marvel that the removal of man's last and supreme frustration would lead to orgiastic outbreaks of aggression, a thought which had been expressed by Johannes von Saaz around 1400. Life would become unbearable and a new savior would have to emerge in order to teach mankind anew the capacity to die.

Science has not come closer to eliminating death but has only combated death by postponement, thus extending the average life span of Occidental man to an unheard-of degree. The possibly detrimental effect of even this change can be envisaged. The aged will soon prevail over the young; impetus and momentum toward bold social action and toward remolding of political, cultural, and artistic forms will be halted by the adherence to the existing order so significant of men over forty; youth will be deplorably crowded in by the adversaries of the new. And oddly enough, perhaps those groups, the average life span of whose members will be short, will have a greater chance of survival. But such warning may be premature; science succeeded in extending man's life span only a short time ago, and history has not yet recorded the consequences of this innovation. Science will continue to respond to society's great demand for the banishment of disease even if this is bought at the price of increased restrictions on the optimal and maximal efflorescences of life. For man still disentangles himself from serious disease at the cost of permanent traces which limit the maximum capacity of the functions for which the unharmed organism is destined. A long life span per se is often considered a good in itself, a mark of distinction (I suspect that the great age attributed to many Biblical figures, particularly of the early times, was an expression of the writer's respect, as if it were indecent to claim of a reverend person that he died at an average age). Likewise modern medicine seems to consider the prolongation of the average lifetime as a good in itself. Yet, since contemporary society is based on man's overspecialization and man can keep his place in the community even when only a selection of his functions is preserved, the threat to society of harboring a huge number of the handicapped becomes blatant only in emergencies. However, the decision for survival or nonsurvival of groups falls always in an hour of emergency.

Notwithstanding the total ineffectiveness of science in

eliminating death, it has profoundly changed one aspect of dying. Whereas before the advent of science—particularly during the medieval ages—man visualized his farewell to life as a frightful agony, contemporary man can count upon a relatively painless death. Freedom from physical pain has become part and parcel of our civilization. Fear of agony—as far as I can observe—has been replaced by fear of protracted invalidism and of the dementia of old age.

The expectancy of freedom from physical pain has had a significant bearing on our civilization. Following the lines of the unconscious, which equates birth and death (Graber, 1930), I proceed to the analogous problem regarding childbirth. Helene Deutsch (1930) has admirably discussed the preponderance of contemporary women who desire painless birth. The far-reaching consequences which the mother's absence—so to speak—during the birth of her child must have upon the relationship to her offspring become evident as soon as one's attention is drawn toward this problem. Helene Deutsch believes, however, that this revulsion against birth pain—being correlated with the vicissitudes of female masochism—may change in future times to a desire in favor of experiencing, with fullest awareness and with maximum inner participation, the final phase of giving life to a new being.

Contemporary man does not want to approach his death in full knowledge thereof. Those situations where society imposes death upon a person impress most people as exceedingly brutal and barbaric for just this reason. Knowledge that one will die at a predetermined moment is considered so unbearable that this phase is considered worse than the deed of execution. Indeed, knowledge of dying is thought to be so unbearably painful that many may even think the death penalty a punishment of moderate severity if it were carried out when the condemned—without being apprised before—is sleeping.

The gruesome problem of capital punishment, its justification by the state and some churches, the attempts at reconciling its existence with Christian ethics, the superstitions surrounding it, and the barbarism of the treatment of the condemned in most countries are most important sources for a psychology of death. Yet that area of research which would be most promising, the psychology of the condemned during the last hours of his lifetime, is scarcely possible by virtue of the insuperable obstacles within the scientist himself. Poelchau, a minister in a Nazi prison, gave a most painful report (1949) of his own inner experiences while witnessing the last hours of the condemned. While his approach was not that of the scientist, it is probable that the scientist would be as little prepared to do objective research in such a situation. Indeed it is impossible even to read Poelchau's book with equanimity.

Problems connected with the patient's knowledge of impending death (Case Two) and the question whether a patient ought to be told of the fatal nature of his disease (Case Three) will be discussed later. In general, contemporary society goes to great lengths to conceal from the patient the certainty of death. This is true chiefly of metropolitan society, particularly of its elite. In Central Europe, at least, there was no reluctance within broad groups of the peasant population to discuss impending death freely in the presence of the dying, who participated as if it were not a personal tragedy. I do not know, however, whether this was also true when death concerned a young person.

Be this as it may, the principle of keeping such knowledge from the patient is quite evident in our society. The practice may go so far that in the case of a nationally prominent personage the information will be kept from newspapers as long as the patient is able to read them. It is true that some physicians are in the habit of telling their patients the truth about their conditions. However, I still consider truthfulness in this situation as being contrary to the present general trend, although there are no statistics for the various techniques.

VII

INDIVIDUALISM AND ATTITUDES TOWARD DEATH

Our practice of withholding from the patient information of impending death is perhaps the most surprising
custom in a century which is proud of its individualism
and allegedly eager to develop the individuality of each
person. The moment of death is still the most important
and most decisive in man's life, far greater than the
moment of conception, which, like the moment of birth,
is beyond evaluation and without individuality. The belief
that the constellation of the planets has a bearing on the
formation of character and on the course of the future life
is the result of an attempt to provide the moment of birth
with individual structure. Narcissistic personalities may
use other means. Goethe reported the beneficial measures
which his grandfather, as Lord Mayor, had introduced in
his native city subsequent to his grandson's having been
born dead and then brought to life with great difficulty. In
this instance a mind who provided for almost every moment of his adult existence the highest possible individuality reached back to mark the very beginning of his
existence, like a *nouveau riche* who tries to prove that his
father was wealthy when his son was born. The moment
of conception is without interest—I do not follow here the
psychobiological aspect of the origin of individuality—
since it is a prerequisite only, a beginning, the cipher point
of a scale which becomes meaningful only by subsequent

51

steps of structurization. Whether conception occurs or not
is of no importance in itself. Life that did not evolve is a
deficit about which there is no consciousness, but as soon
as psychic structurization has started—particularly when
structure has led to the individual's experience of self—
death becomes the meridian point of the scale. But unlike
other such maximum points, this one has a retrograde
effect on the whole scale. On this moment of termination
will depend the value and the meaning of the entire scale.
My view that the recoil of the moment of death upon a
person's life history is characteristic of man might be disputed. G. H. Mead (1932) propounded that the record
of the past in all of its aspects is constantly changed by the
emergence of the new. I believe that Mead's concept of the
present is most pertinent, that man's feeling about the
past as something unchangeable and complete in itself is
not according to fact. Nevertheless, the retrograde effect
which the moment of death has upon the dying man's
past is different from the effect which Mead described
regarding the emergence of the new. Once a human being
is dead his record shares this effect of the new with all
other sectors of the universe; whereas during a person's
lifetime each new action or each further step in terms of
growing structure has a retrograde effect upon his individual past history inasmuch as it molds a record which,
once it is completed by his death, becomes part of a total
and more comprehensive record liable to all the changes
which the subsequent emergence of the new casts upon the
past of the universe.

Yet beyond Mead's theory, my concept of the last moment may appear to contradict some psychoanalytic tenets,
to wit, the claim that the fundamental structure of the
personality is founded with the ending of the oedipal
phase, or at the utmost with the ending of puberty. However, the main sources of psychoanalytic knowledge pertain

to records gained from the observation of people to whom the moment of dying is still far distant. The processes which possibly occur during old age, particularly during the terminal phase preceding death, are with few exceptions (Felix Deutsch, 1936) unknown to us. Actually it is possible that when they face the moment of life's termination some individualities may achieve a structural change which elevates them above their preceding level. Before dying, the patient described in Case Two accepted certain behavior patterns in her husband whom she had reproached for many years, and another patient (Case Three) forgave a relative against whom she had borne a deep-seated antipathy. However, it remained unclear how far the patients' transference to me had a bearing on both accomplishments. Nonetheless, it is possible that in some instances the ego shortly before death becomes more tolerant toward itself and therefore achieves a degree of harmony which previously was foreign to it (Felix Deutsch, 1936). In other words, the knowledge or the vague feeling that the end is approaching may enable some persons to step aside, so to speak, and view themselves and significant sectors of their lives with humility and also with insight into the futility of so much that is taken too seriously so long as the world is near and man is passionately living *in* it.

It is feasible that for some people the terminal pathway becomes significant by an accomplishment which had previously been beyond their capacity. It was impressive to notice, in the two instances just mentioned, that both patients were able to look as if from a distance at areas which had been overwhelming until then. We may describe this as living *beside* the world while they had previously lived *in* it, evaluating this accomplishment as a step of individualization inaccessible to them before. Of course, we may assume that the very opposite tendency will be observed in many more instances. The fact that steps of individualization may occur spontaneously at such a late time does not, in my opinion, contradict the psychoanalytic theory. As puberty by its regressive force permits a partial remodeling of the personality (Anna Freud, 1936) —the rigid structures of the latency period are often partially dissolved and reorganized during that phase—the final pathway may also—again by the force of regression (Felix Deutsch, 1936)—dissolve certain structures and thus permit a last step forward. These accomplishments of course have usually no social significance since the person is not permitted to make use of them. From the standpoint of a purely pragmatic psychiatry, the structural changes during the terminal pathway may not be more than items of clinical information, of little interest beyond their theoretical content. However, from the viewpoint of a psychiatry which puts man's individuality and its vicissitudes into the focus of attention and which looks at man exclusively under the aspect of what he is, regarding societal values as secondary and peripheral, the terminal pathway will be of incomparable interest. A psychiatrist pursuing such a psychiatry will find here an important function to fulfill, namely to help the patient accomplish the maximum individualization of which he is capable. The psychiatrist faces here a grave issue. Should he adhere to the principle of letting bygones be bygones and therefore center his effort exclusively upon the patient's peaceful, that is to say, painless dying? Or should he carry out the last and immutable consequences of those values which are inherent in the patient's individuality? The Catholic Church, as is known, follows the latter principle. Since the ultimate goal of man's life—in her estimation—is to appear before the Creator in a state of sinlessness, the dying person must receive the holy sacraments under all conditions, even when the patient is unaware of his approaching death. I lack experience as to the frequency of internal relief to the patient from receiving Holy Communion as Viaticum. I wish to stress, however, that whatever the statistical finding may be, the religious principle cannot be accepted as objectively valid by secular psychiatry. The meaning which the state of sinlessness has held for Occidental man may find its equivalent now in the state of maximum individualization; nonetheless, the goal of maximum individualization ought never to become a compulsive measure, as has happened with the rites of some churches. Those last few steps of individualization which may be possible along the terminal pathway may or may not lead to happiness; they may or may not facilitate the last farewell to life. Because it is difficult to anticipate which effect these steps may have upon the patient, he will be left to take the lead and the psychiatrist will follow. Of course, in the process of terminal, maximum individualization a person may discover the futility of his past; he may discover that he squandered a treasure and he may be seized by greatest regret. But in combination with the tolerance of which I spoke earlier, this recognition may lead to a triumph of individualization, and the final processes of structurization during the terminal pathway may provide the past life with a meaning which it would never have acquired without them.

Once life has ceased, the deceased person's record becomes petrified and unalterable and this alone would make the moment of death the most important moment of man's life. There is, however, one considerable exception to be discussed briefly. There are persons whose lives appear to exhaust themselves in the function of preparing the way for their offspring. A historical instance of this kind concerns Goethe's father. A study of his biography may well prove that the function and meaning of his life exhausted themselves in casting the mold which served as a frame of his son's magnificent life. In such instances the moment of death is possibly insignificant. Once such a person has set the pattern for his genius offspring, the meaning of his own life has been accomplished and the moment of death seems to lose personal significance aside from the effect which it has upon the offspring. Possibly this is true of the parents of all geniuses. But an argument may be raised here, namely that I have relinquished the realm of pure psychology and overemphasized a special factor.

A large number of people whose existence is of paramount importance to the community sacrifice their individual existence to the social place they occupy. Georg Simmel (1908) has shown that this is the prerequisite of certain professions; for example, the individual life of a priest recedes into the background and his social function is the predetermined cast into which his individuality dissolves itself. I agree with Simmel's conception. If a priest is to accomplish his goal, his ego must give up its own identity, and this becomes its most distinctive mark.

The existence of Goethe's father, however, was related to his son in an entirely different way. He did not give up his own identity but rather emphasized it so strongly in his relationship to his son that most of Goethe's biographers— misunderstanding profoundly the function which he played in his son's life—condemned him harshly for not doting upon his son. Nevertheless, in psychological terms, his life makes sense only if it is viewed in conjunction with his son's position at the pinnacle of German culture, for Goethe accomplished what his father had tried to do and had even occasionally accomplished in a small way, so that the father could say—perhaps rightly—that he himself would have achieved more than his son if nature had given him the latter's wealth of talents.

The father thus experienced in his son not only the complement but also the main part of his own life, and the psychologist faces here the exceptional situation of a man of strong individuality who, when he dies, does not discontinue the record of his own life but still enriches it by his son's continuous production of great cultural values.

However, I think such situations occur so infrequently that one can say it is self-evident that with the moment of death a person's life record has become petrified, and that by recoil this moment sheds an unalterable cast upon all previous life moments. Because of this self-evident principle it becomes an outstanding fact that in our civilization the prevailing tendency is to protect a person from the knowledge of his impending death. One might expect that a person who had lived independently, shaping even trivial life situations in an individual manner, who had refused to take life for granted but had tried to infuse into all manifestations of life consciousness, awareness, and understanding, would abhor the idea of being overwhelmed by death and of departing from life without forewarning. But rarely, I assume, will the answer be heard which one patient gave shortly before his death when he was asked whether he would not want an anodyne: "Nobody shall deprive me of my death" (Heim, 1949). The full awareness of each step that leads closer to death, the unconscious experience of one's own death up to the last second which permits awareness and consciousness, would be the crowning triumph of an individually lived life. It would be taken as the only way man ought to die if individuality were really accepted as the only adequate form of living and if life in all its manifestations were integrated, which would of course include death and the sorrows of the terminal pathway. Yet would there be sorrows upon that pathway if death were really understood as the prerequisite of life? I knew an outstanding man who carried the principle of individualization unusually far. When he fell sick he wanted to be apprised of the nature of his disease. When he was told by his friend, who also was his physician, that cancer had been diagnosed, he continued his meal—to the admiration of those who were present—with apparent equanimity. Yet postoperatively he developed a psychosis.

Notwithstanding the effect of surgery, it is conceivable that he might have undergone this strain without subsequent psychosis if he had not been told of the gravity of his illness. It is remarkable that this man, despite his age and despite his profound knowledge of life, was still full of rebellion against the necessity of death. We might contrast him with Socrates who accepted death, even at the hands of his fellow men, as a logical necessity scarcely deserving protestation.

VIII

REMARKS ON THE PLACE OF DEATH IN THE HUMAN SPECIES

The great effect which I claim the knowledge of impending death may have on psychopathology may appear contradictory when I also claim that man has always an unconscious knowledge of his impending death, at least when the latter is brought on by internal reasons. In raising the question whether a patient should be told the truth about his physical condition or not, I only meant to ask whether he should be provided from without with a husk into which he can fit his unconscious knowledge. Although it cannot be proved empirically that such unconscious knowledge is present in each instance, it is necessary to assume its presence in case mental lucidity has been preserved. I have noticed in some instances that when a patient's condition takes a turn for the worse, he stops asking the physician about the prospect of his recovery. There is one great exception to the assumption of unconscious knowledge about one's impending death. I have observed, very much to my surprise, that patients suffering from senile dementia are completely free of the fear of death. However, this strange phenomenon occurs only in patients who have reached the stage of dementia which is free of delusions, a stage which I call pure dementia. I cannot at this point go into the details of the psychology of dementia senilis. It is the necessary consequence of the disturbance of time experience which arises in the wake of the disease. The representation of the future has become blotted out, and where there is no sense of the future there cannot be any knowledge of death. Fear of something that is meaningless is, of course, not feasible.

Despite the pitiful aspects of the situation, it is nevertheless somewhat comical to observe a senile patient weeping when told that he will have to be operated upon and smiling when told that he will soon die. The prospect of pain and the discomfort of an operation (the meanings of which do not presuppose the category of the future) elicit in the senile patient adequate emotional responses, whereas the far more serious prospect of death cannot cause him any concern since the meaning of death has been reduced to a mere word. In such instances one cannot presuppose that there is an unconscious knowledge of impending death. If it should ever happen that every person evolved senile dementia if only he lived long enough, then we would have to consider the possibility that nature had taken the precaution of sparing man the agony of dying. Fear of death would then be the index of the store of life in the organism; that is to say, as long as man feared death he would still have a rightful claim to life because the zest to live would not yet have been satiated. In the senile patient, apparently, an equilibrium has been established which is not disturbed by the occurrence of death. The senile patient, it can be said, is psychologically dead although he is biologically a living organism.

Thus in the early phases and possibly also in the last phase of human development man's mind is unencumbered by the representation of death. In between man may try—even successfully—to keep his mind unruffled by his knowledge of death, as did Epicurus: "When I am, death is not, when death is, I am not; therefore, we can never have anything to do with death." Here, by logic, death is conjured away. Or death may come terribly close, as to Lessing

(1777), who wrote thus to a friend while his wife was vainly struggling for her life after their newborn infant had died:

> I seize the moment that my wife is lying entirely without consciousness, to thank you for your sympathy. My joy was only a shortlasting one. And I lost him so unwillingly, this son! For he had so much sagacity! so much sagacity!—Do not believe that even the few hours of my paternity turned me into this monkey of a father! I know what I am saying. Was it not sagacity that one had to pull him into the world by iron tongs? that he noticed the stench so soon?—Was it not sagacity that he seized the first opportunity to take off again?—Yet the little curly-head is also dragging the mother away!—For little hope is left that I will keep her. For once I wanted to have it as good as other people. But it turned out badly for me. [See also Appendix, iv.]

It seems that the human species is the only one which knows of death. At least, man's closest relatives, the apes, are ignorant of the phenomenon. It is most impressive to read Zuckerman's (1932) brilliant report on *The Social Life of Monkeys and Apes*. When the overlord, who is the sole proprietor of the females among baboons, shows signs of decreasing dominance, sexual fights are prone to break out among the males who are in dire need of a female partner. Often the prize female who is the center of the fight is exposed to such violent handling that she succumbs to the injuries suffered in the fray. The remarkable observation, however, concerns the fact that the fight continues to rage around the dead body of the victim. "Its owners carried it around by the waist, groomed it, examined its ano-genital area, and often copulated with it."

The horde of apes observed by Zuckerman might easily be taken as a variation of the primordial horde which

Freud (1912/13) tried to reconstruct in *Totem and Taboo*. Whereas, in the history of the latter, death and its representation are of paramount importance, observation of the former shows sufficient evidence that among the ape horde thinking and acting are unencumbered by any representation of death. Thus the life of the human species is gravely complicated not only by the oedipus complex but also by the knowledge of death.

Is it possible that the oedipal complex establishes itself in conjunction with the knowledge of death? Some records, at least, suggest that at the beginning the child is possibly not puzzled as much by the question of where man comes from as by the problem of what will happen to him. In an early psychoanalytic study by C. G. Jung (1910), it appears as if the child's inquiry into the facts of life was precipitated by her noticing the signs of age in the grandmother, and I wonder whether this sequence might possibly contain something typical. However, as Freud has shown, the problem of death is beyond the child's mental capacity. The utmost he can comprehend is the concept of absence which is much further away from reality than is the construction which the child, with the help of his pregenital and phallic imagery, achieves regarding the propagative processes. Refined research into this matter might show that the child's inquiry into the generative processes is a secondary edition of an earlier and short-lasting inquiry into death. Possibly the child turns away from such an inquiry because of the accompanying horror and because of the utter hopelessness and ensuing despair about any possible progress in his investigation. Here a correlate to what was previously discussed in the animal is found in man's ideation. While death is unknown to the animal, man cannot imagine it although he knows it. Since death per se is not represented in the unconscious, man cannot imagine the state of death; he can only visualize it by the representation of peripheral factors.

The libidinal functions and the generative processes are, of course, richly represented in the unconscious and their echo is loud and distinctly audible to the mind. Man feels sexual-erotic impulses, and the possibility of mastering them is implicitly given simultaneously with their occurrence. The gradual convergence of life toward death is not represented in man's unconscious (Bonaparte, 1938), but simultaneously, death must be accepted as a *donnée* over which man has no mastery. It is an assemblage of these and many more factors which makes man's mental struggle with death so difficult. The following outline of sequences, although biologically perhaps valid, nevertheless does not encompass the cluster of psychological problems surrounding death:

Man is born prone to death. Amazingly unprotected by nature against death, depending entirely upon the good will and wisdom of his environment, it is a marvel that he survives the initial phase of his existence at all. As a matter of fact, it is well known that the whole of modern medicine was necessary in order to make this survival a probable event. This incredibly great tendency of the infant toward death coincides with Freud's theory of the full reign of the death instinct at the beginning of life. Dying is an easy matter, the rule, so to speak, and not the exception for the infant. The same is true of the final stage of senile dementia. Thus at the beginning and at the end of life—the end being defined here as a stage of exhaustion of life's potential—the organism bends itself toward death, surrendering without struggle. At the beginning this may be because the death instinct has not yet been fused with and pacified by the libidinal instincts; at the end, perhaps, because the instincts of life have exhausted their beneficial effects and the death instinct has become reinstated into the initial position of dominance. Between these two far distant, but dynamically almost identical situations, a period should lie in which death would appear as a foreign body or, from the biological point of view, as an avoidable accident caused by a complication of stimuli originating either from within or from without and being fatal by quantity or quality. This rather simple scheme of sequences is immeasurably complicated by the evolvement of a structure as highly differentiated and complex as man's ego organization; it is further complicated by the taboos inherent in the oedipal complex—the greatest barrier to the gratification of instincts—and by man's knowledge of death, which makes him the only species capable of suicide. As certain as death is the final outcome of man's life, as uncertain it is whether he will die by suicide or by extraneous causes. Brun (1953) recently adduced among many other arguments against Freud's theory of the death instinct the fact that only 0.63 pro mil. of Swiss adults end their lives by suicide. If the frequency of suicide were an argument for or against the death instinct, then of course Freud's thesis would have been a piece of nonsense from the very beginning. However, I believe that man's *capacity* for committing suicide ought to be considered, and this capacity, I believe, is universal among mankind. Relatively rare as suicide actually is, it must have a deep meaning, since of no one can it be said with certainty that he would never commit it. And strangely enough, in only two phases does man seem to be incapable of suicide, namely during the preoedipal, oedipal and early latency periods on the one hand, and, on the other, in the aforementioned phase of senile dementia, that is to say, when according to theory the death instinct is relatively dominant. The evolvement of ego structure thus has two effects. It increases the potentiality of life's prolongation and it creates the possibility of the organism's destruction by its own planned action. This dichotomy—

potential postponement of death and potential premature death by short circuit, introduced into human life by one and the same structure—is typically human; it is incomparable to anything observed in other species and possibly forms the deepest layer of conflicts in the human personality. The frequency with which the conflict leads to short-circuit solutions is not decisive. If it were high we would not have an opportunity to observe it because man would have become extinct. That man can commit suicide and that the potentiality of such action rests in every person, these are the essential points.

Actually we encounter a series of psychobiological apparatuses—wrongly called self-preservative instincts (Heinz Hartmann, 1948)—and cultural taboos directed against suicide. Some religions declare suicide one of the greatest sins. In some cultures an attempt at suicide is liable to prosecution. The richness of security measures, culturally as well as biologically, against suicide suggests how strong man's tendency must be to succumb to that potentiality. Without taking the contribution of the superego into account, one may say that in most instances of suicide the following two contrary factors may have their bearing in varying proportions. By the act of suicide another person is almost always psychologically killed (Freud, 1909a, 1920b). But it must not be forgotten that in the act of murder also suicide is probably committed psychologically (Alexander and Staub, 1929). By suicide the union or reunion with a loved —though ambivalently loved—object is realized (Friedlander, 1940, among many others). The contrariness of factors ought not to be confusing. It is not easy to defeat the impulse to live. Possibly the ego can array such powerful forces as are necessary to carry out the suicidal intent only by baiting the forces of love with the promise of a supreme gratification. This bait of libidinal gratification has apparently led many an observer to overlook the primary and undisputable fact that suicide remains a self-destructive action, whatever gratification of libidinal daydreams the act per se might furnish. The clinical observation that motives such as the desire to be reborn (Schilder, 1925) or to atone or, as said before, to be united—usually with the preoedipal mother—play a great part only demonstrates how the individual must act in order to achieve prematurely that for which he is destined unalterably. And this point, I believe, is the principal issue. Strange as it may sound, suicide is the result of a rebellion against death. For many—perhaps even for most—people the idea of having to die is unbearable. Partly they respond to this necessity as if it made life senseless and meaningless. By committing suicide they believe they have cheated death as the condemned cheats the executioner and the populace when he kills himself. I believe that for most suicides the act does not mean really dying. Dying for them is something that is suffered and passively submitted to; when actively performed it becomes a triumph, as if the ego has proved itself to be almighty when it is strong enough to cast its own life aside. By converting passivity into seeming activity the ego carries out nature's most stringent command and preserves nevertheless the illusion of independence and of having stepped outside of nature—as if nature cared whether the human life span was shortened by a quarter, a third, or even a half. One aspect of nature seems to be her care that created life perishes in order to give room for new life. Linguistic usage seems to share the conviction of the person who commits suicide. Language—it is my feeling—differentiates between dying and committing suicide. Logical analysis, of course, will see in this differentiation only a qualification of the form in which death took place. Nevertheless we have the vague feeling of being unprecise when saying of a person who committed suicide "he died," as if self-inflicted death were essentially different from biological death. The reaction of society to suicide may be touched upon in passing. I was struck when I noticed that the suicide of an old man, who had been fatally sick for a long time and whose natural death would have been taken as a matter of course, provoked unusually strong emotions in others. Some spoke of him as if he had accomplished a great deed; others reproached him for the exhibitionistic way in which he had proceeded. But there was general agreement that he must have suffered severely, and everyone felt far greater pity for him than if the proximate cause of his death had been the fatal disease because of which he ostensibly committed suicide. Here society's ambivalent attitude is well demonstrated. The person who commits suicide becomes a hero and therefore arouses ambivalent reactions—veneration and anger. Because he defied death he is revered like Empedocles; but he is censored because he took flight. These reactions, of course, are irrational and reflect our own unconscious attitudes regarding suicide: our horror of committing it and our temptation to do it; the condemnation of suicide is often the effect of a strong impulse to perform. Whether suicide is always the result of great suffering I do not know. A famous character such as Werther was pictured by Goethe as having gone through immense suffering and the book moves us—at least today— more by the description of these sufferings than by the tragic end.

The frequency or infrequency, respectively, of the occurrence of suicide is not the decisive factor; rather, that every human being possesses during most of his lifetime the capacity of committing suicide should be made the center of investigation. By and large I would say that in every analysis we have to grapple with suicidal tendencies in the patient (Federn, 1929). These tendencies are ever ready to be activated, and it is only the positive transference which keeps them in abeyance. Every analyst knows this danger and is concerned about it just at those times when the analytic process is accelerated and the negative transference is evident. Solidified ego structures, then, are in the process or on the verge of temporary dissolution and this is a moment when the ego, this guardian *kat exochen* against the self-directed spread of the death instinct, may be itself off guard and weakened. What the proximate motive for suicide may be in the individual instance is not under discussion here; we are concerned with the clinical fact that in almost every patient the actual impulse can be discovered if the analytic investigation is carried sufficiently into the depths of the patient's history and personality. This clinical finding impresses me as one more suggestion that Freud's postulate of a death instinct covered a biological and psychological truth. As there are in our organism latent tendencies toward sickness, constantly waiting, so to speak, for an opportunity to be activated but kept in abeyance by the organism's vast store of defenses, it is possible that there is likewise a suicidal tendency constantly present in latent form but usually well locked up, visible, therefore, only under special circumstances.

Yet one rarely observes—with the exception of melancholic patients—an instance of a patient's consciously racing after death with that intensity and insistence commonly observed when the ego pursues libidinal or aggressive gratifications. The melancholic patient, prostrated wholly by the crushing burden of a fantastically inflated superego, ever ready to give way to an equally intensified aggression, offers such a complex picture that he seems to be inappropriate for a decisive discussion of the death instinct. I once observed a patient who had tried over and over again to poison himself. He definitely was not suffering from melancholia but was diagnosed as schizophrenic by an experienced and well-informed colleague. Although I disagreed with the diagnosis I did not intend to minimize or dispute the gravity of the situation. To my very great surprise, as long as this patient was under my treatment, a repetition of such suicidal attempts never did recur. As soon as a transference was formed (which happened very soon) the suicidal impulse seemed to be blown away. It became quite probable that the urge to commit suicide, which had become almost a compulsion, was active because of unsatiated libido and the long series of suicidal attempts had to be regarded as a constant courting for love. It substituted for a perversion, and the whole process of self-induced falling asleep—that is to say, dying—and being reawakened were so much eroticized that scarcely any aggression against the self was noticeable. (I am not reporting the dynamism which kept this process going but only the energetic relations in the psychopathological end product.) I do not know whether such a clinical picture would weaken one of the arguments Brun raised against the theory of the death instinct, namely that a passionate surrender to death never occurs. I myself would only hesitatingly use such clinical observations in favor of Freud's theory of the death instinct, and I doubt that Freud was primarily motivated by the observation of such rather rare perversions. I would rather assume that the masochism almost regularly found at the bottom of a neurotic symptom may have required far more urgently the revision of the theory of the instincts.

In countering further the argument that clinical observation shows, in general, little of a positive striving in man toward death, I want to hypostatize for a moment the concept of nature: nature did not need to establish in the psychic apparatus particular security measures to enforce death. Since basic forces were relentlessly progressing toward the leveling of tension, nature's problem was, so to speak, to build up a protection against an all too quick attainment of the complete leveling off which is death. It follows, therefore, that clinical observation shows predominantly the richness of the mechanisms supporting life. Freud's theory of the death instinct ought to make the clinical observer expect in the adequately developed adult nothing but manifold security measures against death and a series of apparatuses for the discharge of aggression against the outside world. These two expectations are fulfilled. The rich material of self-directed destruction, as is well-known, is mainly a recoil of aggression which originally was destined to be channeled against the environment but was reversed in its direction by further acculturation of the ego due to the integration of a superego.

IX

DEATH AND THE PLEASURE PRINCIPLE

Death is the only event concerning the whole psychobiological organism which is predictable beyond dispute
once birth has taken place. Though this is a truism it is
a far-reaching one. Logicians teach that it is wrong to say
the sun will rise tomorrow. If we want to be exact we have
to state—so the logician rightly informs us—that the sun
will rise tomorrow if the present cosmic conditions are
in force at that time. Such a form is necessary if predictions
are to be meaningful. Strangely enough, the prediction of
the death of organisms is the only prediction which does
not require equivalent qualifications. F. C. S. Schiller
(1935) has correctly disputed the traditional syllogism
which leads to the conclusion that Socrates is mortal. Nevertheless, I believe that the mortality of organisms can be
predicted without qualification since life and death are
different aspects of one and the same process. In strange
contradiction to this knowledge, the ego cannot imagine
the state of its own death.

Yet man's eternal life can be the content of a thought
and can also be imagined in conformity with man's incapacity to imagine death. One feels inclined to say that it is
not necessary for man to imagine his own death because it
is the only certain event which will occur beyond any dispute. With due permission for teleological thinking, one
may find a deep purpose in this incapacity, since, if man

could imagine his own death, this might destroy the ego's paramount function as a barrier against the death instinct's premature attainment of its goal.

In other words, would man not make far more frequent use of the capacity of laying hands upon himself if he could really imagine the state of death? In two famous passages allusion was made to this possibility. When Socrates says in the *Apology*: "If you suppose that there is no consciousness, but a sleep like the sleep of him who is undisturbed even by dreams, death will be an unspeakable gain," he expresses the idea which Hamlet, marveling about man's attachment to life, expresses in the reverse: "To sleep, perchance to dream, ay there's the rub." Both seem to agree that the imagination of a state of unconsciousness and its identification with death would have an extreme attractiveness for man.

Socrates and Hamlet disregarded momentarily the fundamental fact that a state of death cannot be imagined. Apparently the ego is inhibited under ordinary circumstances in striving toward a goal which it can represent only in thought but not in its imagination. I am omitting here temporarily the energic aspect of psychoanalysis and have stressed only a fundamental fact of preconscious and conscious functions, whose value, however, must not be underestimated in their great contribution toward impeding the ego's surrender to death. This stress upon the ego's disinclination to strive for the unimaginable will elicit the argument that the state of sleep cannot be imagined either, although the ego gladly tries to attain it. Sleep, however, occurs before an ego has been formed. Furthermore, as has been shown (Anna Freud, 1950), the child struggles against sleep in a certain phase of ego development, namely when he becomes aware of the world of objects and starts to engage himself actively in it. The ego must learn to integrate the biological function of sleep which is fully formed during the initial phases of its development. Only the certainty that the ego will find the world of objects again makes sleep a pleasurable process. The slightest doubt about the prospect of reawakening actually results in grave sleeping disturbances in the adult (Fenichel, 1942). Finally one must mention the ego's unique relationship to this biological function. It is essentially helpless if we disregard the artificial digestion of soporifics. Whereas the ego can actively support and assist the gratification of all other biological needs by effort, irritation, or stimulation, it can do almost nothing in order to induce sleep other than tempting complete exhaustion which very often is a cover-up for a self-destructive tendency amounting to a suicidal attempt.

The ego's attitude toward death seems ambiguous. Death almost always comes both too early and too late— too early because the ego has rarely realized all of its potentialities, and too late because individual life has been a detour leading finally to what it had been at the beginning: nothingness. This antinomy inherent in man's feeling about death finds its echo in the symbolism with which man has surrounded death: death is at times the redeemer, at times the revenger, then again the force of injustice which kills the young and lets suffer the old; at times he is visualized as the great democrat who does not heed hierarchical superiority or spare the wealthy, the King, and even the Pope. These mutually contradictory feelings about death, which have been found so profusely since Christianity took hold of the Occident, are not universal. A less differentiated ego probably repudiates the idea of death without hesitation or compromise whenever it concerns the self or an unambivalently loved person but welcomes it, again without hesitation or compromise whenever it concerns the ego-alien, the foreign, the enemy (Freud, 1915a). This clear-cut distribution of positive and negative attitudes toward death can nowadays perhaps be found occasionally in children but not in adults. Feelings of guilt, the mutual penetration of love and hatred, the barriers against the uninhibited discharge of aggression, the deep injuries man's narcissism has suffered by the discoveries of science (Freud, 1917), and many other factors have left their indelible traces upon man's feeling about death although the ancient and primordial abhorrence of it is still noticeable. Yet notwithstanding this abhorrence, there is the remarkable ease with which the ego risks its own destruction in order to achieve its goals. Ambition, competition, the craving for prestige and for adventure lead man often toward exposure to the gravest dangers.

Puzzled, one may ask what the profit of such daring actions may be, if they are so likely to cause death. The frequent recurrence of one pattern inclines us toward considering it a rule: the fear of castration is so great that the destruction of one's self appears preferable. Man's reaction seems to be, with surprising frequency: rather dead than castrated.

Two components of the castration complex are involved. The possession of the penis promises and guarantees the experience of greatest pleasure and the possession of the penis provides also narcissistic gratification. The social area in which man's motivation derives momentum from the castration complex is vast. Almost all those situations in which competition with contemporaries or defeat by others lead to internal situations unbearable for the ego are genetically derivatives of the castration complex. Clinically one can observe that men who have attained relative freedom from the castration complex in their relationship with women still are under its sway in their relationship with men. Freud's description (1937) of the paramount obstacle in the analysis of males finds confirmation in daily observation. The traumatic situation, as is well known, occurred when it dawned on the boy that there are beings who do not possess penises and when he compared the smallness of his organ with the size of that of adult males, further when he feared or wished that the father would make out of him a girl and use him sexually. Here a deep sexual desire comes in conflict with a narcissistic motive, namely, the pride in masculinity (Freud, 1918).

The narcissistic component of the castration complex transgresses its original scope and becomes one of the principal sources of male narcissism. Its later efflorescences are so intensive that many a psychologist overlooks its origin and wants to derive man's main motivation solely from craving for prestige and self-respect. Indeed, many patients are so intensely attached to prestige values that it requires much patience and astuteness in order to obtain also the biological factor (castration complex in the narrower meaning of the term). It is most impressive and likewise puzzling to observe male patients—the same can be easily found in the biographies of nonneurotics—risking their existence in order to make sure of their superiority over competitors. Delinquent patients will destroy their whole careers on the spur of the moment in order to prove to themselves and—in their fantasy—to their environment that they can defy their fathers and are not afraid of them (Fenichel, 1939).

When the intensity of the complex is above average, the variety of social situations which fall within the scope of the castration complex appears to be infinite. What is said here of male psychology is encountered in women in the relationship to the child. Barrenness or loss of a child results, with most women, in a similar conflict as that observed in men when traumatized by an event which unconsciously means castration.

We encounter here a situation of fundamental importance in a discussion of the psychology of death. Apparently man cannot tolerate life without the prospect of pleasure. Concomitantly one can also observe an approximate readiness to die when maximum pleasure is experienced, pleasure which the ego feels cannot be surpassed.

It is my impression that at the height of true orgasm, when for moments the ego is lost, and during the subsequent short time of complete satiation, when the ego is almost inaccessible to external or internal stimulation, a person is ready to surrender to death without struggle (Ferenczi, 1924). The future is then no longer represented and any action of meaning or importance has become inconceivable. In an early phase of psychoanalytic theory a similar problem played a significant role in regard to the formation of the theory of sexuality. Freud (1905a) emphasized at that time the well-known situations in the lives of some animals who become easy prey when they are in a state of sexual excitement. (I wonder whether the state of defenselessness induced by sleep incurs the same dangers.) Yet this biological situation seems re-established internally in man when he reaches that level of gratification implicitly inherent in the orgastic capability (Freud, 1909c; Keiser, 1949; Needles, 1953). This constellation is reflected in language. A particular instance occurs in "The Canonization" by John Donne. In the explication of this poem Cleanth Brooks (1947) makes this point, noting that "In the sixteenth and seventeenth centuries 'to die' means to experience the consummation of the act of love." I feel inclined to believe that this factor also—besides the many other factors usually mentioned—has its bearing upon the fact that in our society most men do not attain the full orgastic peak; the average ego can only tolerate an intensity which is far below the potential maximum.

Likewise I have observed in the few deliveries I have witnessed a brief period in which the woman has been overwhelmed by a passionate triumph incomparable to anything that could be experienced in other circumstances. Here also I had the feeling that in this moment life had reached a peak from which the rest appeared utterly meaningless and negligible. In that moment, perhaps, a woman is also ready to surrender without regret and pain to deprivation of a future. Puerperal depressions may contain (aside from the well-known involvement of aggression and guilt feeling) a deep biological factor arising from the self-evident truth that a woman has reached the maximum of her creative potential in the moment when she has given birth to a living child.

Be this as it may, the fact—which for many may be a truism—that life becomes intolerable without prospect of pleasure contains no small psychological problem. Understandable as it is that only the prospect of pleasure keeps the basic processes of ego formation going, that the transformation of the pleasure principle into the reality principle requires the promise of pleasure pending though postponed, it is difficult to fathom why a mature ego which has integrated the fundamental necessities of life, which has experienced most of the great pleasures life can provide, still needs the prospect of some pleasure in order to continue its existence. I am not speaking here of the pleasure-unpleasure relation in the melancholic patient. I am referring to the basic fabric of the ego which requires the attainment of pleasure if it is to fulfill its functions.

It is most impressive to watch what this ego can achieve. It can go through the greatest deprivations; its capacity to bear pain is incredible; its versatility and sagacity in bending reality to its own purposes are infinite, and again it will not be deterred by maximum sacrifices in fulfilling this function. But all these almost miraculous achievements are based on the prospect of some future pleasure. When this prospect—illusionary or realistic—crumbles, the whole ego organization crumbles likewise and death becomes the only solution, regardless of what the biological life potential of the person may still be. Here the ego, in my estimation, shows quite openly the last vestige of its origin: it shows that it arose totally and completely from drives. Far as it may go in accepting the reality principle, it cannot overstep this last limitation. Boastingly as some may have claimed that they have succeeded in casting off all sources of profane pleasure, that worldly love has lost its meaning, and that all their efforts are absorbed in meditation and contemplation of God, no one—as far as I know—would claim that he could live without pleasure; for in such moments of supreme elevation beyond the world as we know it and of supreme turning toward a deity, the new state implicitly becomes a source of greater pleasure than the individual had known prior to the attainment of that state. And also, the stoics and cynics of ancient antiquity who made themselves independent of the lure of secular pleasures still derived pleasure from this new state of alleged immunity.

The disorder of melancholia has been used as a clinical proof of the existence of a death instinct (Federn, 1930; Weiss, 1935). I believe that this proof is not succinct since the clinical picture is so much complicated by the turning of sadistic drives against the ego (Brun, 1953). I surmise that the clinical fact of the ego's need for pleasure, if it is to function, and the frequent preference of death over castration may be clinical observations preferable to those yielded by the melancholic patient for a discussion of the subject matter. Jones (1927a) introduced the concept of aphanisis into psychoanalytic terminology. He signified with the term a state in which the ego would suffer "the total, and of course permanent, extinction of the capacity (including opportunity) of sexual enjoyment" beyond castration. Castration, if measured by aphanisis would mean only a partial loss. I believe that the concept of aphanisis is an important one. Its elaboration may lead to a better comprehension of the representation of death in the various psychic systems. Though death cannot be represented in the unconscious, aphanisis can. The anthropological fact (Rivers, 1911) that some peoples do not draw the line between life and death, but between health on one side, sickness and death on the other—as it is expressed in their vocabulary—may support this view. Aphanisis then would include sickness and death, that is to say, all states in which the gain of pleasure is impossible.

In the following I would like to use the term in a way which is different from Jones's. Aphanisis may include the absence of all potentialities of pleasures (the sexual and nonsexual ones) or the absence of all pleasures except those derived from the penis. I am referring here exclusively to male psychology. In women the constellation is far more complicated and less transparent than in men.

We can describe the following clinical alternatives:

(1) The ego may accept aphanisis in order to preserve the penial pleasure, a state one can observe occasionally in perversions where feelings of guilt force the ego to give up all pleasures except the forbidden perversion leading to orgasm.

(2) The ego may accept castration in order to escape aphanisis. Feelings of guilt enforce genital inactivity for the sake of keeping almost all other avenues of pleasure open.

(3) The ego strives for the preservation of all avenues of pleasure, but risks aphanisis, that is to say death, in order to assure the integrity of the penis and superiority over other men. Defeat means castration in such instances and death is preferred.

This third alternative is of interest here. Whatever the imagery of death may mean in the individual instances, the clinical fact remains that often forces which easily lead to self-destruction become activated with a presumptive threat to the penial integrity. I believe we are dealing here with the same destructive forces which would also unfold their deleterious effect if the ego were supposed to function without actual enjoyment or prospect of pleasure. Whether the total deficit of pleasure or its prospect, respectively, would lead to suicide or a psychosis, or a suicide-like exposure to danger, would not make a difference in the context of this discussion. The main point is the sudden damaging effect upon the ego, a damage which is perpetrated by something instinctual in case pleasure is abolished or threatened with abolishment. I believe the clinical observation compels the assumption that one of the functions of the ego is to make innocuous these injurious forces which can be observed clinically as soon as basic pleasure mechanisms are destroyed or threatened with destruction.

X

DEATH AND EGO FORMATION

I want to refer again briefly to Freud's comprehensive construction that life was wrested from lifeless matter by the as-yet-unknown operation of stimuli upon inorganic matter. "Perhaps the process was," Freud (1920a) continues, "a prototype resembling that other one which later in a certain stratum of living matter gave rise to consciousness." That is to say, each new psychological acquisition was also wrested from a preceding state through the operation of external stimuli. As a matter of fact, it seems that this process of new acquisition by the operation of external forces can be observed to a certain extent in each instance of ego development. The constant operation of the environment upon the child's drives converts them gradually into an ego. Although this process is greatly facilitated by inherited factors of maturation (Heinz Hartmann, 1939), the ego has not yet been wrested from living matter as consciousness has been and therefore special stimuli must operate upon the child in order to enforce the development of ego structure; whereas living per se leads to the establishment of consciousness in the human species. That is to say, consciousness has become a permanent institution; whereas ego structure must be reacquired in each individual anew and therefore requires specially patterned stimuli. The basic process of ego development, however, may make the theory of a death instinct more or less prob-

81

able. It is appropriate to quote here a philosopher who viewed the development of the ego under the aspect of the contribution which death makes to it. Georg Simmel (1918) suggested that if individual life went on indefinitely without ending in death, the ego would never acquire that state of differentiation which it actually shows. The fact of death forces the ego to search for the discrimination between life and its contents, a thought similar to that which Freud (1915a) had previously expressed in connection with the situation in which the idea of a division of man into a body and a soul was conceived (see above). Oddly enough, Simmel connects this ability with a basic requirement of ego development, namely the necessity of bearing frustration. He writes:

> The disproportion which exists between our drives and potentialities, on the one side, and the concrete fulfillments, internal and external, on the other, must belong to the motives conducive to the formation of a continuous ego. If our wishes were always completely fulfilled, then our acts of volition would die with this fulfillment and a new act with a new content would start; the inner process would be completely exhausted in its relationship to reality; the ego would not lift itself from this intertwining with reality which would accompany it [the ego] at every turn. This lifting, however, occurs when the will survives its contact with reality, because the latter cannot fulfill the former when the ego with its act of volition [*das wollende Ich*] still exists where reality is no longer. A harmonious, consistently contented relationship between will and reality would suck into itself ego consciousness and would make much less discernible the ego in its own proper course. The *No* and the *Too-little* of external reality vis-à-vis our will causes the will to have an effect far beyond its contact with reality so that the ego becomes conscious of itself in this situation, and

above all of the continuity which stems exclusively from its own impulses. [See also Appendix, v.]

Viewed under the energic aspect of psychoanalysis, this means that only the frustration of drives can furnish the energy with which to build an ego and only in the situation of frustration can an ego become conscious of itself. Simmel is perfectly right in interpolating this basic requirement of ego development in his discussion of death, since death is the ultimate and potential barrier to any act of volition which does not will death. Yet each act of frustration raises aggression in the infant's organism which is not yet regulated by an adaptable ego structure. That aggression is a necessary intermediary link in the chain of events leading to the formation of ego structure makes Simmel's remark so important in our discussion. The ego is apparently built by an infinite aggregate of frustrations; in this process that aggression which is raised by frustration is fused with the instinctual demand which has been frustrated. The two—the aroused libidinal energy and the aggression elicited by frustration—unite and probably neutralize each other. In this way a store of neutralized energy is built up which can be used for the formation of ego structure. This model can serve as an approximate visualization of some archaic ego defects encountered in patients whose early developmental phases were characterized either by excessive gratifications or excessive frustrations. In both instances there will be a relative lack of either one of the two energies, and therefore the process of neutralization must suffer, which in turn will make itself noticeable either in a weak or in a faulty ego structure. I am referring here to only one of the many prerequisites of ego formation (Hartmann, Kris, Loewenstein, 1946). Freud (1915b) when describing the metapsychology of that process which leads to the infant's discernment of internal

and external reality—one of the basic steps in ego formation—suggests as a central factor the difference in gratification and frustration which is produced by the same action
of the infant. In other words, when the stimulation originates within the infant, flight does not lead to reduction of
tension, but when the infant is exposed to external stimulation, flight will succeed.

In the aforementioned scheme we see how a drive is not
permitted to re-establish an earlier state, thus causing displeasure which in turn raises aggression. But aggression
against what? Not against the outer world since the latter
has not yet found representation in the infant. The aggression must be directed against the state of displeasure itself
which, however, is part of the infant. Actually we are
forced to assume that early aggressions—prior to the infant's discrimination of without and within—are self-
directed, a situation comparable to the dog's gnawing at
those parts of his skin which are anesthetized (von Uexküll,
1926). To all external appearances the infant when scream-
ing, fidgeting and kicking—that is to say, when angry—discharges energy which looks to the observer like an aggression against external reality. Yet when it is seriously
considered that this objectively existing reality has not yet
found representation in the infant's mind and that these
discharges evaporate into a psychologically self-contained
system, then it may become conceivable that in the infant
the mobilization of aggressive energy has a different effect
than it customarily has in the adult.

The emphasis I have put here on frustration as a driving
force toward early ego formation should not lead to an
underestimation of the possible role which pleasure plays
in ontogenetic development and which it possibly also has
played in phylogenesis. In considering Freud's theory,
which culminates in the statement that death was prior to
life, one may hypothetically add a factor which at certain

levels assisted the formation of ever higher structures, aside from the operation of external stimulation. Pleasure might have been a premium that lured life further and further away from its origin, when in the earliest structures of life the pleasure mechanism was barely evolved at all (Ferenczi, 1924). At least there is no indication that plants or unicellular organisms can experience pleasure or displeasure.

Such an interpretation of Freud's theory is also suggested by Schilder (1927) when he writes: "It is a basic immanent thought of psychoanalysis to regard the living organism as an unfolding [Ausfaltung] of the instinctual, if you will, as a symbol of the psyche." I believe I remember reading somewhere in Schilder an even more succinct formulation, namely that the libido creates its organs of discharge—an idea which, though it cannot be proved with present-day means of investigation, has its merits and also finds a place in biological tradition. Although Freud (1920a) rejected "a general impulse towards higher development" in the world of organisms, I believe one cannot refute offhand the construction that the libido, following a tendency to find new and more highly structured apparatuses of discharge, might have been effective as a propulsive evolutionary force. The assumption that a higher degree of differentiation also leads to a steeper or higher gradient of the course taken by libidinal genital processes seems well justified (Ford and Beach, 1951).

If a tendency toward greater pleasure should have held the place of an evolutionary motor concomitantly striving against the primary aim of the death instinct, this would make it even more understandable that the ego necessarily succumbs as soon as all potential avenues of pleasure gain are blocked. Thus constructions necessary at present in order to visualize the early steps of ego formation do not seem to contradict Freud's theory of the death instinct,

Furthermore, the psychopathology surrounding the castration complex and its ramifications in the male personality impress me as almost proving this theory.

XI

REMARKS UPON THE FEELING OF IDENTITY
AND MUTATION OF THE WORLD

In investigating the psychology of action, the observer's attention is usually occupied with the great variety of motives which form the internal incentives of actions as well as with the great variety of external stimuli and their patterns which by their bearing on the subject elicit actions. The interplay between external and internal stimuli, the result of which can be observed in actions, is indeed a fascinating problem.

However, we perhaps do not see that despite the great variety of actions taking place within an ever-changing external and internal milieu, two factors can be discovered which do not change but remain rigidly constant, namely the feeling of identity of self and the feeling of the identity of the world—the former being an index of the way the subject experiences itself and the latter being an index of the way the subject experiences reality.

There is a remarkable similarity in the structure of the two experiences. Although the subjective contents of the ego are constantly changing, nevertheless a factor remains unchanged, namely that barely describable core in which our self-identity rests, the feeling that whatever might happen to us something still remains the same in us, and that throughout all vicissitudes something in us cannot be changed—that the subject remains identical with itself

87

within the broad stream of sensations, perceptions, images, and actions which vary with each time moment.

Likewise, those sectors of reality with which the subject is in contact change constantly either by the subject's own activity or by other causes; nevertheless, the subject has the feeling that this everchanging world remains identical with itself. Strangely enough these changes—internal ones as well as external ones—are necessary in order to maintain the feeling of identity of self and of external reality. If the ego felt no change at all within itself, it speedily would have the feeling that it had lost its identity. *Mutatis mutandis,* this is also true of external reality. In order to facilitate communication, I want to speak of a mutation which occurs when reality appears so profoundly changed that the subject no longer experiences the world as identical with the world he had experienced before. Thus we distinguish changes well circumscribed and constantly occurring around us, which do not affect the identity of reality, and mutations which correspond with a changed identity of the world at large.

It is reasonable to inquire into the sources of the subject's feeling that the external reality remains identical with itself. In part this feeling may be suggested by certain reality factors. The world changes in accordance with the seasons and the hours of the day, changes which are quite considerable, but reality finds its way back again and again to an appearance which it has had at a previous time. The conclusion, then, seems justified that these changes have concerned only the outer layer of reality, that the inner structure of reality has persisted throughout the changes observable within the colorful and conspicuous stream of phenomena, and that therefore reality has remained identical.

Important as this and other external factors may be in contributing to man's feeling that the world remains identical, I do not believe that these external factors would suffice to evolve in man the feeling of the identity of reality. I would rather assume that the dawning feeling of one's own identity leads to the evolvement of the feeling that the external reality preserves its identity despite any action undertaken by man.

At least, in many instances one can observe that the subject's feeling that a mutation has occurred is preceded by a weakening of the feeling of the identity of self. I want to quote only one example which appears typical to me. Older people—almost regularly—complain that the times have changed, that the younger generation is essentially different, that the world is no longer what it used to be. These remarks—which indicate a threatening mutation rather than describe an extreme mutation—are rooted in the subject's inability to integrate the process of aging which takes place in himself. The subject increasingly encounters in himself phenomena in which he cannot recognize his own former ego. This gradual estrangement of his present ego from his former ego, the vast preference which the subject feels for this former ego, and his reluctance to accept or integrate his present ego lead to the feeling that the world has undergone a mutation. Prior to the onset of this aging process such reality changes are usually accepted as incentives for actions or for general adjustive processes but do not lead to the experience of a mutation.

In my estimation, the feeling of the identity of the world goes beyond recognizing the familiar or recognizing the familiar within the unfamiliar (wiedererkennen). Even in situations in which a subject is bewildered by the influx of entirely new perceptions, this does not necessarily affect the feeling that it is the same world which is encountered.

Likewise a subject does not need to recognize himself in his present condition in order to maintain the feeling of identity of self. The feeling of identity of self as well as the feeling of identity of reality are more fundamental than any cognitive process. A strange dichotomy is encountered here. It seems that the feeling of identity of the world is a necessary prerequisite for our daily operations or perhaps for action in general. If we had the feeling that the identity of the world could be discontinued by our actions and that after a particular action had been performed we would not meet the same world we had known before, we probably would not be able to carry out that action. When we act, we have the feeling that we act only upon a partial aspect of the world, one which does not affect the identity of the world as we know it.

This of course is quite contradictory to the finding of science that there is one total world which continuously changes, never remaining identical with itself from one moment to another.

Thus the feeling of the identity of the world becomes a frame of reference indispensible to action, a background which is almost always taken for granted and into which the single actions are woven—a firm and resting platform, so to speak, which we need as a starting point for our daily operations.

Quite possibly, in pathological conditions characterized by the patient's inability to act, such as in catatonia and severe obsessional neuroses, the patient has lost the feeling of the identity of the world and this may be one of the reasons why his capacity to act has been temporarily reduced to zero.

Be this as it may, there are situations—outside of the direct realm of psychopathology—in which the subject has the feeling of facing a world which has undergone a mutation. This happens usually when he has suddenly, and without previous warning, lost by death a person whom he has greatly loved. Then the world may definitely become one which is entirely and essentially different from what it has been before, with the feeling of the identity of the world abolished at least temporarily. It is noteworthy that this mutation is not produced by the projection of a change in the feeling of the identity of self but is enforced by an event in the external world. The death of love objects threatens the feeling of the identity of the world. Although this feeling may also issue from the sudden loss of property deemed indispensable to the owner, I still believe that there is a fundamental affinity between this type of mutation and death. Property can, in such instances, be shown to have been the substitute for a past love object.

The feeling that death has caused a mutation found a permanent and far-reaching expression in the Gospels. The whole Christian religion is based upon the conviction that the world before and after the Savior's Crucifixion was essentially different. Likewise religion quite effectively tries to heal the fracture line caused by the feeling of mutation in the bereaved person's ego; it promises a reunion with the deceased in a life after death.

In considering the place which the feeling of the identity of the world has in the human universe, we may also find a new characteristic of those events which have a traumatic effect upon man. It may be surmised that the effects of trauma in the life of the adult may be accounted for by the extent that they threaten or actually change the feeling of the identity of the world. Part of the neurotic symptomatology may serve the function of denying that the sense of the identity of the world has been lost and thus may establish a continuity where actually a discontinuity has occurred. Neurotic symptoms may serve, among other things, also to ascertain that the present and the past are identical.

Here we touch upon a fundamental issue in the political history of Western society in which the rate of societal change has acquired an acceleration incomparable to anything mankind has ever experienced before. It becomes increasingly difficult to maintain the feeling of the identity of the world. The resultant feeling of discontinuance is a source of threat and anxiety. The increasing appeal of conservatism and the consequent tendency toward the acceptance of a dictatorship—in whatever form—are also rooted in the tacit desire to put a brake upon a developmental speed which is beyond the power of integration at the disposal of the single individual. Yet this longing to ascertain that there is no discontinuance between present and past stems from man's struggle against the fear of death. The feeling that past and present are identical implies the unconscious conviction that this identity will extend also into the future. It is a consoling reassurance that the ego is protected against future annihilation. The necessity to believe in the identity of past and present seems to manifest itself acutely when man is permanently exposed to extreme danger.

Bruno Bettelheim (1943) reported the seemingly senseless concern of prisoners in concentration camps that nothing should be changed in their home environments. It seems that in a situation of greatest danger to their lives, the necessity arose to make sure that a sector of reality which was charged with intensive emotions did not change its identity. This sector seems to have served as a representation of the world at large and helped in devaluating the evidence brought forth by their immediate environment that reality had undergone a mutation.

It is also well known that most people feel the desire to visit the places at which they spent their early childhood. When such visits are made and it is discovered that these places have been considerably altered or even destroyed, a deep shock is felt. I know an instance of a man who had stood up well under the impact of his displacement to foreign countries and the partial loss of family, but who was struck by the full awareness of these events only when he returned to his place of birth and found it destroyed by war. Then and only then did he feel his world had really changed.

Thus it can be observed that in man a silent struggle is going on for continuous reassurance that the world remains identical. The strongest reassurance of course is provided when the ego can convince itself that the world of childhood has not perished but is still in existence. Then the fear of death can safely be dismissed.

I have stressed here a retarding, conservative factor which—within the sphere of action—is carried into man's life by his fear of death; yet it would be a one-sided approach if a factor which is almost the opposite were not equally emphasized.

The experience of a world altered by the death of an object intensely loved, the knowledge—conscious or unconscious—of the future destruction of one's own ego, the fracture lines which discontinue the identity of the world, all these factors demonstrate to the mind the extent to which the world can be changed. Here the imagery of death sets an intensive stimulus for action, and man desires to do actively what he has to suffer passively: the goal of creating a mutation of the world becomes his paramount ambition. Actually one can observe historically that the more man's belief in a life after death is weakened, the bolder his actions become. Science which more than any other doctrine has raised man's doubt of the existence of a soul, has simultaneously provided man with instruments capable of destroying and creating worlds almost at will. Man's orbit of action can be reduced to a minimum of self-preservation and even fall short of this minimum, or it can hypertrophy and then spread far beyond this small orbit to embrace the whole surface of the planet and penetrate into the existence of well-nigh each and every one of his fellow men. His self-preservation, then, may be likewise endangered by this hypertrophy of activity. Yet in each of these extremes the impact of the meaning which death has upon man can be sensed. Man's action seems to be extended between two poles: the maintenance of the identity of the world in order to evade death and the mutation of that identity in order to convert the prospect of pain into the presence of pleasure. If man's existence were not subject to death he possibly would become a completely inactive being.

XII

REMARKS UPON THE DEATH MASK OF BEETHOVEN

After having grappled with problems of death as a force intrinsic to the organism, a few remarks about the moment of dying may follow. Much has been written about the subject. The moment itself—for self-evident reasons—has inspired awe and stimulated imagination. I assume that most reports of quasi transfiguration or allied phenomena before death are of a legendary nature. Although most existing reports about the last moments of human life are embellishments necessitated by the beliefs of the writer or of posterity, it is conceivable that in the last hours of agony psychic processes occur which deserve investigation because of their uniqueness.

Research into the matter is made difficult at present since the mind of most dying patients is not lucid because of the dispensation of drugs. The only contribution I want to make to the matter concerns a remark about the variety of facial expressions of the dying or dead person. The expression of peaceful sleep seems to prevail. However, there exists one death mask which gives occasion for some deliberation. This is the mask of Beethoven. It is significantly different from any other death mask I have seen or any facial representation by sculpture or painting, for that matter. It would be wrong to describe it as an expression of pain, grief, sorrow, or agony, although all these factors may be involved to some extent. To my feeling, the face expresses a state in which pleasure or the possibility of pleasure or the hope for pleasure or the prospect of pleasure have irrevocably vanished; that is to say, it concerns the aforementioned state in which—as I think—death has to occur either by internal reasons or by suicide. If the human face in the moment of death should show terror, fright, anxiety, disgust, despair, or suffering, this would not reach the stage which I have in mind and which I think took on manifest expression in Beethoven's death mask. All these emotions, insufferable and void of pleasure as they may be, do not belie potential pleasure in the future. If they occur with great intensity, they may burden the psychic apparatus beyond endurance and lead to death; but then the psychic apparatus has proved itself to be too weak and death is inflicted by infirmity. The expression on Beethoven's death mask is incommensurable with any question of strength or weakness; it expresses a state incompatible with existence.

Some have tried to explain this expression by means of the effect which the autopsy had upon the face. I repudiate such an explanation, but understand well that the interpreter felt compelled to search for an explanation beyond the realm of psychic life, since he had never seen such a face before. Although in Occidental culture the attempt has been made innumerable times, it is remarkable that no sculptor or painter has ever succeeded in creating this facial expression.

Faces showing Christ or various martyrs before, during, and after death have been sculptured and painted by the greatest artists, with sublime artistic accomplishment and with intense religious devotion, but in all these artistic reproductions which I know, there is always a libidinous factor recognizable. Notwithstanding its superb artistic portrayal, when the expression of extreme suffering is presented in art, it shows—to my feeling—the admixture of masochism. Beethoven's death mask is free of this admixture; life has become utterly depleted of libido; there is no more pain or grief or despair in this face but only something for which no language has a term because it is outside human life. Immersing one's mind in the sight of the mask, one obtains the impression that the view of this sculpture makes it unnecessary ever to look at any other sculpture of a human face, since the ultimate of what can be said about man has been put here into a visible form. This impression may be of interest in view of the lengthy disputations regarding nature and art in aesthetics. In the sight of the mask one is inclined to admit the superiority of nature above anything man can create. (Then too, no artist could ever create such a mask because it is utterly impossible for the living to identify with such a state.) As long as man can suffer he can suffer only by activating the ever-present store of masochism; that is to say, automatically libido is mobilized. The fact that only in Beethoven has the human face reached a stage which—as far as it can be documented—no other human being has ever attained must be explained by those who know the intricacies of his biography and of his creations. It seems to me that in the latter he reached that limit of a dimension at which human life is still feasible, and therefore it would be understandable that in his own life he also reached a limit at which, under average conditions, human life is prone to collapse. The other outstanding feature of the death mask is its utter freedom from any trace of love or hatred. Love and hatred are indices of relations between the person and the world. But for this face the world has vanished. An inner force, unrelated to any sector of the outer world, has taken possession of man. What the medieval world vainly tried to express by the symbolism of the skull has here taken on factual form. It is the incarnation of death. Possibly a future epoch psychologically more gifted than

ours will be able to discover in this mask a proof that the
death instinct is a psychobiological reality.

I felt more sure of my interpretation of Beethoven's
death mask after I came across the following paragraph
(Sullivan, 1927):

> Beethoven's work will live because of the permanent
> value, to the human race, of the experiences it com-
> municates. These experiences are valuable because
> they are in the line of human development; they are
> experiences to which the race, in its evolutionary
> march, aspires. . . . The great artist achieves a relative
> immortality because the experiences he deals with are
> as fundamental for humanity as are hunger, sex, and
> the succession of day and night. It does not follow
> that the experiences he communicates are elementary.
> They may belong to an order of consciousness that
> very few men have attained, but, in that case, they
> must be in the line of human development; we must
> feel them as prophetic. Beethoven's late music com-
> municates experiences that very few people can nor-
> mally possess. . . . They correspond to a spiritual syn-
> thesis which the race has not achieved but which, we
> may suppose, it is on the way to achieving.

This aspect of Beethoven's work reverberates also in the
expression of his death mask, which is beyond the border-
line of empathy.

It is worth while to add what Beethoven's great prede-
cessor said regarding the way he felt about death. When he
was informed of his father's last illness, Mozart wrote to
his father (April 4, 1787):

> Since death (properly understood) is the true ulti-
> mate purpose of our life, I have for several years past
> made myself acquainted with this truest and best
> friend of mankind so that he has for me not only
> nothing terrifying anymore but much that is tran-
> quilizing and consoling!

And I thank my God that He has bestowed on me the good fortune to provide the opportunity (you understand me) of recognizing death as the *key* to our true blessedness.

I never lie down in my bed without reflecting that perhaps I (young as I am) shall never see another day; yet none of all who know me can say that I am socially melancholy or morose. For this blessing I daily thank my Creator and wish it from my heart for all my fellow-men.

[Quoted by Turner, 1938.]

If this was Mozart's true attitude toward death, then one feels inclined to speculate that it was the very opposite of what I believe can be read as the last message which Beethoven left to the world in the mask of his dead countenance.

XIII

DEATH AND SELF-PRESERVATION

In a discussion focusing upon the psychology of death one cannot avoid the introduction of the collective factor, which holds an essentially different place here than in the psychology of love. Whereas with the establishment of an ego, man in present Occidental society takes over full responsibility for the selection of his love objects and their care and the way of gratification of his libidinal desires, his struggle against death has for a long time been taken out of his hands. This process has been accelerated through the modernization of society and will probably continue to an unpredictable degree. Man is no longer responsible for his safety. Society has evolved specialized institutions for that function, and when man is endangered or threatened by annihilation, a simple appeal to the proper institution ought to re-establish the former equilibrium of security. This surrender of self-preservative functions to society has reached in our times an extent which even the recent past would have considered unbelievable. In practical terms this means that any adult can stop at any time the fulfillment of those obligations which he carries in terms of the preservation of self. Society will fill out the gap he has created and replace this deficit.

It was inevitable that such a development would leave a deep effect upon the personality of modern man. This can be best discussed in the context of man's struggle against disease. In primordial times society had evolved specialized institutions for this function in the form of the medicine man, and it may be that there has never been a period when individual man felt fully responsible for his body. Be this as it may, the medicine man of primordial times and a modern physician can be taken as two extremes of techniques which had an identical purpose, namely, to restore health, that is to say to establish the states of freedom from physical discomfort and of unencumbered functions. If we disregard the physical aspect of the two techniques and limit ourselves to a psychological consideration, we shall—I think—see as the greatest difference the degree of participation to which the ego of the primordial patient was drawn into the therapeutic process in contrast with the relative or even complete lack of participation of the modern patient in the identical situation (Ernst Simmel, 1926). It is perhaps permissible to say that the primordial patient could not be cured against his will. The primordial physician had to infuse the patient's ego with stimuli which incited the therapeutic processes. Modern medicine has reached the point where therapeutics are developed with such refinement and therefore are so precisely tuned to the disturbed biological process, that the patient's personality can be totally excluded from the therapeutic process. There are, of course, still areas where the modern physician inadvertently follows the footsteps of his primordial colleague. As an illustrative example, the treatment of peptic ulcers can best be quoted. Morton Gill (1947) has shown impressively that well-nigh any therapeutic measure—even injections of water—has a curative effect on that disease as soon as the patient evolves faith in the treatment, but that even the best expert treatment is of no avail if it does not elicit in the patient this belief. One may, therefore, conclude, as some have done—what will be anathema for any decent internist—that the dietary measures centering upon the ingestion of milk had their beneficial effect because of their accidental coincidence with widespread fantasies most people have about this liquid—a liquid to which, after all, every human being believes he owes his life.

But this state of affairs is exceptional, only an isolated instance among the biological methods which modern medicine has evolved almost to perfection. Yet in view of this perfection one would expect contemporary man to rejoice; cheerfulness and a new *joie de vivre* ought to seize the human species since freedom from one of the greatest fears our ancestors knew ought to liberate untapped forces. Yet the psychiatrist notices quickly that all that modern medicine has achieved is to make it more difficult for man to die, whereas man's preoccupation with his body, his worry about disease have not decreased; it may even have been augmented. Thus disease plays, if possible, an even greater role in contemporary society than previously and this, no doubt, is a paradoxical effect which no one foreseeing the recent progress of medicine would have dared to predict. Yet man seems to be vaguely aware of the destructive forces which are latent and ever ready to spread in his organism, and all the assurances he can obtain from the study of recent life and death statistics are brought to naught by the immutable place which sickness holds in human life.

The meaning of organic disease has not yet been deciphered. It seems to be a necessity in the human world. While it is tempting to link this necessity of the human organism to become sick with the assumption of a death instinct, yet sickness gives so often a new lease on life that this argument loses much of its initial impressiveness. Ehrenberg (1923) has shown that the potential of life is often greater after a disease than before. Diseases do not always bring the organism closer to death but instead may postpone the final event, as the simple fact of acquired immunity shows. The effect of disease upon man's creativity is indisputable; Thomas Mann in his *Magic Mountain* has given lasting form to the idea that a disease may lead to the enrichment of life.. Disease per se may apparently serve both life and death. Perhaps the ultimate function of disease is to give the death instinct a temporary discharge, so that life may resurge unencumbered. Possibly man would die far earlier than he does if no place were provided for disease. Perhaps we should look at disease as catastrophic-like events of regeneration comparable to revolutions, which are also indispensable complications to societal development despite the aversion most people feel for them. But, just as in the course of a revolution the whole state may be destroyed by a process meant to rejuvenate it, sickness also may destroy the whole organism although its original function might have been only to give the organism a new lease on life.

XIV

REMARKS UPON DEATH AS A PSYCHOLOG-
ICALLY DETERMINED EVENT

The aforementioned historical process of the ego's increasing surrender of self-preservative functions to social
institutions is a process which the ego does not select but
to which it must submit automatically and which goes on
relentlessly, possibly leading to an undermining and final
destruction of society. This process, I believe, has also had
its impact upon the prevailing conceptions of death. Since
institutions outside of the ego are held responsible for the
preservation of the individual, a total collapse of the functions of self-preservation, such as in death, could not be
viewed as an event which is rooted in the individual's personality. Thus death comes to be accepted as a psychological event only in case of suicide. However, I wish to
postulate tentatively the assumption that death—in whatever shape or form it may appear—is always a psychological
event, growing out of the individual's total life history and
the ultimate result of his individuality. I am well acquainted with all the arguments which can be raised
against this extreme position of psychic determinism. What
can possibly be the connection between a given life history
and the chance unloosening of a screw in a passing car,
which skids and causes instantaneous death to the pedes-
trian? Thousands and thousands of well-documented instances can be adduced which prove beyond a doubt that
the delay of a few seconds, a step to the right or left, might

have prevented death. Indeed, when man-made death may reach hundred thousands of people in a few seconds or when millions of people may die in a short time because of epidemics, inundations or earthquakes, it seems preposterous to postulate that in these instances each person who perished was individually in a state out of which his ultimate fate was born—that death was the organic conclusion of each life history rather than an inorganic event, foreign to the various psychological states of these people at the time of catastrophe, carried accidentally by a supra-individual, unselective force into their lives. In view of the record of history, my assumption must be declared to be the silly misapplication of the otherwise correct principle of psychic determinism. It may be feasible—it will be said—that future science will prove that the principle of psychic determinism is applicable to all those instances where the fatal conclusion occurred in the direct context of the individual life. It may be feasible that death by organic disease always grows out of a total life history, that accidents with personal involvement, such as the fatal fall of the mountain climber, may be always the effect of an unconscious actively engaged in the preparation of the lethal end, but to claim the same principle for the occurrence of mass death and of accidents utterly divorced from any thinkable unconscious involvement must amount to the introduction of mystery into the psychology of death or the resurgence of a religious dogma which was so touchingly expressed in the simile of no sparrow's falling to the ground against the Father's will.

Despite these self-evident and therefore very convincing arguments, I suggest that a final conclusion not be drawn before the matter has been examined by reliable research. Common sense—and all arguments I have enumerated are of such nature—has been disappointed by science in matters of even greater self-evidence. The question is still moot. It has not been investigated. At present one can only speculate about it. The arguments against the assumption appear irrefutable and those for it rather negligible. But despite man's frailty, his easy vulnerability and his innate infirmity vis-à-vis cosmic forces, organic nature, and the organized destructiveness and hostility of his contemporaries and of the society in which he has to live, man still might be the master of his destiny without knowing that he is. There is still the faint possibility that man could die only when the inherent forces of life have lived out their potential or when an inner complication forces the ego to turn the balance in favor of the ever-ready forces of internal destruction. With unending monotony we observe, whenever we study clinically the biographies of the living, that the responsibility for their hardships, their successes, their pains and joys, their failures and triumphs rests ultimately somewhere in the interplay of various psychobiological forces which we call the human person, and that whenever reality has seemed to impede the unfolding of personality for a long time, this happened by concealed co-operation of the person thus harmed: should we then, just in conjunction with the most decisive, final, and ultimate event of death, assume an exception and say this one sometimes depends entirely on forces alien to the human person and sometimes occurs, at any instant, irrespective of what man has been or is or still could be in the future? Possibly life and death are organized in this way, but before we commit ourselves one way or the other, it should be clear that either point of view is now the outcome of prejudice since science has as yet kept aloof from the psychology of death. However, it scarcely seems possible, in such matters which touch upon our most personal sentiments, to suspend judgment as wise men so often do when empirical investigation has not yet unearthed the facts upon which to base rational judgment. I wonder to what extent it may be necessary for the evolvement of a true psychology of death to base such a psychology axiomatically upon the supposition that death in man is always the end product of his total life history and can never occur unrelated to the dynamic constellation within the personality (Wilder, 1937); that is to say, what appears to the naked eye as the accident, the physical effect of which ends life, is only the proximate cause which is embedded as a precipitating factor in the broad stream of the vicissitudes of the death instinct. The death instinct and the strength of the counteracting institutions would then decide upon the final effect.

I want to quote an example of how in the face of death it may dawn upon a mind that this death is embedded in the dying person's stream of the unconscious and belongs to him in a personal way (Poelchau, 1949). Before he was executed by the Nazis, Dr. John Rittmeister, neurologist and psychiatrist, wrote in his last letter to his wife:

> Is not perhaps this kind of life's end the right one, desired, and aimed at by the unconscious—I who already at the age of fifteen was heavily impressed by Giordano Bruno's destiny and dying? My life also was a struggle to find truth, meaning and an idea, before anything else. . . . [See also Appendix, vi.]

XV

DEATH AND THE MASSES

This theory may appear less offensive to the demands of common-sense thinking when it is applied to man's encounter with death in certain historical constellations. The individual's co-operation with or resistance to the course of history has been little studied, and the historical record reports only the effect resulting from myriads of individual actions. But how these individual actions fit into the general historical event is, I believe, not known. In the context of this introduction, those historical periods are of particular interest in the course of which the sentiment of impending death becomes universal and seems to be integrated by nearly every member of society. Comparable to the superstitious beliefs of compulsive patients, the conception of the millenium has great bearing upon Occidental society. When the first millenium after the birth of Christ approached its end, Occidental man was seized by the fear of and the hope for the Lord's return. The end of the world was envisaged, which meant man's final end had arrived. With the approach of the end of the second millenium the conviction again has spread that the days of man are counted, and that this time his end will be prepared by his own ingenuity. If one compares the present idea with the sentiments prevailing in Occidental man a millenium earlier, he must concede that the fear of the atom bomb—rational and realistic as it may be—is nevertheless also a rationalization. With a clocklike punctuality, almost predictable, the same fear has recurred at a time which coincides with Occidental number mystics. Apparently societies are seized periodically by a universal fear of mass death. Are the individual actors, then, on the stage of history particularly prone to die? Do we become infected by the historical emotional climate even in the deepest layers of our personalities? Again science is silent and we can only resort to suppositions and assumptions.

One cannot leave the challenging subject of the illusion, fantasy or imagery of impending mass or societal death without thinking of one of the most surprising and puzzling mass phenomena, namely the well-documented self-destructive tendency of masses. Although this phenomenon belongs to the study of history and sociology, nevertheless it may find its rightful place in this context since notwithstanding the arguments which can be raised against the thesis, it may be stated that this self-destruction issues from an accumulation of personal individual tendencies among the members of society.

The most striking symbolization which the self-destructive tendency of whole societies found in Occidental imagery is that of Cassandra, who correctly predicted that Troy would fall if the Trojans acceded to their impulses but who nevertheless was overruled and even held to be demented. In contrast to Greek mythology, Christ had to be betrayed and crucified Himself in order to fulfill the predictions of the prophets.

It is wiser to return to the myth of Cassandra, which is better suited to a discussion of the reality of mass psychology than is Christian eschatology. The myth tells that despite Cassandra's sensible reasoning the more or less undifferentiated mass, under the guidance of unscrupulous leaders, threw its weight onto the scale of error and misjudgment, a fatal mistake repeated over and over again in the course of history but with particular frequency, if I am not mistaken, in that of the Occidental community.

Strangely enough, the history of the masses shows the sway of the death instinct with particular clarity and obtrusiveness. I wonder whether those who so urgently clamor for direct clinical evidence of this instinct possibly would be satisfied if they were faced with the facts of mass behavior collected and presented under this aspect. Quite possibly they would object that the various members of the mass are compelled to act without possessing insight into a highly complex situation, that therefore they are forced to follow the highest bidder, who usually is the most unscrupulous leader. What the members of the mass want is power of the collectivity with its ensuing security and also gratification of their own needs. If the decisions of the day were to be made rationally, each member would have to devote his time to the accumulation of so much knowledge that the societal process per se would have to stop. Also it will be said that societal decisions of historical consequences cannot be rationally made at all because there is no science of history available in the sense that the natural sciences permit predictions based on empiricism.

It may be said that every person—whether irrationally motivated when acting under the full sway of mass sentiments or rationally motivated when basing his decision upon the study of facts—has to proceed upon prejudices, the only difference being that this is quite openly done and easily accessible to observation in one instance and discernible only after some inquiry in the other. Mankind has not yet found a frame of reference on the basis of which the probable effect of specific measures can be predicted. Therefore, the choice of measures is an area in which the effect of instinctual processes can be observed.

Whenever science has succeeded in discovering the probable effect of actions, and such discovery has been integrated into behavior, an instinctual process becomes concealed. The latter may continue, but it has vanished from direct observation. This, by the way, is one of the reasons why so many of Freud's discoveries can be observed directly in societies in which science has only a limited bearing on behavior.

But, the reasoning will be, is there no other alternative than that between instinctual and scientific behavior? Of course there is, but behavior based on science is different from any other alternative by the very fact that whatever the motivation for scientific behavior may be and whatever instinctual forces may be discharged in it, the latter cannot be recognized in the behavior pattern per se, whereas in all other behavior patterns the instinctual factor is— to a larger or smaller degree—discernible. If we consider now the directions mass behavior may take, the self-evident statement can be made that by chance mass behavior may coincide with that which science—if such existed—would suggest. In other words, when relying on instinctual impulses the ego depends primarily on the nature of these instincts which prevail in the final formation of actions. Since mass action has so often led to self-destruction, I believe that despite the desire to have power, security, and gratification simultaneously, man's self-destructive desires are strongly at work in mass behavior. It is quite surprising to learn from history how often just those who would have been excellent leaders are rejected (Irving Stone, 1943), and how stubbornly those who mean well are despised by aggregates of people under the domination of mass sentiment.

It is worth while to quote here a sentence of Trotter's famous treatise (1919):

We seem almost forced to accept the dreadful hypothesis that in the very structure and substance of all human constructive social efforts there is embodied a principle of death. . . .

Trotter added this statement to his original treatise probably under the impression of Freud's thanatology. It seems that the libidinal distribution which takes place in the individual person when he becomes a mass member is particularly dangerous in terms of the release of self-destructive energies. The great libidinal gratification which the mass situation provides, the regression, the reduction of the personal superego (Freud, 1921), and the apparent defusion of instinctual energies ensuing from those factors all seem to create a dynamic situation which is particularly liable to endanger the individual and concomitantly also the mass of which he is a member. In accordance with Freud's theory these are situations where usually untapped stores of the instinct may be released in the form of aggression directed either against all that which is not part and parcel of the mass itself or against the mass itself. This quick interchange or even coincidence of aggression toward the mass-alien on one hand and self-destruction on the other gives renewed evidence of Freud's postulate that aggression against the external world is converted self-destruction. When such problems have become accessible to research, psychiatry will make contributions equivalent to those biology has made, and this part of science will become an equally important adjunct to mankind's fight against death. Yet much time must pass until rational investigation can reach these deeply buried forces which decide man's destiny.

XVI

ON A POSSIBLE EFFECT OF MODERN MEDICINE UPON ARTISTIC CREATION

In returning to individual life I want to mention a problem closer at hand and more promising in terms of the research possible at the present. The biological methods of prolonging life have reached such a point of excellence that not only can death by "accidental" infection be avoided but even death by a disease which is deeply rooted in the biological structure and possibly preformed in the early stages of the developing organism. In our days I think it has happened for the first time in history that a great writer and artist was saved from death which had threatened from the very matrix of the organic substructure (Mann, 1949). As so many sensitive artists are, Thomas Mann was aware of the time when his life was to end since the disease was not of an "accidental" nature but well rooted in his life structure. But this foreboding of impending death, correct as it was since it came from life's deepest sources, was nevertheless deceptive since medicine had learned in the meantime to combat even such sinister dangers; thus we can witness what a great man will create at a time which is actually beyond the point he was biologically destined to live. Questions which often have been asked arise again, such as what music Mozart or Beethoven might have created had they lived longer. It was said that both had reached the creative pinnacle. But if Goethe had died after having written *Werther,* we

113

also would surmise that this early creation of a genius could not have been excelled by any subsequent creations; what we probably would have overlooked is that after a genius has exhausted one style or a medium of expression he creates new ones, employing them in their turn until he has realized the potential inherent in them. But what happens to the genius when the psychobiological matrix of his existence is artificially changed, when the moment of death predestined by the psychobiological structure is artificially postponed? Can he give form only to those stragglers which had fallen aside earlier when the creative impulse rushed along and the writing hand could not keep up with the speed of the creative mind, or does he form out of this artificially gained, unforeseen time a new creation, which surpasses everything he had created before? The literary document in which Thomas Mann reported upon his silent struggle with death—possibly the first fruit we owe to the life-saving operation—would give an occasion to debate some of the problems involved in man's recently acquired ability to postpone death. If the operation had not taken place, Thomas Mann would still have lived for an undetermined period of time. I assume he would have ended the novel of *Doktor Faustus* under all circumstances. But who would dare speculate whether this creation would have been more, or less, magnificent than it is if it had been written to the end under the agony of impending death? Would there have been time and concentration left to write his report upon the writing of *Doktor Faustus* or something equivalent to it? The report (Mann, 1949) as it stands now is in parts a magnificent work, moving at times—in my estimation—to the heights of Tolstoy's "The Death of Ivan Ilyitch." Yet the tragic height of the work is suddenly interrupted when the author reaches the point where he is admitted to a modern hospital. Then the mystery of death vanishes under the impact of the array of technological paraphernalia. The immensity of death which pervades the preceding pages is suddenly reduced to the dimension of a simple industrial process. The tension differential between the two parts symbolizes very well what might happen to great art when the reality of death is conjured away by the reassurances of scientific therapy.

XVII

PROBLEMS OF EUTHANASIA

I must apologize for the many digressions into the unknown which forced me to relinquish at times the scientific attitude and to come dangerously close to a belletristic approach, but the psychology of death is of such importance and so direly neglected that I could not resist the temptation to bustle about among the many, as yet unsolved, problems. In returning to the more sober clinical aspect of the question, one encounters, of course, the grave problem of euthanasia. As is well known, euthanasia is legally forbidden and its practitioners prosecuted—as far as I know—in all countries which pretend to follow the principles of the Old and New Testaments. With the development of modern pharmaceutics it was inevitable that euthanasia should come to be practiced to a very large extent without being detected. How widespread it is I do not know, but I believe euthanasia is far more common than most people know, and more common than those who do know admit.

Euthanasia is forbidden in our society on the grounds that there is a prohibition against killing, which principle—we are told—must be upheld because it is part and parcel of the Decalogue revealed to mankind by Divine Grace. As Jahoda (1948) points out, and I believe quite rightly: "the prohibition of the Decalogue: 'Thou shalt not kill' represents—like any penal law—nothing but an objective state of affairs which becomes a crime only when

116

it is realized by the individual against the law and with evil intent." Jahoda continues that human life per se is not considered inviolable in the Old Testament since in quick succession to the Decalogue the lawgiver demands capital punishment for actions which are considered by present society as no crime at all, such as cursing one's parents, or considered as crimes of minor gravity, such as homosexuality. A study of the Old and New Testaments would not, I believe, unearth any convincing argument against a law which would permit a physician to shorten the suffering of a fatally sick patient. Most arguments against euthanasia, such as the assertion that the physician can never be certain of the fatal nature of the patient's disease, are spurious; the rate of error would compare favorably with those instances in which judicial power errs by sending to the gallows those who are not responsible for their crimes. Also the argument of possible abuse is spurious since any law may be abused, and it is up to the lawgiver and the law-enforcing agencies to protect society against the abuse of existing law. If euthanasia is really against the Christian doctrine, then—I must conclude— capital punishment is also. It is an arbitrary and illogical decision to take one person's life against his will but to deny death to another when it would become a privilege and a relief. I would go so far as to say that even if the theologians could proffer better proofs than they do at present for the divine source of the Decalogue and for the sinfulness of euthanasia, a physician would—under present conditions—have to burden himself out of Christian charity with the sin of euthanasia. A deity which permits human beings to be exposed to such awful sufferings as are caused by some diseases must be called unjust in forbidding man's charitable impulse to curtail such sufferings, and it is feasible that man's sense of justice and charity compels him to offend the will of the Divinity.

Actually some of those physicians who uncompromisingly deny patients the beneficence of euthanasia are not superior to their contemporaries in their general ethics, and it is quite possible that this moral stringency is often a concealed manifestation of their sadism. I hasten to add that this is by no means meant as a rule and that in turn one definitely can find among physicians practicing euthanasia fantasies of omnipotence and a deep-seated ambivalence. Euthanasia is not always born out of charity but may mean to the physician's unconscious the gratification of a murderous impulse.

However strongly I am convinced that euthanasia is not an offense against ethics as they practically prevail in contemporary society and that it is not incompatible with Christian ethics when the content of the whole Bible is considered, I believe nevertheless that the tendency of modern ethics may go contrary to the acceptance of euthanasia. In other words, in the course of the nineteenth and twentieth centuries some sublime thinkers have evolved thoughts which go beyond the ethical content of the Bible, and it is conceivable that Occidental society after having passed through the throes of the present crisis may evolve —on the very basis of the works of these thinkers—an ethical system which will succeed better in the pacification of human aggression than either the Old or the New Testament has evidently been able to do. According to these new ethics, human life may become really the *summum bonum*—which it definitely is not in the two Testaments— protected against any interference for whatever reasons and under whatever circumstances. Then, of course, euthanasia would become inacceptable and unethical. But these new ethics would not only protect human life, in whatever forms it should appear, against any kind of destruction; they would make the freedom from suffering, unless voluntarily submitted to by the sufferer, an equally binding ethical demand.

Psychiatry—in my opinion—contains the seed for just such a technique. It is conceivable that through the establishment of transference, through an approach which mobilizes the archaic trust in the world and reawakens the primordial feeling of being protected by a mother, the suffering of the dying can be reduced to a minimum even in case of extreme physical pain. Here the psychiatrist would take over directly the function of the priest or the minister and simultaneously prove the superiority of psychiatry over the religious approach, which comes to a quick end when man has lost his faith in God. No doubt, here is a situation where he will be glad to find sincere religious feelings in the patient, since they usually facilitate the farewell from this world unless the primitive fear of fire and brimstone sheds pain even on these last moments. In view of the difficulty of the task of attending psychiatrically the dying, and in view of our ignorance about the psychology of death, the psychiatrist will gladly give way to the man of God whenever the latter can reduce mental pain on the deathbed, but in view of the increasing reduction of true religious sentiments in Occidental man, the frequency of a demand for the psychiatrist during the terminal pathway will grow.

The man of God is in real difficulty when the dying man declares that he does not believe; he can only repeat arguments which every member of Occidental society has listened to innumerable times, hoping that the fear of death, latently or manifestly present in all of us, will make his mind more pliable to the improbable during the last hours of his existence. Scarcely anything impresses us more as a denial of and distrust in the alleged kindness of God than the last-minute attempts of some church representatives to win dying patients over to the side of their brand of dogma.

The psychiatrist will support the religious feeling when present and will not try to impose his personal type of conviction. He will primarily heed the patient's individuality, adapting his procedure to the patient's past and tuning it to the potentialities still resting in him. Thus one could say that the psychiatrist possesses potentially a variety of procedures—limited only by the variety of individualities.

When the psychiatrist approaches a new problem, he can be sure he will find stimulation and answers in the field of literary arts. Let me quote a passage by Gottfried Keller in order to give an example of psychiatric euthanasia:

> Once the little ten-year-old son of a neighbor was incurably ill with lingering sickness and neither the minister's admonition nor that of the parents had succeeded in consoling the child in his pains and fear of death, since he would have liked so much to live. Calmly smoking his pipe, Landolt sat down at the [boy's] bed and spoke to him in such simple and suitable words of the hopelessness of his situation, of the necessity to resign himself and to suffer for a short while, but also of the gentle deliverance by death and the blissful, changeless repose which is allotted to him as a patient and God-fearing little boy, and of the love and sympathy which he, a stranger, held for him, that the child changed from this hour on and bore his pains in serene patience until he really was delivered by death. [See also Appendix, vii.]

There is no need to evaluate this technique from the psychiatric viewpoint. It is one of the many possibilities that exist. If it were applied in reality it would show much courage on the side of the psychiatrist.

The question which must be discussed here is whether psychiatry will be able to live up to the requirements of the new ethics which I have previously envisaged and, if so, why so little has been done in the past. The answer is sad and simple. In thinking and acting man follows the law of inertia or the pathway of least resistance. As long as we accept techniques requiring little effort but producing quickly the semblance of a solution, man in general just does not rise above the occasion but follows custom, unsatisfactory as the quality of the end result may be. A new materialism, in the reprehensible meaning of the term, holds psychiatry at present in its sway. For example, as long as shock treatment and surgery are permitted to be used in the treatment of schizophrenics, almost no psychiatrist will undergo the burdensome task of struggling with the patient's mind for its recovery. As long as the prison is available as the final domicile of the delinquent and the criminal, why should society provide means of reorganizing the personality of the lawbreaker?

As long as an injection can discontinue the patient's sufferings and thus assure a peaceful death in unconsciousness, why should one make the dreadful, cumbersome, and risky detour of providing the patient's mind with a mental solution which will help him rise above the frailty of his physical condition?

The new ethics as I envisage them will not know the prison and will take exception to the present pessimistic view that social behavior can be enforced only under the threat of pain and isolation; it will concede physical interference with the human brain—this most exquisite gift of nature—only when pathology is demonstrable; it will permit the agonized mind to become drowned in narcotics only when it has exhausted its vast store of mental and emotional solutions. The new ethics will have to overcome the lure of the sham solutions which require almost no effort at all. This, however, concerns mainly the societal aspect of the problem. In the meantime those who are re-

pelled by the present routine solutions and are striving
toward individual solutions of individual conflicts must
work—within the small islands of their activities—at least
for an approximation toward those techniques which later
on may be evolved to that degree of precision and efficiency
which might facilitate their general acceptance in the
future.

PART TWO

Three Case Histories

INTRODUCTION

While the following three clinical reports do not live up to the aim set forth in the preceding essays and do not, perhaps, present the reader with much which he did not know before, they should serve to illustrate the clinical fact—which, as far as I know, is not disputed by anyone—that the psychiatrist has his rightful place at the side of the deathbed. In all three reports the subject matter will be the history of the respective patient as well as the question of how his mental sufferings may be reduced by psychiatric techniques.

Yet in each report special aspects will also be emphasized. Case One is interesting because here it so happened that the psychiatrist could make an important contribution to the physical treatment. In Case Two the psychiatrist's contribution to the dying patient's environment will be discussed. In Case Three the dangers to the psychiatrist himself when dealing with a dying patient will be emphasized.

All three reports are concerned with quite unusual situations. A psychoanalyst whose judgment I value once said that the unusualness of the case is almost always the reflection of a disturbance in the analyst. In the instances here I plead exception. The mere fact that the psychiatric treatment concerned dying patients makes the unusual unavoidable.

Although my contacts with all three patients—if measured by the intensity of the psychoanalytic treatment—

must be called superficial, the outline of a technique which possibly may find frequent application could be seen. I believe that the technique of the treatment of the dying patient must center around what I want to call "the gift situation." The psychiatrist must create at the proper time the correct situation in which to give the right gift. Since physicians in our society are not expected to make presents to their patients, such an act is considered by the patient as an unusual and unmerited favor of destiny (Perroux, 1954). Of course, the gift can have a beneficial effect only if it occurs at a time when it is experienced by the patient as a symbol, that is to say, when he has formed a strong positive transference. The particular exigencies of the technique require the most strict avoidance of any admixture of negative transference in the patient's relationship to the psychiatrist, but without these negative feelings being directed against others. The patient must obtain from the beginning of contact the impression that he can rely totally on the psychiatrist and that there are no limitations to the extent to which the psychiatrist will go in order to assist him. Also, the psychiatrist must not wait until the patient verbalizes his wishes but must fulfill them unexpectedly and to the patient's surprise. To a certain extent the patient must learn that the psychiatrist knows better what the patient wishes than the patient himself. Then the gift will be experienced by the patient as the physician's giving him part of his own life, and the dreadful stigma of being selected for death while life continues outside will be converted into a dying together (Jones, 1911, 1912), greatly reducing the sting of death or transforming it into an impending rebirth which may convert the reality of death into its opposite.

At all times the need of psychic assistance to the dying has been recognized, and society has usually assigned this function to the one who had the right of serving as an intermediary between man and a deity. If the psychiatrist should take over this function in those instances in which the priest or minister is unable to fulfill the task, he would continue—from the historical point of view—what has been accomplished previously by others. However, it would become necessary to evolve for the psychiatrist a frame of reference since the frame of reference of his predecessors is not usable by him.

CASE ONE

The mother of a patient of mine asked to be permitted to see me from time to time after her son had left treatment. She claimed she was in no need of any psychiatric treatment but was searching for the opportunity of conversing occasionally with an "intelligent person." Since it was my impression that she was in reality in need of advice and guidance, I accepted her proposition.

She was in her late fifties, mother of three sons and with three grandchildren. She had been born in England and married to an uncongenial husband given to chronic alcoholic abuse. She was a type of woman who is encountered less frequently as time goes on but whom it is always delightful to meet. Victorian at heart, she nevertheless had preserved enough independence to be critical of her own philosophy of life without, of course, being able or willing to change it fundamentally. Of sharp intelligence, she combined good literary tastes with wit and appreciation of witticism. The foremost motivation of her actions was the fulfillment of her duties which she extended far beyond the socially necessary and which had led to a painful curtailment of her own pleasures. Her life lacked those pleasures most of us expect to gain in life.

She had been brought up by a rather unsophisticated or, better, uncultured mother, who had made her, her father's and her siblings' lives a real hell. Suppressed in her individuality, ungratified in her affection for her father, and forced to live up to the arbitrary standards of a sadistic

128

mother, this woman's immigration brought her welcome relief. Yet quite in keeping with well-known facts of psychopathology, she had married a man who was the opposite of her own character and who provided her essentially with the continuation of her earlier experiences. She had never loved this man but was deeply moved when he expressed his affection since—as she claimed—no one had ever before told her of feeling love for her. When, after the engagement, she met a man for whom she felt love and who responded affectionately, she nevertheless thought it to be her duty to marry her fiancé, fully aware that he was utterly incompatible. Thus having children, attending them, caring for them became the mainstay of her existence. Indeed she was proud of them, enjoyed their successes and bemoaned their failures. She never demanded anything but was ready to go to extremes in her assistance to them. Gardening and Dickens' novels were her other sources of pleasure, which occupied her increasingly since her sons had reached adulthood.

To a certain extent she reminded me of the patient whom Anna Freud (1936) described in her study of altruism, although my patient had not gone so far in surrendering her individuality as the one described by Anna Freud and had retained a store of conscious demands and wishes which, however, she barely permitted herself to express and whose fulfillment she would not have dared to request from her environment. As can be imagined, it was fascinating to see the problems unfold which were rooted in this Victorian, neat, altruistic lady protected by a well-organized and solidly structured character based on the firm and reliable integration of values. At the beginning she centered her conversation upon the son who had required treatment and who was a source of great worry for her. But in presenting her relationship to him, many of her own conflicts could be drawn into the discussion and soon the conversation flowed around her as the center of our common interest. At a time when I had not yet known her —her son reported it in his treatment—cancer of the breast had been diagnosed. It turned out that she had noticed a tumor for a long time but had felt reluctant to consult a physician, a trait highly significant of her. The expenses for surgery and hospitalization threw the family budget off balance and no money had been available for the son's treatment. In order to secure the necessary funds his mother had suggested selling the family house.

I had interceded and the house was not sold. I believe that this was the beginning of the formation of her transference to me, although she did not know me at that time. As it later turned out, this house with its adjacent garden played an enormous role in her emotional life and their loss would have left an irreparable cleft in her life. Therefore my insistence that the house be preserved came to her as a great relief and she looked on me, prior to personal acquaintance, as a kind of protecting guardian. As can be well imagined, our conversation turned soon toward her past operation. I was surprised to hear that she was not examined at regular intervals for a possible recurrence of her physical condition. When I strongly suggested that this, in my opinion, was an indispensable measure, she raised the argument that the physician would think she was a hypochondriac. She voiced this objection repeatedly when the question of a medical examination came up. Although she was assured by others that she had to be examined at least semiannually, she could not quite discard the apprehension of being considered a hypochondriac. Since she was not in analysis, I could not get at the bottom of this unwarranted fear. I assume that it was partly the outgrowth of her Victorian-puritanic tradition not to emphasize physical matters in life and to disregard the body; it probably also was a strong attempt at denying the possibility of the return of a fatal disorder from which she had been told she had been rescued; but it must also have been connected with a deep masochistic tendency which was manifested in the general structure of her biography and also in her procrastination in seeking medical advice when noticing a tumor. This kind of masochism—which also played a role in Case Two—is often fatal to the patient.

It is remarkable how often patients request medical advice when their complaints are based on psychogenic etiology, and how often they hesitate to go to a physician in the presence of a physical one. It seems as if many patients had one desire in mind, namely to hear that the body is in good condition, that the vague awareness that this may not be the case deters them from facing a situation which might destroy this expectation. But the desire to avoid a fear-arousing situation would not by itself explain this complication.

It usually occurs in patients whose masochism is unquestionable. They conspire secretly at their own self-destruction by concealment of symptoms usually under the pretext of modesty, shame, or humility. (In Case Three we shall encounter a different clinical type of masochism.) After a period of arguing the matter she promised, however, to submit semiannually to a checkup. Her physical complaints during this time concerned neuralgic pains in shoulder and neck which—according to the physician—were the sequelae of surgery. Although she had to be reminded from time to time, she faithfully kept her promise and later did not put up too great a resistance to periodic examinations. Approximately three years after a simple mastectomy had been performed and about two years after our acquaintance had started, she reported a dream. This in itself was unusual since we had never before discussed her dreams. In her dream, which referred to a recent event, she saw her newborn grandchild, who had died shortly after birth, in a coffin. From her associations it became clear that the background of the dream was a wild triumph over newborn life that had to perish, whereas she was permitted to live. I had the feeling that such a triumph was absolutely foreign to this Victorian, essentially inhibited and dutiful lady, and although her regular checkup was not due for a few months, I insisted that she be re-examined instantly. A recurrence of her malignancy was found and the patient had to be operated upon again.

The patient's relapse offered a sad opportunity to realize some goals of psychotherapy. Although she lacked confidence in the surgeon who had attended her at her first operation and although she had not felt at ease in the hospital, she nevertheless thought it her duty to stay with her physician and therefore thought she could not avoid undergoing the second operation under circumstances identical with the first. My insistence upon her being operated by a specialist in one of the leading hospitals forced her to give up temporarily her humble and unassuming attitude. She quickly formed a strong attachment to the new surgeon and had the feeling of broadening her existence by the privilege of conversing with him.

The surgeon was not only outstanding as a specialist but was also a remarkable human being, sophisticated and with artistic tastes which were similar to those of the patient. The feeling of being close to and appreciated by a benign father substitute was a succor for old wounds she had suffered in the relationship with her father. Consequently, when her husband showed the first signs of a fatal disease, she was able to establish new object relations which made her look at his approaching demise with relative calm.

Her husband's death was followed by feelings of guilt which, however, could be kept at a minimum. Now she had attained the situation of freedom for which she had been longing since her marriage and early youth. Her sons

were independent and did not warrant the constant wor-
ries of former years. The tragic implications of the Second
World War were quickly used by her to indulge in customary ways, but this period also went by without incur-
ring for her any loss. But her husband's death had left her
with relatively small funds, and the probability arose of
her becoming dependent on her sons. Although it was clear
that they felt responsible for the patient's welfare and were
glad to support her, if only because of her unswerving devotion to them throughout the years, the patient again felt
unworthy and worried about the prospect of receiving
these natural signs of filial gratitude. Yet her resistance to
pleasure and to the gratification of natural selfishness was
weakened. The only serious problems of this period concerned her jealousy of her favored son's wife, which took
on the form of a partly justified, yet essentially exaggerated
critical attitude. Psychotherapy was the least successful in
regard to her feelings about this woman, but perhaps it
was wholesome for her to find a well-rationalized discharge
of aggression in this relationship.

It was not difficult to help her in organizing the free
time which she now had. She took up painting, extended
social contacts, and satisfied her literary tastes. Yet nothing
could persuade her to fulfill her greatest wish: she felt a
deep longing to see her England again but justified her
reluctance to travel by noting the expense involved. I was
convinced that this was only a rationalization, but it was
evident that here her capacity of readjustment had found
a limit. Although this step of independence and open indulgence in pleasure concerned a natural and well-justified
wish, it would have been beyond the limitations enforced
by her basic masochism.

When I moved away from the city where she resided,
our relationship was reduced to regular correspondence
and occasional visits whenever we happened to be at the

same place. All seemed settled until I was informed that metastases had been discovered in the chest, which had necessitated hospitalization. Her lifetime was considered a very limited one. I could not leave to visit her but sent flowers and received the following reply written in a fading handwriting:

> Thank you, dear, the roses are exquisite—don't worry about me—I have a splendid trained nurse on doctor's orders—he says I may have this summer but he can't tell. Fondly with best love and memories of ten happy years.

The only other service for her I could think of was an appeal to her physician whom I did not know—the surgeon so greatly admired by her had died in the meanwhile—to prevent her being exposed to suffering. The answer was not encouraging. He told me of members of his family who had gone bravely through the same tribulations and of necessities from which a patient cannot be freed, but soon thereafter I received information of her death which made me think that her sufferings had not been excessive.

Two problems which are quite independent of each other ask for discussion. One is the remarkable fact that an impression which was gained from a dream led to the discovery of important physical pathology; the other concerns the psychiatric treatment of the dying patient.

I

It appears necessary first to ascertain beyond doubt whether or not my insistence upon the patient's immediate checkup was really precipitated by the dream which she told me, and the subsequent associations, but not by other factors. To my best recollection, the patient had not mentioned in that hour any physical complaints which would have been different in any way from those of preceding interviews; to the contrary, since she was preoccupied with the recent tragedy of the loss of the baby grandchild, she even spoke less than usual of her neuralgic pain. Nor was there anything in her physical appearance that might have suggested the necessity of a re-examination. My advice was based merely on an intuitive flash that such a triumphant outbreak as the patient showed—of elation in view of a great tragedy, following a sad dream—should be taken as a signal of greatest danger. Afterwards I concluded that I might have preconsciously thought that only the feeling of an impending catastrophic downfall could induce this highly socialized personality to discard her well-integrated morality and indulge in a triumph which would not have been so remarkable in a different type of personality structure.

Be this as it may, there are the following possible explanations. First, the simultaneity of dream and malignancy might have been a pure coincidence. There may have been no correlation whatsoever between the two; instead, my ever-ready apprehension may have been activated by any unusual occurrence. The possibility of a coincidence cannot be disproved, and this may be the correct answer to an inquiry into the matter. Yet I know for certain that I had never insisted—either before or after— that this patient have a physical recheck unless it concerned the half-yearly examination promised by her. Second, the patient may have responded to a condition of internal irritation caused by the renewal of the malignant disease (the dream might have been a derivative of that irritation), thus proving again what many (Freud, 1900; Stengel, 1935; and others) have demonstrated, namely that knowledge about the body, inaccessible to conscious thinking, may nevertheless enter the dream. In this instance the manifest content would not have directly revealed the disease—as in the clinical examples of Stengel—instead, the dynamic constellation leading to the dream would have been the effect of a reaction to that deeper and unconscious knowledge. My own unconscious, then, would have responded to a process which actually occurred in the patient's unconscious, but which found indirect expression in her associations to the dream. Third, it may be assumed —and for this possibility I am indebted to Dr. Julius Bauer of Los Angeles, who called my attention to it—that the patient had palpated a tumor or a lymph gland, an observation which she either had neglected to mention or had forgotten. Then the dream would have been activated by a day residue, a hypothesis more sober than the second eventuality which might strike the internist as mystical.

I think present knowledge does not permit a decision as to which one of the three eventualities comes closest to truth. The third eventuality might have been clinically examined *a posteriori,* had I not learned of it only after the patient's death.

Whatever the truth might have been—inasmuch as this patient had no valid reason at all to consult her surgeon and the latter had no valid reason to set an earlier term than usual for the next examination—the situation reminds us that the psychological observation of a patient might be an indispensable adjunct to internal medicine.

The function of psychological observation as a diagnostic tool has been well known, and I emphasize it now only because the reverse process is widely discussed nowadays, namely, that psychological processes may be inferred from psychobiological symptoms. Instances of the diagnosis of a physical disorder in the course of an analysis occur frequently, although the psychoanalytic technique makes a physical examination impossible. Jones (1927b) reported such an incident. A patient in his thirties complained of a "pain in the neighborhood of the anus when going to sleep" and wanted to explain this symptom as paraesthesias. Yet, since various features made Jones suspect an organic disorder, he requested an immediate consultation with a surgeon, who found a rectal carcinoma. The problem I raise concerns a graver and psychologically a more interesting question, namely the possibility of inferring the presence of physical pathology when it does not appear as a physical symptom at all.

A clinical instance which belongs in some degree to this sort of problem, and which impressed me as particularly instructive, may be recorded. A psychoanalyst was called to treat a patient in her early forties who had been amenorrheic for over three years. She was referred by an outstanding gynecologist who excluded premature menopause or any other physical origin.

The analysis proceeded satisfactorily, inasmuch as considerable material was offered by the patient and many factors were revealed which correlated with her main physical symptom. After a year of treatment the analyst had a very definite impression that the psychogenic background had been discussed sufficiently to warrant a return of the cycle, but the symptom stubbornly remained uninfluenced despite a favorable course of the psychoanalytic treatment itself. In view of this state of affairs the analyst came to the conclusion that the symptom must be of physical etiology.

Another gynecologist was consulted and a granulosa cell tumor diagnosed, after the removal of which menstruation recurred. The analysis was continued for the character disorder which required therapy.

Here again we encounter a situation where the analyst was guided by formal characters of psychic processes rather than by his medical knowledge. The formal characters cannot be taught or learned; their recognition depends on a certain feeling about the meaning of total situations. Medical knowledge and its concomitant thinking, which are restricted to the observation of symptoms, may even obviate the intuitive response to these formal characters, and I have occasionally observed that nonmedical analysts have a particularly fine feeling for the barely noticeable differences between physical complaints brought about by psychogenic and those by physical etiology.

Some psychiatrists believe that the diagnosis of psychogenic vs. physical etiology of a symptom can be made from the history of the symptom. Nothing is more wrong and more dangerous than such a belief. There is, of course, a high percentage of patients whose histories will lead the physician upon the right track, but as will be seen in the history of Case Three, this trust may lead to quite erroneous conclusions. To be sure, there are rare instances of symptoms which cannot be produced by physical evolvement. Freud (1893) has shown one such syndrome. But this I think is rather exceptional.

II

When I received the patient's last written message (see page 134), I felt moved. I had the impression that the preceding time of psychotherapy had given her something which—strangely enough—provided her with a peaceful outlook upon her impending death. This unknown something had been unintentionally created by me, since I had not foreseen this tragic turn but had accepted the assurances given postoperatively by the respective surgeons. I assume that the patient had experienced the period of psychotherapy as a gift from me, given out of affection, if not out of love. It was apparently fortunate in terms of the requirements of the final pathway that I never had charged her a fee. This had been done because her financial situation would not have permitted the additional expense of psychotherapy. Further, I do not think her pride would have permitted recognition and admission of the necessity of psychotherapy even if adequate funds had been at her disposal. Not paying a fee gave her the opportunity of rationalizing most of the therapeutic interviews as casual meetings, and of mentioning only sporadically the plight in which she would have been without psychotherapeutic assistance.

It was also a fortunate circumstance that in our society professional services or services of any kind, for that matter, imply when free of charge an act of love. The feeling of being loved without having to pay the usual compensation for it in the form of obligation—and the latter may be only the obligation of having to love in return—that is to say, the feeling of obtaining unmerited or unwarranted, but spontaneous, love seems to be a kind of antidote against the agony of death, in some instances at least.

I do not want to give the impression that here a religious or a particularly ethical aspect has been introduced into psychotherapy. I do not believe such a psychotherapeutic measure requires more love than many other professional situations. The peculiarity of the psychotherapy of the dying patient is different from others only because of the necessity for providing the patient with the experience of a certain feeling which we have when we meet intensive love, in order that the patient might be relieved of his otherwise unavoidable grief and sorrow. In order to avoid misunderstandings, I add something which ought to be self-evident—that we are concerned here with the feeling of encountering sublimated love, perhaps better called affection. The remotest impression of meeting passionate love in the therapist would destroy the beneficial effect, because any admixture of passion would necessarily produce the impression of selfishness and also activate feelings of guilt of a dangerous kind. Whether the need to feel en-wrapped by a sublimated form of love which does not require any counterservice is genetically connected with certain experiences within the mother-infant relationship or whether it touches upon fantasies which the adult forms about this relationship I do not know; it could be that within the regression which sometimes occurs in the dying patient (Felix Deutsch, 1934), there is a longing for a past pleasure in which the feeling of maximum security was also provided; or it may be that a longing for the fulfill-ment of a fantasy of that sort is reawakened.

On the other hand, one may assume in the instance of this patient that a childhood fantasy of and desire for a father turning helpfully toward her and loving her—a fantasy never even approximately fulfilled in her child-hood—was gratified by a father image in a sublimated and therefore guilt-free way. Yet probably—in view of the pres-ent tendency to consider the mother-infant relationship as the first and ultimate force giving form and structure to the later character—the former assumption will receive acceptance more readily (Coleman, Kris, Provence, 1953).

I think we are on relatively safer grounds if at this point we again recall Freud's theory. The dying person is ex-posed—so one must deduce from his theory—to an im-pending release of intensive, self-destructive energies, and to bind them by his own libidinal resources transgresses biological limitations. He therefore may need the accre-tion or influx of libidinal quantities in order to compen-sate for his own deficit.

Sublimated libido which is turned toward an object—perhaps the highest form of love—seems to serve that pur-pose the best. It would be of interest at this point to know what the correlations between disease and libidinal needs really are. There are sicknesses which have a stimulating effect; patients suffering from them feel a greater need for sexual satisfactions than usual. But most libidinal functions are prostrate in a sick body. Freud's descriptions (1914, 1920a) of the functional distribution of libido in the state of pain can also be applied to the state of the dying patient. The libido is then totally drawn into the process of binding the death instinct activated in the pathological processes, leaving no surplus to maintain those functions which, under ordinary circumstances, are fed by libido. When the organism is engaged in the last and supreme effort to combat this destructive force, any distraction of the libido from this goal would cause damage, but the accretion of sublimated libido from without apparently eases the patient's struggle.

Thus one function of the psychiatrist in this clinical situation is to provide the optimal libidinal accretion. I am trying to construct here a sort of ideal model of the dynamic situation in the psychiatrist during the last phase of treatment. Although clinical reality will depend on so many variables and imponderables that it appears futile even to consider the multitude of variations, nevertheless such a model may have its usefulness.

The chief manifestations of this sublimated love will be—besides the readiness to help and the anticipation of the patient's needs—sorrow and pity. These two emotions ought to evolve automatically in the psychiatrist. In face of the impending extinction of a human life such involvement is almost unavoidable, and moreover the patient has a rightful claim to these emotions. However, sorrow and pity must never grow into grief and despair, which are the proper emotions of the members of the patient's family and of his friends. The dying patient rarely receives from his family the psychic assistance of which he is so direly in need. Grief and despair burden the patient, undermining his fund of psychic resistance against the impending cataclysm. Sorrow and pity provide trust, courage, and consolation; grief and despair undermine the patient's morale merely by the likelihood of the patient's becoming infected by them and evolving the same emotions. Grief and despair imply the finality of the situation and obviate the other attitude which the psychiatrist—paradoxically— must also evolve, namely the belief in the indestructibility of the patient's body and mind. In all of us the archaic belief in the immortality of the soul is still dormant. We probably never outgrow this animistic belief completely, although it has no place in the scientific frame of reference which guides the physician in his practical pursuits. Yet this dormant belief that the soul cannot perish comes in good stead in dealing with the patient on the terminal pathway. The belief must only be extended to include the patient's body also in order to serve its purpose. In that part of the psychiatrist's personality which is in direct contact with the patient this belief must be deeply rooted. Yet my emphasis upon the necessity of the psychiatrist's animistic belief that the patient must survive physically and spiritually should not be misunderstood. It does not concern anything that needs verbalization or could be verbalized, just as sorrow and pity do not need verbal expressions but will be felt by the patient if these emotions are sincerely present. The psychiatrist's partial conviction of the patient's survival, of course, should not lead to any action that might minimize the gravity of the patient's situation. No more is necessary than the internal emotional conviction that the living body and mind of this patient cannot be converted into something dead. Only when the patient falls into the terminal coma and is unconscious may the psychiatrist relinquish this magic belief.

To return to the introductory remarks on thanatologies: if the psychiatrist were dealing with a patient who has integrated the idea that death is the matrix of life and that in dying he fulfills life's primary law, then a reactivation of the archaic animistic belief in the psychiatrist would become not only unnecessary but would even impede the great achievement of which the patient would be capable.

However, different clinical necessities may require a split attitude in the psychiatrist. The necessity of maintaining simultaneously two attitudes which seemingly exclude each other makes the technique difficult. On one hand the magnitude and the gravity of the situation must be fully recognized, acknowledged, and accepted by the psychiatrist. It is immaterial whether the patient knows consciously or not that death is impending. Somewhere within him there is such knowledge, and the psychiatrist, even when he is merely present, is always in contact with the patient's unconscious. If a psychiatrist were to behave toward a patient who has no conscious knowledge of his impending death in the same manner in which he behaves toward one suffering from a disease with a benign prognosis, he would probably not elicit a favorable transference reaction. Despite the patient's alleged—and from the point of view of consciousness, his true—ignorance of his condition, I believe that most patients would sense the incongruity of the therapist's behavior. Again I do not have in mind any particular verbalizations but only the attitudes which are at the basis of the psychiatrist's direct dealings with the patient.

On the other hand—as I mentioned before—the psychiatrist must not waiver in his conviction that the patient is ultimately immortal. The resultant behavior of the therapist must be contradictory, but strangely enough it is not experienced as contradictory by the patient. Just the opposite seems to be true; it fits into the patient's expectations and therefore strikes him as harmonious and logical.

III

The patient wants to obtain the reassurance that no serious harm will befall him, but simultaneously, he wants to be treated in conformity with the gravity of his situation. Thus the psychiatrist's seemingly contradictory behavior is correlated with contradictory expectations in the patient. A clinical example may demonstrate the intertwining of these aspects.

Case Three died without conscious knowledge of the fatal nature of her disease but was convinced—in conformity with the content of my communications and those of the other physicians who treated her—that she suffered from a minor disorder. I had treated the patient prior to the onset of her terminal disease, customarily sending her monthly statements which had not been small, the patient having been of considerable wealth. When I met her again she was fatally sick and I treated her during the terminal phase without ever mentioning the payment of fees. Now under ordinary circumstances this would be a strange procedure, and logically the patient should have inquired about it. However, during this period she took for granted my not bothering her with financial obligations and did not draw any conclusions, although one might have expected that this circumstance alone would have aroused her suspicion that an essential change must have occurred in her condition. On the other hand, when I found out that she had not subscribed to the monthly programs of her favored broadcasting stations, I sent her as a gift the annual subscriptions. This gift casually conveyed to her an idea which implicitly covered a considerable extent of the future and had the intended effect.

Here the disparity between therapeutic measures can be demonstrated in a particularly poignant fashion. A dying

person should not be molested with avoidable trivialities
of daily life such as payment of fees (I follow here only
the technical advice of Federn regarding the psychotherapy of acute and intensive depressions) and in this
respect I treated the patient with the sorrow and pity required by her true clinical situation. I believe it would
have been a mistake to send the customary monthly statements, although common sense would stress the risk caused
by the possibility of suspicions being aroused in her by
such omission. On the other hand, while it was objectively
a waste to subscribe to annual publications for a person
who would live for only a few weeks, it was a reality-
adequate action in so far as it provided a channel through
which the therapist's animistic conviction of the patient's
immortality could be conveyed.

This incident illustrates again the manifold functions a
gift may fulfill in the clinical situation of impending death.
In this instance it helped the patient to maintain a strongly
represented future. The Christian religion, as do many
other religions, points the direction here. It tries to banish
the psychological uniqueness of death by denying its essential difference from life, namely the discontinuance of
a present and of a future.

The religious dogma is, with relatively rare exceptions,
not an essential help to the psychiatrist since the belief in
the immortality of the soul, although deeply rooted in
man's unconscious, is only rarely encountered nowadays
as a well-integrated idea from which the ego could draw
strength. What is usually encountered is only a vague feeling—if not a mere *façon de parler*—not structured enough
to protect the ego from being flooded by despair vis-à-vis
death. Furthermore, other weak points in the eventual
protection by religious convictions have to be considered.
If the patient harbors a grain of doubt or skepticism, this
may convert that which should protect the ego into an

additional burden. Actually under such circumstances the psychic vicissitudes along the terminal pathway would be less tragic without the interference of religious beliefs. In particular, those religious convictions which lead the ego to believe in its irreparable sinfulness may produce unsolvable psychiatric complications. But in view of the general decline of deep religious convictions, this problem will not be followed up. The psychiatrist has the task to create—within a frame of reference acceptable to the patient—an emotional atmosphere which the priest or minister would either demand from the patient on the ground of certain dogmas or expect to find in him as self-evident insights into the nature of man. The example I mentioned earlier shows that this atmosphere can, under favorable circumstances, be created by measures which are simple and which appear trivial if viewed from without. When using noninterpretative tools, psychotherapy often appears quite simple. Yet if we investigate the preconscious and unconscious contents which are stimulated by the seemingly trivial and thus become linked with them, it is questionable whether such measures ought still to be minimized.

A principal point involved is the anticipation of the patient's needs and the necessity of not waiting until the patient has verbalized that which he is wishing for. In Case One my task was facilitated, since by virtue of our previous relationship the idea of the gift was formed and ready. The flowers I sent probably had more the effect of reminding her of the past and of making distinct an idea present for a long time than of creating a new facet in our relationship. Therefore the feeling of not being alone but of belonging to somebody—thus sparing her the isolation which lies in agony—could be activated with relative ease.

One may feel inclined to make the factor of unambivalence the cornerstone of the therapeutic relationship to the dying patient. Such a statement needs a qualification. An unambivalent relationship is usually not described in terms of the extent to which the wishes and needs of a love object are fulfilled. Relationships in which one encounters an unusual degree of self-sacrifice, going toward an almost complete gratification of all the wishes of the love object, show often a considerable core of ambivalence at the bottom.

In many instances that which seems to be wish fulfillment strangely enough leads to a weakening of the ego in the person who receives the gift and therefore contributes to his later downfall. Unambivalent love—I think—cannot be measured by the wish fulfillments granted to a love object. Unambivalent love also puts up demands and expects a return for a sacrifice. Denial of a wish fulfillment is quite compatible with unambivalent love. Yet the frame of reference within which the therapeutic relationship between the psychiatrist and the patient who approaches death takes place is plotted out between different categories. The patient has—in accordance with certain axiomatic-like societal principles—a claim to have his wishes fulfilled inasmuch as they do not transgress the limitations set by law and custom nor involve harm to others.

The latter factor concerns usually those who have personal ties to the patient and who must weigh the preemption which the service rendered to the dying takes upon the future. The series of conflicts which may be aroused in this situation are well-known. The following incident shows the solution a cynical person invented. The wife of a wealthy man was seriously sick. One morning she told her husband that in her dream she had seen the angel of death, who had said he would spare her if her husband would buy her a particular piece of jewelry. It is unnecessary to say that it was an extremely expensive one. Thereupon the distressed husband went to the jeweler, bought the piece but stipulated that he might return it in case his wife should pass away.

The psychiatric technique is different from the duties of the patient's personal environment. Aside from the advisory duty, the psychiatrist must foresee the situation where his wish fulfilling function finds its rightful place. A wish fulfilled at the patient's request has scarcely any therapeutic effect since the psychiatrist in this instance behaves like the patient's environment. Whenever a psychiatrist fills out a real gap—if, let us say, the patient actually is deserted and is not attended by anyone who is the object of his natural affection—he does not act as a psychiatrist in the proper sense of the word but fulfills a general human duty which does not require any discussion in this context.

But it is rather typical that the persons in the personal environment cannot adequately fulfill their natural obligations toward the dying patient, because the envisaged death of a loved person will inevitably create intensive conflicts in the patient's environment. Here is an important area which rightly belongs to the psychiatrist's responsibility.

The patient's environment is distracted by its own grief and despair—including the defenses against them—since both emotional reactions are probably related to the unavoidable ambivalence under which human nature labors. This measure of natural ambivalence—as it may be called —is enough of a burden to the patient moving upon the terminal pathway to require in addition a relationship which is free of that admixture. Freedom of ambivalence amounts in this clinical situation to the capacity of giving to the patient those emotions which he needs. As I have said, they are sorrow and pity and the confidence that the patient is immortal in the present crisis. A gift may easily become the symbol of that triad.

It is an often-recorded fact that during the Revolution, French aristocrats went on dancing until shortly before they were taken to their execution. Whatever the psychological background of such behavior in the face of death —it was unquestionably a victory of denial—I surmise that this seeming reconciliation with bitter fate was facilitated by the knowledge that death was in this instance a mass event, destroying not only the self, but everything cherished, admired and loved by those who were facing annihilation. Parts of our egos rest in what we love. Freud described this by the term of narcissistic cathexis. When objects heavily charged with narcissistic energies are destroyed, parts of us go with them; thus we die a partial death. To the French aristocrats who had witnessed the fall of their society, their own deaths might have become a trivial event when measured in terms of the preceding societal cataclysm. From this, one may conclude that the envy of the living is also one source of the pain involved in dying. Death as an event befalling the *me* in isolation, when life goes on for all those surrounding the patient, may create an unbearable frustration; whereas death as an event destroying the *me* and all the *you's* one loves might paradoxically reduce the pain. The opposite has been more often described, the consolation and solace the dying obtains from the perpetuation of his own self in his offspring. Then death is successfully denied because the destruction of the own person is invalidated by the existence of progeny. This mechanism, however, can be successfully activated only in the absence of significant ambivalence. Whereas the ambivalence of the surviving person toward the dying and the dead has been often described, the ambivalence of the dying person must also be considered. We are dealing here with a vicious circle. The dying person feels the ambivalence of those who will outlive him; that is to say, the unconscious triumph that

death has halted before one's own person but reaches out
for the other is unconsciously perceived, and thus the
ambivalence of the dying person toward the living is
stimulated which, in turn, increases the fears of the surviving.

The psychiatrist can appease this conflict of ambivalence
in the dying by giving him the feeling that part of the
psychiatrist is dying with the patient. On a small and
symbolic scale we are copying here the death of the
pharaos, when the godlike prince took everything he loved
into his grave with him. When the physician becomes the
principal object of the transference of the patient's affection, when he simultaneously maintains a position which
is free of that implicit triumph so characteristic of those
who outlive the patient, and when he also provides the
patient with the feeling that his death is more painful to
the psychiatrist than his own would be, then the psychiatrist becomes a source of incomparable succor to the
agonized patient who, thus comforted, may experience his
own death in a masochistic way, without rebellion. Then
the patient may convert the dire necessity of "I have to
die" into "I am dying for you." Death may then even become a process of a narcissistic gratification, in the manner
of the martyrs, for whom death was a highly active process
leading to the victory of the Church over the evil of
paganism.

The task of the psychiatrist as outlined here cannot, of
course, be fulfilled entirely because it transgresses individual capacities. If it can be achieved in some approximation, very much has been accomplished. Since in this
clinical situation the therapeutic emphasis is far less upon
what is done and said than it is upon what the psychiatrist
himself is feeling and therefore can make the patient feel,
the physician's own attitude on and feeling about death
become of paramount importance. If death means a rou-

tine event of a merely biological occurrence for him, the psychiatrist cannot fulfill his obligations toward the patient upon his terminal pathway.

One of the greatest difficulties seems to lie in the necessity for the psychiatrist to activate attitudes which seem contradictory. This problem has been encountered earlier in connection with the demand that sorrow, pity, and belief in the patient's immortality ought to be present. But it goes even further. Despite the giving of sublimated love in the form of affection, this affection must not be "realistic," as it would be when the physician loses a loved person of his own private orbit. Then sorrow and pity would probably grow into grief and despair and the physician would change from a helper into a danger to the patient. Thus the sublimated love must never transgress a certain intensity, and yet it must never appear to the patient as an emotion *in abstracto*.

Another contradiction exists also between the physician's full awareness of the dread involved in the certitude of death for this particular individual and the insight that this impending annihilation of life is an organic event per se, deserving no other response but the one with which we bow to all other necessities of life. If these two—surely contradictory—attitudes are not well balanced, the patient will either feel rejected and unloved or be drawn toward extreme acting out.

The necessity of simultaneously maintaining contradictory attitudes, difficult as it may appear, does not impress me as an insuperable task. The ego is accustomed to participate in contradictory attitudes and pursuits. Usually one discovers irrationalities behind such contradictions, but an adequately differentiated ego must be able to tolerate a certain degree of irrationality (Heinz Hartmann, 1947), and it is part of mental health to share and participate in the unavoidable irrationality inherent in human life and

the life of groups. Thus the ego is capable of the simultaneous activation of attitudes which from a rational point
of view are contradictory. In the clinical situation I am
describing here, it is necessary to use this capacity of the
ego for a constructive, that is to say, rational purpose. To
speak in concrete terms: in regard to the conviction of
the patient's immortality, the ego would use an archaic
wish of the id and a conviction which is part of the repressed part of his personality; in regard to sorrow and
pity, the ego would respond to the undeniable facts of
reality. In making use of contradictory attitudes in this
therapeutic situation, the ego would carry only an organizing principle (Heinz Hartmann, 1947) into actions
which are often chaotic and performed without awareness.

Still more, however, the psychiatrist's own thinking and
feeling about death will count. A great danger may derive
from the psychiatrist's religious convictions regarding
death and its meaning. The slightest pressure toward making a patient accept a concept of death which is alien to
him may cause irrevocable damage to the transference.
In certain situations (Case Two), the meaning of death
or life respectively must be discussed; however, the psychiatrist's duty is not to convey his own beliefs, ideologies,
or convictions but to construct that frame of reference
which will best serve the patient's needs. It would prove
unspeakable arrogance and superciliousness if anyone
should boast that his own personal convictions necessarily
coincide with such requirements.

The platform from which the psychiatrist can operate
at all is—in my estimation—the insight into the essence
of death, that is to say, its being simultaneously the prerequisite and the fulfillment of life. Yet human nature is
of such kind that this insight can be barely applied by
man to his own imminent death. Likewise, when death
threatens those who have eminent emotional importance,

only secondary consolation can be drawn from this philosophical position. Yet in a professional situation in which ego mastery prevails over impulses, this insight is of invaluable assistance. The undeniable fact that life goes on, however untimely death may appear in the individual instance, is correlated with the aforementioned attitude that the patient is essentially immortal biologically as well as spiritually. The regret, however, that life requires the annihilation of all the individual forms in which it manifests itself leads to that sorrow and pity which the dying person so urgently needs.

The last remnants of ambivalence may vanish if the therapist can rise to the greatness of the moment by recognizing that the tragic conflict between Eros and the death instinct, which occurs in each individual, does not necessarily exist in nature at large but that possibly life and death appear—when viewed in the great context of organic life covering this planet—to be in a state of harmony supporting each other and serving each other. Though death is more ancient than life and is its prerequisite, its forces require the spread of life; life, in turn, has led to the formation of ever superior structures during the millions of years since organic substances have been wrested from the inorganic state. Yet these marvelous organic structures would not have developed if death had not converted innumerable generations of antecedent forms into inorganic matter. What man necessarily must experience as struggle and conflict leading to pain and suffering in the individual forms of life manifestations may be embedded in a supraordinated matrix of harmony. If the clinician can make himself part of that matrix at the side of the patient's deathbed, he might be able to unfold the maximum therapeutic effect. But whose mind, we may ask, is great enough to rise in truth to such insight into the cosmos in which life and death take place?

CASE TWO

A married woman in her middle forties, the mother of three children, was referred for consultation. She had previously sought professional advice for her children but was told that she should first discuss her own problems with a psychiatrist. Her situation, indeed, was desperate. Being a biologist herself, she was aware of the limited time which she would be alive in view of a spread of cancerous metastases. Her previous history contained elements which aggravated this desperate present and made it indescribably tragic.

The youngest of three siblings, she had grown up in a small community of Eastern Europe and had at an early age shown the unusual qualities of her personality. Her intelligence was superior; her mind active; her energies unbounded; her willingness to help others extraordinary. Her appearance was attractive and her face beautiful. If it is added that her outlook upon life was optimistic and that she usually was prepossessed by her cheerful spirits, one could have rightly said that nature seemed to have lavished all good things on one person.

When she gave me the general outline of her life history, there was no indication that neurotic symptoms had played any major role in the past (this impression was changed, however, by subsequent information). She had always been able to live up successfully and effectively to the requirements of the often very difficult situations she had had to go through. She received her education away

154

from home and lost all support because of the political upheaval in Europe. On her flight from Hitler she went to France, where by manual labor she barely eked out a living until she could come to America. Here she made a splendid adjustment, got her Ph.D. and became a respected and successful biochemist, devoting herself to cancer research. She had married a well-known architect and given birth to three children, two girls and a boy, whom she adored and who—in her estimation—had developed splendidly. Thus it seemed that everything necessary for a harmonious and pleasing life was established and also that this life had not been made possible just by fortunate coincidences but was the result of her unbounding energy, which knew how to take obstacles and never flagged despite the ups and downs reality had imposed upon her.

The destiny of her relatives, whom she had left in Europe, was different. Both her father, a successful physician, and her mother had disappeared, probably killed like almost all of her relatives with the exception of her brother. But all these tragedies were borne by her without outspoken neurotic reactions and without conspicuous suppression of emotions. She acknowledged the extent of the tragedy intellectually as well as emotionally and gave free vent to her rage and sadness, both of which are the natural companions of those bereaved by the senseless annihilation of their loved ones. Her reaction was slightly different when she was informed that her brother was killed. This loss had not been incurred in the course of historical mass events but was brought on by the personal vengeance of a husband enraged by his wife's unfaithfulness. Her brother's death—so it seemed—provoked a neurotic reaction limited exclusively to internal processes and not finding its way into manifest behavior. Although during the time of mourning for him an occasional idea of suicide entered her mind, it was never accompanied by any serious intention, appearing solely in the form of a thought which did not cause any emotional perturbation.

Several years prior to my meeting her, she had had a tumor in her breast. It was removed and proved to be benign. Later she had another tumor in the same breast, and, as before, a biopsy was advised by her surgeon. The day of the operation was fixed, the room in the hospital reserved, when a friend objected to her being "cut up so much," and advised her to consult another physician first. The patient took up that suggestion and was allegedly told by the consultant that she was in no need of surgery. The patient felt relieved by such advice, although she had not particularly dreaded the operation. The consultant requested to see the patient semiannually. For several visits, she was told that no operation was required. Then after a few consultations the surgeon's opinion changed, and he requested an immediate surgical intervention. The patient responded with rage, feeling that she might possibly have been misled by the consultant whom she had trusted unhesitatingly. She changed physicians, was operated on and a malignant growth removed. Despite all medical precautions, metastases developed in the skin and in the other breast. The patient was doomed and she knew it. Since her chief worry concerned the fate of her children after her demise, she had asked to be given the name of a reliable child psychiatrist. She herself was referred, in turn, to a psychiatrist. This was, I believe, a sound procedure, inasmuch as it would have been incorrect to attack her children's problems in isolation from her own unavoidable psychological involvement, although in terms of current standards there was no area of ostensible psychopathology noticeable in the patient. Indeed, she seemed to have accepted the fact of her impending death better than could be expected, while she continued to hope that modern radiation and hormone therapy might postpone the tragic event to such a late date that her children would have reached an age at which the loss of a mother might cause less injury.

While she was deeply grieved by the tragic prospect of her future, no signs of a pathological depression or a melancholia were visible. Thus her own comportment and emotional reaction seemed free of psychopathology except for the absence of one emotion which should have been present if the fictitious yardstick of normalcy were applied. For she claimed not to feel any anger or hatred against the consultant who had so ill-advisedly counseled her against surgery. Nonetheless, the knowledge that the gruesome catastrophe could so easily have been avoided increased her bitterness—strangely enough, we are sometimes more lenient in our reproaches against destiny when our downfall has occurred by absolute necessity.

So far as could be ascertained in our first meeting, no psychopathology which would justify psychiatric treatment was visible. Indeed, even if such psychopathology had been encountered, there is a question of the psychiatrist's place in such unfathomable tragedy. Each single factor seemed destined only to aggravate her plight. Had she been old, had she been without children, had she lived an uncreative life, had she been a passive, dependent person, any such circumstances would have been islands, albeit small ones, on which to build something of a rationalization which would possibly be helpful to the patient as well as to the psychiatrist in his endeavors to mitigate the patient's grief. But she was young. She had a husband and children to whom she was indispensable; she had a broad area of socially significant professional activities and had never learned to submit to the powers that be. In addition, she knew that a casual conversation with a friend had be-

come by freakish accident the signpost to her grave. Moreover, she was excellently trained and observed the progres-
sive signs of her disease with an uncanny objectivity. As
was fairly certain from the beginning, she lacked that
wholesome function of the mind of forming illusions and
fantasies when sagacity and wisdom have reached a blind
alley. It is well known (even of physicians, to the surprise
of their colleagues) that for those suffering from a lethal
disease the capacity of self-deception by overlooking symptoms or drawing false conclusions is often quite extensive,
but in this instance no point was observable at which one
might see the evolvement of self-deceptive illusions.

Realistic and rational as she had been in almost all previous life situations, so the patient continued to be in this
final one, although one would have wished that nature
had proffered a last consolation by means of the irrational.

Well aware of the impossible situation in which the
psychiatrist found himself here, the patient played her
hand with full force. One of the preconscious motives for
so doing—as became evident in the course of the first
interview—was the humiliation she felt at the idea of having been referred to a psychiatrist. Although she denied
this vigorously in later months, it was clear that she had
harbored that contempt for psychiatry which is significant
of so many contemporary biologists and physicians, particularly those who are outstanding in their respective
specialties of physical medicine. She told me that she would
not have hesitated to advise others to seek psychiatric help,
but the idea that a psychiatrist should be called in order
to assist her was inacceptable and humiliating; thus she
referred to a problem which would become important
later, namely her inability to accept passivity or, to phrase
it more clearly, situations in which she had to submit
passively.

I had the feeling that she had built in her mind the image of a supercilious, condescending psychiatrist who would disregard her arguments, convinced that she had a neurosis. In keeping with my real impression I told her that I did not know whether I could help her at all, that from what she told me it was evident she was not suffering from a neurosis, that her attitude and self-mastery were most admirable, that I doubted I would be able to bear up so bravely as she did in a situation of equal stress, but that despite the risk of wasting her time she might continue to come and visit me for a while, giving me and herself a chance to find out whether our conversations might possibly ease one or the other point in her present distress. She promised to do so, and from then on the question of her coming or not coming never became a serious problem, although she needed, during the first few weeks, the repeated assurance that she had not been sent to me because someone had suspected or observed irrational behavior or because I thought she was suffering from a psychiatric disorder. In comparing my own resources of endurance unfavorably with hers, I had apparently facilitated a positive transference in the first interview.

I want to raise a question here which may occupy us later in a different context, a question of ethics concerning the sincerity and honesty of the psychiatrist's statements to a patient. I do not refer at this point to the question—so often debated—of whether a question of fact such as the patient's prognosis must always be honestly answered. I refer to a broader context such as the above, when in comparing myself with the patient I admitted my own inferiority. I spoke the truth in that particular situation, but I know, too, that I would have made the remark if it had not been in accordance with reality.

There are two groups of disorders whose treatment, in my opinion, cannot be adequately conducted if a psychiatrist introduces, on ethical grounds, the principle of complete honesty. These are the groups of delinquencies and of schizophrenias. A description here of the therapeutic techniques necessary for the two groups of disorders would lead too far afield, but it may be said that they often require of the psychiatrist an almost complete initial acceptance of the patients' symptoms as valid and correct reactions to external occurrences. The psychiatrist has to pretend such opinions initially if he wants to establish a positive relationship with the patient at all. I once met a psychiatrist who flatly refused to proceed in such a way with a delinquent boy because he considered this behavior a lie and therefore an action unacceptable to him. The Latin saying, *de gustibus non est disputandum* can perhaps be applied with even greater justification to ethics and I did not try, nor would I have known how, to convince my colleague. But I want to justify these ethics nevertheless, since the point may come to the reader's mind at various passages in these pages.

My reasoning is rather simple: it is unquestionably unethical to thrust a knife into a person's belly, but the surgeon does it repeatedly. *Mutatis mutandis,* this is the state of affairs in which the psychiatrist finds himself. The surgeon is excused from customary prohibitions because his knife does not harm the patient but saves his life. The psychiatrist's pretended convictions do not harm the patient either but are a station on the road to the patient's recovery, when he will be able to listen to the truth and benefit from it.

In other words, psychiatric ethics do not only permit the psychiatrist, but make it incumbent upon him, to convey to the patient those meanings (and emotions) which are necessitated by the patient's psychopathology. Therefore the frame of reference—during the initial treatment phase —is not necessarily a reality which has objective existence. As evolved by Freud, the classical psychoanalytic method of treating the neuroses is characterized by the coincidence of the two. The analyst conveys to the patient everything that he observes in the patient. The frame of reference in this instance is the aggregate of all the psychic processes that occur in the subject undergoing analysis.

The uncompromising honesty of the analyst who uses the classical method was not born of any ethical deliberation, but it has been justified by its expediency and appropriateness. It is the only way which will enable the patient to rid himself of his symptoms. In the confusing variety of syndromes outside the well-defined area of transference neuroses the situation is quite different. In the aforementioned instances of the delinquencies and schizophrenias the aim of the technique is to get the patient into a state which will allow the same uncompromising honesty which characterizes the classical treatment of transference neuroses. The clinical situation I was facing in the case of this patient was different in yet another sense. If I had been compelled by clinical necessity to tell her an untruth, I would not have the chance of replacing this later by a corrected statement. Thus in this instance an ethical problem was introduced which is absent in most other therapeutic situations. Nevertheless, I am convinced that the aforementioned principle of organizing all therapeutic steps strictly in accordance with the patient's needs preserves its validity in the circumstances of this patient.

What was my task in this instance? Under less unusual circumstances I would have thought it my function to preserve the patient's morale by providing illusions of possible recovery—as happened in Case Three—but here any attitude of minimizing the gravity of the situation by even the remotest allusion would have been offensive to the patient and would have destroyed any confidence in my honesty or intelligence.

Although I had to take a rather pessimistic outlook on

any possible contribution on my part to the patient's welfare, I gained the impression fairly early that the patient's sickness possibly endangered her children, inasmuch as shortly before her own end she might commit suicide after having taken their lives, thus becoming a victim of a wave of despair about leaving her children in a world which in her opinion would be pitiless and unfriendly since it left them unprotected by maternal affection. I found myself here in a peculiar situation. Nothing of this kind was ever verbalized by her, directly or indirectly. Nor could I inquire whether my suspicion was justified or not. Any direct approach toward the subject was utterly impossible in view of the horror attached to the possibility of such an action. Whether or not she had ever harbored, consciously or unconsciously, this intention or a fantasy of the sort, any allusion on my part would have necessarily put an end to her further visits to me. Thus, although I had no evidence for my forebodings, I thought it my duty to keep this grave problem uppermost in my mind. Aside from the general knowledge that a person going through a crisis of such magnitude might develop an explosive reaction at a critical moment, there were some details which justified my apprehension: I had to consider that the patient's grief centered around her children and that she showed a strong tendency to visualize her impending death as an event which was exclusively tragic for her progeny, with an almost complete denial of what it meant to herself. This showed that her narcissism had been displaced from her own person upon her children, a psychic process occurring in nearly every mother, but which had here taken on a dangerous proportion. Tragic as it necessarily is for children to lose their mother, nevertheless I had the impression that the patient exaggerated. She spoke as if the children were quasi-doomed, without anyone to take care of them. She minimized her husband's contribution and claimed he did not know how to deal with them. Briefly, she pictured her children's future in the darkest colors, demanding that a person be found now who would be able to take over for her after her demise. She wanted that person to live with the family. Thus the children would have at hand, immediately after the mother's death, a substitute to whom they were accustomed. At the same time, however, she claimed that it probably would be impossible to find such a person and—as it turned out later—when such a person was found, the idea was intolerable to her. Evidently the extreme pity for her own children—amounting to the attitude that the lives of motherless children are ruined forever—was self-pity which had been shifted to her children. In such guise this proud person, unable to admit her despair about her own destiny, could give vent to her true feelings. It also must be added that the patient had shown from her youth on an overconcern for children. Prior to her marriage the crying of a child or his suffering was unbearable to her. The fact that a neurotic component was present regarding her general relationship to children increased the impression that danger might be lurking in this area.

The partial confluence of child and own person, so often the key mechanism of maternal altruism, could have worked toward destruction in this instance, as it sometimes does in cases of melancholia. On theoretical grounds it is reasonable to assume that at the basis of her concern there was a narcissistic overevaluation of her own importance, as if she wanted to say: "Only I can take proper care of my children," which in turn probably had grown out of a selfish impulse: "No one else should possess my children."

The technical problem involved was very difficult for two reasons: First, it must not be verbalized for the reason I mentioned before and also because its verbalization might precipitate the becoming conscious of the impulse and thus cause the weakening of the restraints of the ego. Second, the problem did not concern the patient's welfare but that of others who were not under my direct care. In general, psychotherapy concentrates exclusively upon the patient's needs and advantages in the broadest sense of the word. Other people's welfare finds consideration only in terms of what it means in the patient's life. It would be against the principles of psychotherapy if the therapist gratified his own altruistic impulses at the expense of the patient's recovery. This does not mean that the patient is supported in his selfish strivings or encouraged to gratify his egoistic impulses; it amounts only to the preliminary exclusion of ethical axioms in order to enable the patient to evolve spontaneously his own altruistic strivings. In the clinical situation discussed here this consideration was missing since the patient was not to be granted the benefit of enjoying the fruits of unselfishness. The only goal, if the patient's needs were to be exclusively considered, would have been to reduce the sufferings incurred by her approach to death. Yet this might have meant the patient's final union with her children in death.

Common sense might easily repudiate the acknowledgment of any problem in this context, and as a matter of fact the clinician has no other choice in his practical dealings but to prevent such a tragedy under all circumstances. But this does not refute the fact that we are dealing here with a theoretical problem of no small import. This will become even clearer when I discuss the allied problem of the patient's possible suicide. Early in our acquaintance she declared that she had the fullest confidence in her treating physicians and would undergo without objection any further surgery or other therapeutic measures suggested by them, but added that she would not tolerate under any circumstances a protracted period of lingering in a hospital, tortured by pain and filling her time by passively waiting until she died. She had observed such instances repeatedly and was filled with horror at the idea of going through the same stages of gradual decomposition until freed by death. Therefore she was determined to commit suicide when the time came for her final hospitalization. She had made preparations for that eventuality, raising many arguments to prove the reasonableness of her intentions.

Now, to prevent a patient's suicide is the self-evident duty of a psychiatrist and needs no further justification or discussion. However, in this instance the whole problem acquired a new perspective. Here, a patient whose life could not be saved, who was destined to rot away under great psychic and physical pain, was determined to end her life a few weeks before her natural death. If our thinking and feeling about suicide were not burdened by traditional, prejudicial, and sentimental concepts—that is to say, if we could be rational about such a matter—indeed there would be no problem involved except for one factor. Had the patient ever deliberated on the effect of her suicide on husband and children? Would not the difference of effect upon them, depending on whether she died by natural causes or by her own hand, make worth while the prolongation of sufferings? Aside from this complication, I do not see any rational argument that could have been raised against the patient's reasoning. Of course, objections drawn from various religious systems abound, but this patient had no religious ties and did not believe in the immortality of the soul. Nevertheless, I felt exceedingly averse to accepting the patient's proposition and was determined to prevent her suicide. Yet it must be admitted that my determination was based on irrational grounds, and I raise the question—without being able to answer it—whether the psychiatrist has the right to impose his own way of feeling upon a patient's decision when this is exclusively the patient's own affair. I could argue that a suicide would not be in the style of the patient's past life, thus making myself the executive of her own superego, since she had made it her principal business to live up to the fulfillment of her duties and to give her best to those whom she loved and for whose welfare she felt responsible. Notwithstanding the fact that if she had been unmarried the idea of her suicide might have been slightly less shocking to me, the aforementioned reasoning would have been a rationalization. The generosity of "permitting" another person to commit suicide probably transgressed my limitations. Here frontiers are discussed where rational thinking loses its power and nothing remains but the hope that one's own unconscious might not lead the therapeutic will astray. It must also be considered that in our society a patient's suicide is, often quite wrongly, held against the psychiatrist, and the possibility that a patient's suicide, occurring for whatever reason, would injure one's professional narcissism cannot be excluded. I could imagine that another psychiatrist might have helped the patient to achieve her goal in a way which would have prevented detection by others; he might have given her the consolation necessary for ending her life with a minimum of conflict. Such freedom of action and independence from the view of one's own time will be a possibility for only a few and cannot be expected from the average therapist.

Aside from such problems, grave in terms of their social implications, many of a personal nature came up. There was the patient's imagery concerning her disease. The human mind does not respond to sickness in terms of its objective properties; instead, each patient usually evolves his subjective imagery in accordance with the unconscious meaning which the diseased organ, as well as the type of disease, has for him. However, some disorders elicit typical reactions. It is well known that in diseases of the venereal type shame, humiliation, and feelings of guilt are the customary patterns of response. Also, a disease like cancer often evokes typical imagery. It became clear that the patient would have suffered less if her sickness had been a heart disease, although a severe heart disease might have shortened her span of life even more than the malignancy. A cancerous growth creates the imagery of a disease which relentlessly and progressively devours the patient from inside, whereas a heart disease apparently gives the feeling of a chronic stage which will be discontinued eventually, but by accidental complication rather than as the result of a merciless course.

The element of being devoured creates an atmosphere of gruesomeness and uncanniness which is absent in most other diseases. This factor was particularly emphasized by the course which this patient's sickness took. From time to time she discovered new nodes in the skin. The breast became completely filled with cancerous tissue; breathing became impeded by the formation of serous fluid. The abdomen protruded—as the patient thought by ascites—by the enlargement of the liver which had also become the seat of the malignancy. Of course, the imagery of an internal enemy that gradually takes possession of the body and thus replaces what once was one's own body can scarcely be escaped. A comparison of the prognosis of her disease with that of a heart disease seemed to bring temporary relief. Probably the mere comparison and the ensuing verbalization helped somewhat to remove the uncanniness.

It was more surprising to discover behind the patient's initial attitude, which covered up her aversion to psychiatry or psychoanalysis playing a role in her own life, the magic belief that the uncovering of psychogenic factors might possibly put a stop to the progression of the malignancy or at least retard its inroads. She quoted some case histories and pointed to possible psychogenic implications leading to the malignancy in those instances. In scrutinizing her own history she raised the question of whether her brother's violent death might have had a bearing on the constellation which finally led to her own disease. As a matter of fact, the deaths of relatives played a role in all three cases reported here. In Case One, a half sister, much older than the patient, had been institutionalized for many years because of a paranoid psychosis. The sister had developed cancer and in her psychosis laid on the patient the curse that she should suffer an equally dreadful fate. In Case Three, the prolonged illness and final death of the patient's husband were of the greatest importance preceding the time of onset of her last illness. (Though it might be tempting to use these coincidences for a psychosomatic theory of malignancies, I believe on theoretical grounds—not to be further discussed here—that this would be a grave mistake.)

When the patient suggested a theory pointing in such a direction, she put me in a dilemma. Here, by good luck, she herself surprisingly offered the opportunity I had been seeking for evolving illusions which might raise a spark of hope and contribute to the maintenance of her morale. On the other hand, there was the possibility that since she was so well trained and experienced in biology, and since the categories of her medical thinking were derived exclusively from this source, she was trying to test my reliability by holding out a bait. Would I take it and in turn hold out the prospect of a recovery which she knew was impossible? Would I reveal myself now as one who believes in psychiatry as a panacea as she had accusingly claimed so many did? Even if I had been certain that there was no intention of the patient's testing me, I think I would not have responded positively to her suggestion.

The wholesome effect of charlatanery on so many persons who feel sick is, I believe, based not only on the convictions of the charlatan and quack. Both are necessary evils in a society in which the well-trained and scientific physician leaves a gap which he cannot fill because of the many problems which have not yet been solved and which are therefore neglected in the present organization of medical treatment. The charlatan and quack are sociological necessities in terms of the ungratified desires and longings of the many who turn away in disappointment from bona fide medicine. To a certain extent the psychological needs of a human being who finds himself in such desperate straits as my patient could be cared for by a charlatan who would induce an absolute belief in his miracle cure. Such belief would, of course, have been impossible for my patient. Little as she was accessible to religious illusions, she was less likely to accept manifest quackery. When a new drug was used, I found she had studied the literature about it, and she would inform me of its limitations. Yet in principle I must admit that I would not see any objection to sending a patient, under such conditions, to a man known to the profession as a charlatan if his charlatanery were of a kind acceptable to the particular patient. As a matter of fact, a problem of that type actually came up in the course of this patient's treatment. It was necessary to keep alive the little optimism which was still simmering in her by intensifying the physical treatment to the available maximum. I depended in this respect upon the group of physicians who conducted her physical treatment. When it looked as if soon no new therapeutic measure could be introduced, I suggested that the patient go out of town for a few weeks to be treated by a regular member of the guild, close to the top of the hierarchy, who recently had made claims of having used a new drug against cancer with success but whose claims were rejected by the profession.

The treating physicians objected and fortunately other

measures could be instituted which kept therapy active enough to prevent the patient from becoming aware that all hope had been abandoned. Why, then, would I hesitate to allow a patient to believe that psychotherapy could have a significant bearing upon the course of a malignancy? There are different kinds of deception which might become necessary in the treatment of a patient. I am not thinking of quackery in this context but of the deceptions which are part of accepted medical practice. When an internist tells a patient that a certain treatment will help although he knows that the patient is lost, this deception will not be called quackery but an unavoidable step to spare the patient mental pain. The internist can safely use this deception if he uses some tact and circumspection, since his type of treatment is destined to take care of the patient's disease and since laymen and experts agree that injections, drugs, and radiation have a beneficial and often curative effect. In other words, this kind of deception has a great chance of alleviating the patient's anguish because he knows that such means actually do cure many physical diseases; thus the probability of the patient's accepting the physician's claim is great.

If psychotherapy were used for the same purpose there would be many dangers. First, the reliability of the technique cannot be compared to that which uses physical means of treatment for purposes of suggestion. The chance of a delayed doubt marring the initial success is considerable, and no impediment is more difficult to combat in psychotherapy than a disappointed promise or hope instilled by the therapist. Second—and this I consider the more important factor—the psychotherapist depends on the patient's co-operation to a greater extent than the medical man who operates with the means of physical therapy. Antibiotics spread their wholesome effect almost independently of the patient's willingness to recover. Yet psychotherapy cannot work against the patient's unconscious longing for the persistence of his symptoms, and in all graver cases the latter must be attacked first before the therapy of the symptom proper can be started. If the validity of psychotherapy as a therapeutic tool against a certain disease is acknowledged and the patient's symptoms do not subside despite the psychotherapy which he receives, the danger of a rising feeling of guilt in the patient is great, and the psychotherapist may suddenly face a patient who accuses himself that because of *his* lack of co-operation, because of *his* resistance, his condition becomes worse from day to day. I have actually observed such situations in cases of infectious disorders and heart diseases, so many of which are attributed to a psychogenic etiology by members of the school of psychosomatic medicine.

If physical treatment does not lead to the expected result, the patient does not find a reason to accuse himself—instead he may accuse the physician or the ignorance of his times—but in psychotherapy the situation is far more fragile and complicated. While deception is medically justified if it reasonably assures a strengthening of the patient's ego, it must be discarded if there is a chance that it may lead to an undermining of the little resources still at the disposal of the patient's ego. Under such circumstances deception becomes comparable to charlatanery and quackery, even though they occasionally give temporary relief.

In the case of my patient, the first clinical situation in which psychotherapy could actively intervene to her benefit concerned her attitude to some emotions. She turned with great vigor against the impulse to cry. In keeping with her independence, activity, and self-reliance, she looked askance at weeping. When talking to me and concentrating upon her great plight she could not help but react with more intensive emotions than were habitual when she was at home, distracted by children, husband, and household duties and her scanty professional activity, which—by the way—she felt forced to give up completely about this time. Soon she noticed that she was upset only when she was with me, whereupon she apologized, and tried to suppress this. She felt ashamed that the trembling of her hands became visible when lighting a cigarette and felt humiliated by the tears which came when we turned toward the subject of her disease. Emotions which manifest themselves in tears and trembling were experienced by her as pure signs of weakness. She justified her aversion to the manifestation of emotions in the customary way, that is by referring to their uselessness.

Although in this instance the anticipation of such a result would not have been justified, she apparently felt better at home after such releases. Nonetheless, it took quite a while before she accepted the truth that her condition justified pity from others, as well as self-pity, and that it was difficult to imagine who could have been entitled to tears if not she. It was a great step forward when for the first time she could cry outside of the psychotherapeutic situation. This occurred in the presence of her treating physician; yet she could never be brought to the point of releasing her grief in the presence of her family. When she felt like crying at home—which rarely happened—she went to the bathroom and afterwards pretended to maintain the radiant mood which had been characteristic of her before the time of her illness.

The absence of tears in the presence of her children may be justified in terms of a rational purpose, but she behaved in the same way in the presence of her husband or other adult family members. Of course, an unbearable emotional climate was the consequence at home. Constant outbursts of tearful complaints in hysterical fashion would have been more easily bearable than the pretense of adequate functioning by this seemingly even-tempered woman whose true emotional state was written upon her face. I believe that the fight she put up against sadness and tears could not be explained primarily by a defense against emotions in general or in particular, but rather by an avoidance of the feeling that she had been totally defeated in life. I got the strong impression that the main conflict raged around the problem of activity vs. passivity. Consequently she also had to minimize her emotional response to the consultant who had brought so much misfortune upon her by his diagnostic mistake. If she had felt real anger or rage against him, this would automatically have made him an object of considerable proportion; by claiming that she did not feel any particular negative emotion about him, she really succeeded in minimizing him and the consequences of his derelict behavior.

Fenichel (1939) speaks of the counterphobic attitude; by analogy, one easily could say of her that she had a counterparanoid attitude. If any reality situation favored a paranoid reaction it was the one she had gone through. A capacity to form paranoid reactions was present, but it was remarkable to notice in which situation this came to the fore. During the time of treatment I encouraged her to take up professional activities, since her life had come close to being filled out by waiting for her demise. This necessitated her taking a course; and although she really was in no need of further instruction, she agreed. During the course, she felt that another participant, a man, was unjustly treated by the lecturer. Her reaction was excessive. She took the part of the person allegedly mistreated and humiliated, defended him vigorously and expressed her deep resentment when she met me, making plans what she would do if the event were repeated. This was all the more remarkable since the man who allegedly had been so mistreated did not show any sign of resentment and did not complain at all when the patient discussed the incident with him. No doubt, the patient showed here a reaction which was quite paranoid; however, it did not directly concern her contact with the world; it concerned a humiliated, frustrated man who was forced to reveal his weakness publicly.

It is my impression that this patient had an unconscious, but very sensitive, feeling that a paranoid symptom was the result of a weakness in ego structure. She was interested enough in the maintenance of her social image as a strong and undaunted woman to shift her paranoid inclinations into the service of others and to use her altruism as a shield. The paranoid idea replaces a rent in the ego structure, an area where the ego feels defenseless and inferior. In the paranoid idea the greatness of the object is exaggerated— unless object and ego coincide. With her reaction to the lecturer she implied that some weak men need protection against assault; with her reaction to the consultant she implied that no man could really assault her.

Yet her attempt at suppressing her aggression against the consultant seemed to me a danger point transgressing her tolerance. In a long discussion she tried to prove how justified her insatiable rage at Hitler was, but insisted that she felt no anger at the consultant. He had after all tried his best and his motives had been of a noble nature. These rationalizations were in contradiction to the way she had spoken at her first interview when her true feelings were unmistakable. On that occasion she had sarcastically spoken of the godlike fashion in which the man had acted. Although in every textbook—as she reported—it could be read that tumors in the breast should be investigated surgically, although every interne learned this and she herself had known it well, the consultant had pronounced dogmatically that the customary procedure was not necessary in this instance.

Yet with some encouragement she brought out her rage and finally decided she would consult an attorney on whether she had any chance of suing for malpractice. Again she had to rationalize this with an altruistic motive: if a sizable amount of money were to be paid, her children would be well provided for. She knew the law well on that subject and thought she had no chance of success. I encouraged her, nevertheless, to seek advice, knowing well how favorably she responded to any opportunity for being active. I made sure that she went to a reliable attorney. She came back from the interview relieved. The lawyer had told her that he was against the court suit. From then on the consultant did not reappear in our conversation. The dynamic background of this development was not clear. Psychotherapy may have had some influence upon it. I had tried to show her that if her rage at Hitler was justified, then rage at the consultant was justified also; her way of reasoning that the consultant had been free from any malicious motives, that is to say, the technique of *tout comprendre c'est tout pardonner,* could also be applied to Hitler.

How this equation between Hitler and the consultant affected her unconscious I do not know. I would surmise that in part it was taken by her as a permission to be angry, therefore removing an inhibition in her. In part, it may also have seemed to her that I had taken her side uncompromisingly, thus drawing her closer to me. The decision on whether to sue or not to sue was difficult to make because—as is well known—physicians hesitate to testify against a colleague. Perhaps she interpreted my extreme statement as meaning that I would be ready to testify in her favor if I were in a position to appear in court. Of greater influence might have been my insistence of her seeing a lawyer. There I could demonstrate by action that I was serious about her title to anger. It is conceivable that in this patient who depended so much upon activity for her well being, the little release she may have found in discussing the legal situation with an authority was, so to speak, a point of crystallization which brought the unconscious and free-floating aggression to rest. Nevertheless, I wonder why the patient did not respond more strongly to the poor prospect of any one physician's testifying in her behalf. Whether she had suffered a harm which afforded legal redress I do not know, but certainly her history contained enough elements for forming the conviction that she had been subjected to an injustice. And from there it was not far to the expectation and demand that any one of the physicians who conducted her physical treatment with devotion, care, and sacrifice should also sign an affidavit asserting that her sickness was caused by avoidable neglect. As far as I know, this alternative never came up. Aside from pride and the aforementioned counterparanoid attitude, I think, an unconscious or preconscious fantasy— which nevertheless might have contained some realistic core of truth—was responsible for her quick desistance from proceeding against the physician who supposedly had damaged her so severely. At least once she alluded to the possibility that she had not given the most exact information to the consultant. As is well known, the diagnosis of such tumors depends also on whether they change their size in the course of the cycle. The patient thought she remembered trying to convince herself that the growth was smaller at times than usual and that she had informed the consultant of what she allegedly had observed. Yet when she spoke of this to me, she claimed that looking back she doubted that this was so, that she must have tried to disregard the almost imperceptible increase. Her report suggested the possibility that this secret plotting with death followed the temporary lull in her zest of life after she had been told of her brother's death. One of the basic patterns of her life was unquestionably formed in her relationship to that brother, who was eight years her senior. When she was still a little girl her parents had said that she should have been a boy and he a girl since she was so active and independent, whereas he was rather withdrawn and passive. The whole family constellation had apparently been favorable for the evolvement of the assets she had received from nature, but it also contained—as so often happens— the seed of her downfall. Her father was fifty years old when she was born, her mother, thirty-four. A sister, twelve years older than the patient, died from diphtheria when the latter was five. The father apparently took her as a substitute for the deceased child. Furthermore—as can be easily imagined—the aging man must have found particular delight in this precocious and charming little girl. Thus she received extensive gratification of her oedipal strivings. In the biographies of outstanding men one frequently finds the family constellation of an old father and a young mother, and I wonder if this constellation did not also contribute to the patient's developing to a certain extent along masculine lines. However, it would be wrong to overstress this aspect of her development and not to notice that the development of her femininity did not suffer by any means from this masculine admixture, which manifested itself mainly in the necessity for being active. Be this as it may, the sudden change by which the patient came to be her father's favorite was produced by death, and though it evoked her optimism (Freud, 1917b), stimulating a favorable ego development, it must also have left the shadow of a deep feeling of guilt. Thus when she heard the news of her brother's tragic death—he was killed, so to speak, because he had loved—a score of ancient conflicts must have been reactivated.

This might have been the acute and mostly unconscious background of her uncanny conspiracy for her own destruction. All of the accusations she raised against the consultant could—though only under the aspect of the psychology of the unconscious—be also raised against herself. If everyone knew that tumors of the breast necessitate a biopsy, why didn't she? She had had full confidence in her treating physician and there was no realistic reason for further consultations. She said she was not afraid of surgery and had easily gone through her first operation. Apparently her unconscious led her into danger from the beginning. The possibility that later on she became actively engaged in digging her own grave cannot be refuted. One gets here a glimpse of another type of masochism. However, I do not want it understood that I am implying in any way that this patient was responsible for her tragic end.

It is not essential for this question that her death may have been the result of her masochism or may be regarded as an unconscious suicide; it is part of medical duty to know that the human species is under the domination of such instincts and that it is just as much the obligation of a physician to combat them as it is to support the forces of life. The ways of the death instinct operating within the boundaries of the psychobiological unit are silent and intricate; the individuals who become entangled in its vagaries are usually helplessly involved and cannot extricate themselves by effort or sagacity. In such moments their lives depend on outside help. The therapeutic task is most difficult. It is facilitated when the patient verbalizes a suicidal impulse, but the therapist's responsibility transgresses by far such situations, whose dangers can easily be recognized. Far more serious are those situations in which there is no substantial danger signal. A clinically mild depression, a bizarre dream, a sudden resurgence of a lugubrious childhood recollection may under certain circumstances be sufficient reason to advise a patient to avoid situations in which the unconscious so easily can affirm its intent. Once the danger is seen, it usually is not too difficult to paralyze it. I have always considered it most significant that the two suicides in my practice came to me as a surprise; I had not foreseen their eventuality. The physician's awareness of the danger apparently contains in itself a therapeutic effect, as if the warning "do not do it," implicitly present in the therapeutic situation as soon as the therapist contemplates the possibility, provides a barrier against the patient's submitting to the self-destructive tendency, activated for whatever reason.

I think that this factor must be also considered in discussing why this patient did not commit suicide. As I mentioned before, she was determined to end her life prior to the last hospitalization, but she considered it her duty to preserve herself as long as possible for her children's sake. Every day gained was a benefit to them, she said, and would find them stronger and more capable of bearing up under the final trauma of losing their mother. Her plan to bring into their home the person who would later take over her functions sounded reasonable enough. She urgently asked to be provided with her successor. She enumerated many dangers which she believed were lurking with regard to her children and envisaged the bleakest future for her offspring unless a remedy were found in time. At such points, when mulling over the possibility that no proper substitute might be found, she came close to expressing the unconscious impulse she might have had, namely to take her children with her from life. She then was prone to say it was regrettable that she ever had given birth to children, or that it would be better if her children were sick and would not have to live long. In all the discussions about the children's future she did not mention—except for a single instance—the possibility that her husband could ever remarry after her demise.

By good luck I found a person, Mrs. N., who was ready

to enter the patient's household and who seemed to fulfill almost all the stipulations the patient had made. But it became quickly clear that it was impossible for the patient even to meet Mrs. N., let alone have her live in the home. The patient agreed with me that the effect of the presence of Mrs. N. in her household could only be compared to that of the patient's having her own coffin standing in her bedroom. It was decided that since the presence of the woman would be intolerable, the patient would call her only later, when her sickness had obviated on her side any active participation in the children's lives and had made Mrs. N.'s assistance indispensable.

But from then on Mrs. N. became an important part of the patient's fantasies. She became, so to speak, a steady companion. The patient conducted long imaginary conversations with her and told her what to do with the children, how to treat them, and to what to pay special attention. The function of these fantasies was apparently twofold. First, she created and integrated here a mirror picture of herself that would survive her and continue where she would have to leave off. Second, since—as the patient knew—this person was distantly related to me, she became a substitute figure for me. In her unconscious the patient was gradually handing her children over to me. Once she reported the fantasy that I would adopt her children.

Here we encounter a mechanism which is opposite to that which was described by Freud (1917c) as underlying the process of mourning. In mourning the ego achieves the task of gradually withdrawing those libidinal charges which are attached to the representations of the lost love object. By this work it frees its libido for the purpose of turning it toward new objects. To a certain extent the logic of emotions would have required that this patient accomplish the usual aim of the work of mourning before the actual loss of the love objects had occurred. Here is a point of general validity of the psychology of dying, particularly of those who consciously know of the approach of death. Their plight would be eased if by pre-mourning, so to speak, they had divorced themselves from their love objects, accomplishing this aim shortly before their demise. Then at the time of dying they would have withdrawn their interest from the world and could accept death as the natural consequence of the energic constellation in that moment. But the ego cannot achieve this under ordinary circumstances.

First, the libido withdrawn from love objects would not find substitutes as happens in mourning after the loss of a love object; second, the process of withdrawing the libidinal cathexes from love objects is barely possible while perception conveys the fact of the existence of the love objects, and thus the ego is stimulated to renew the charge which it logically should withdraw in the face of impending death. Devoutly religious people apparently can go through such sequences. They divorce themselves from all they love in this world and charge the image of God with the libido thus freed. In the moment of dying they have bid farewell to the world and are exclusively devoted to the expectancy of the new world, which they believe they are on the verge of entering.

Pfister (1930) investigated thought and fantasy processes which occur with great frequency in persons who suddenly face seemingly inescapable death. He found that the thinking of the person who is certain to die in the next moment goes back to early childhood and refers to situations in which dangers were overcome. It works its way from those activated recollections to the present, ending with a pleasurable, sometimes hallucinatory, imagery regarding the future. Since only a few seconds are left to the person, all these processes are sketchy and not more than a few details come to awareness. But surprisingly many informants report having had the feeling that their whole lives passed in stage-like manner before the inner eye, whereby the own person was seen acting in the way early childhood memories are often preserved. Pfister drew some very important conclusions from this material which I do not want to discuss; however, I would like to add an impression which I obtained from his material. It seems that the ego in the moment of supreme danger constructs a new personality by appearing to re-experience the whole past—with emphasis upon situations of successfully warded-off dangers—and then by continuing into a future which is happy, beautiful, and completely bare of the horrible disaster which the person now approaches in reality. In order to construct such a new and surviving personality, the ego must—like taking a run for jumping—first go back and pick out those situations in which it survived despite great dangers. When in this process of reconstruction the ego reaches the present, it deviates from reality, replacing the self which will be annihilated in the next moment by one that approaches a beautiful future.

This mechanism of creating a new personality when suddenly faced by extinction does not occur in every person, but I believe one could notice it in the patient whose history I am presenting here. Mrs. N. became the patient's own new ego that would survive and take care of her children. Whereas in mourning the ego frees itself from the tie to an object, that is to say, an object relationship is discontinued, in the creation of a new ego the patient achieves the illusion of an ego that will continue and preserve cherished object relationships. This process of an ego creation—aiming at rebearing oneself—was facilitated by Mrs. N.'s having the same sex as the patient and by her being related to me.

The fantasy of an imaginary companion had other meanings also, one of which will be presently discussed. From her excessively pessimistic prognosis regarding her children's future and from her unwillingness to encounter Mrs. N., the person who could alleviate these fears, one may conclude that the patient wanted to preserve the conviction of being irreplaceable in her children's lives. I believe the recognition of the fact that the children might develop adequately despite her demise would have produced a depression, if not a total collapse of her capacity to endure the bleak prospect of her own future.

Her ego was caught here in a seemingly insolvable dilemma. The idea of her children's future state being one of neglect and lack of affection was intolerable, while the conviction of being an indispensable and irreplaceable part in her children's lives was one of the principal bonds which kept her tied to this world. Any change on one side of this equation had to be followed by a change on the other, in accordance with some immutable law of the unconscious. Nevertheless, an approximate solution had been found in the shape of the imaginary companion. Mrs. N. gave her a wish-fulfilling fantasy with which she could fill her mind in order to combat the pain of reality without touching her realistic relationship to her children, which thus remained unthreatened by any competitor. Furthermore, since this imaginary figure was closely associated with me, the fantasy amounted to an elaboration upon the idea that her children would be cared for by a person who had for her the meaning of a father. Her father would probably have been the only person to whom she could have handed her children without conflict. Indeed, one finds frequently in the little girl the fantasy of bearing children for the father yet losing her life in the process and suffering a well-deserved punishment in that way. Thus accidentally a favorable constellation and the possibility of a libidinization of the idea of death had been created for her.

Also I had found here a lever regarding the time factor. When I had to leave for a few weeks and the patient wanted Mrs. N.'s address in order to communicate with her, if necessary, during my absence—thus expressing her fear that death would overcome her before my return— I expressed my approval of her meeting Mrs. N., but added that this would be accompanied by great excitement for her and therefore they should meet in my presence after I had returned. Here again was a possibility to show by action my opinion regarding the patient's life during a certain span of future time (cf. my remarks about this technique in the preceding report) which is more convincing than verbal reassurances. About the latter a patient never feels certain because he thinks, and rightly, that if the opposite were true no one would tell him anyway.

After the preliminaries of our professional contact had been settled and the patient's visits to my office had become part of her routine, two main tasks arose: first, to gain time; second, to prepare her for the ultimate phase of her disease.

At that time the patient's appearance and comportment did not betray in everyday contact any conspicuous sign of her disease. She walked energetically, her movements were vigorous and decisive, she looked well fed, and her facial expression was radiant and friendly. Her subjective complaints during most of the time were pains in the shoulder and fatigue. The latter probably was caused by the sedation she took as well as by the disease. One had the impression during this period that every day which the patient had spent without undue sorrow or grief was a gain and the main goal was to bring her, without any untoward psychiatric incidence, as closely as possible to the ultimate phase so much feared by her. It was clear that management and technique would have to be changed as soon as she entered that ultimate phase. There was the danger—as intimated before—that the patient would spend the time until reaching the ultimate phase in an atmosphere of waiting for her death.

The present has a different meaning in the structure of psychological time than it has in the structure of physical time (Georg Simmel, 1918). In the latter it is reduced to a pinpoint, in the former it has extension, which varies in accordance with age, mood, and other factors. For the little child the next day is often far-off future, whereas an adult may look at the next week as still belonging to the present. In historical time, the present may even cover years and decades.

From occasional remarks the patient made, her need to visualize, free of the danger of death, what may be called her biological present became recognizable. This biological present covered in her case and under her circumstances approximately three months. As soon as she became convinced, in discussion with her treating physician, that the endocrine and radiation treatment which she received would carry her far beyond this time limit—actually the patient lived for sixteen months after I first met her—that is to say, as soon as her biological present became purified of the idea of death, she regained an outlook upon the present as a field of activity. All the measures which were taken in order to facilitate the patient's maintenance of activity can easily be imagined and do not need enumeration.

The second task, namely that of preparing her for the ultimate phase, proved far more difficult. Her exquisitely great resourcefulness in responding and adjusting to difficult reality situations was opposed by an equally great resistance to and refusal of acceptance of the tribulations of the ultimate phase. One may even say that the great asset which she possessed in the form of a high adjustive potential vis-à-vis reality difficulties made her such a bad prospect for the premortal period. Evidently she could accept her impending death only as a proximate result of her own activity, but not as an event that would be imposed upon her. Possibly dying by her own hand did not even mean death to her. Here was an area where direct psychoanalytic intervention in the form of interpretations was indicated. The underlying conflict pertained to a vigorous defense against feminine masochism so excellently studied by Helene Deutsch (1930, 1933). The imagery of lingering in a hospital, of rotting away, of being kept alive artificially until death could no longer be postponed, and of then being subjected to an autopsy made her shudder in horror.

Depressing as the ultimate phase of the cancerous patient is, nevertheless the patient's gruesome imagery went beyond the confines of reality, being fed by secret sources of her deep masochism—a masochism which had been banished from her personality make-up by its conversion into an admirable capacity for *active* reality adjustment. That the accent was put upon activity can be seen from her total incapacity to anticipate the possibility of adjusting to the ultimate phase.

I felt reminded of the ancient myth of Alcestis, wife of Admetus, King of Thessaly. When as a young man he fell fatally sick, the Fates agreed to spare his life under the condition that another human being be ready to die for him. His subjects, his friends, and even his aged parents shuddered at the idea of such sacrifice; only his faithful wife, Alcestis, decided to make the supreme step. The similarity between this patient and Alcestis was established since both of them suffered from the knowledge of the moment when they would die, which Euripides expressed in the following lines of Alcestis: "And I must die. Not tomorrow, nor tomorrow's morrow comes this misfortune to me, but even now I shall be named with those that are no more."

Yet there was an essential difference. Alcestis' death was self-willed and contained purpose. The patient experienced her impending death as accidental and utterly senseless. Although Alcestis had made a free decision (was it really free or was it enforced by the necessity to conceal ambivalence?), she suffered by her fate, lamented, and asked for pity. Indirectly she requested a reward from Admetus when she said: "Well! Do not forget this gift, for I shall ask—not a recompense, since nothing is more precious than life, but—only what is just. . . . marry not again." She justifies this demand by her children's prospective welfare and refers to the evils children customarily suffer from stepmothers.

The patient—if speculation be permitted—was a personality who would have acted as Alcestis does in the myth; if she could have discovered a grain of purpose in her sad fate, she probably would not have hesitated to endure her sufferings to their natural end. In her conscious ideology she did not maintain the view of ancient Greece that "nothing is more precious than life," but rather it was the absence of purpose, as will be presently seen, which caused her to recoil from waiting for her death.

Indeed this last phase did not offer even the slightest chance for the release of any activity, but condemned the patient to remain in a pure state of passivity. At this point, one of the few neurotic symptoms, which had been present prior to the onset of the terminal disease, must be mentioned. Her history made it evident that the regular occurrence of anxiety before addressing groups and the few attacks of anxiety provoked in other situations were directed against exhibitionistic desires. The core of the conflict lay in her aversion to her breasts, which she believed to be too large. The gruesome imagery regarding a vegetable-like existence and an autopsy was also evoked by the fear of being looked at, of being defenseless against what was visualized by her as a hostile inroad. Thus here also—as in so many other clinical instances—defenses against masochism were combined with those against exhibitionism.

Objectively, too, the phase preceding the ultimate one was a phase of suffering and passivity, at least the onlooker would describe it in such terms, but in closer scrutiny one could observe that the patient had converted it psychologically into a rather active one. Operations did not keep her in the hospital for a long time. She was up and around after a surprisingly short time and resumed full activity at home even when laboring under great pain. Furthermore, the mastery over the fatigue and exhaustion customarily following X-ray treatment offered another outlet. Likewise, the absence of hypersexuality, despite intensive endocrine therapy, was experienced by her as no small triumph. When the considerable defenses which she must have built against the libidinal upsurge gave way and she was exposed to intensive libidinal urges, she was quite desperate. Fortunately the verbalization of the difficulty sufficed to reinstitute the defensive apparatus and after a few days she got hold of herself and never complained again about untoward sensations. Thus one could observe that this whole phase which appeared outwardly like a chain of constant suffering was converted into a phase of highest activity by her successful denial of those consequences which necessarily follow such suffering. One could even say that as long as her condition permitted movement at all, this sufficed as a protection against the danger of surrender to her deep masochistic wishes. Rightly the patient anticipated that she would have to go through the ultimate phase without the protection of these defenses.

Also the image of being overcome by death, of not being able to ordain arbitrarily the moment of its occurrence, had a masochistic meaning for her.

I first countered her arguments in favor of suicide by referring to the consequences which this would have for her children and her husband. Was she not aware, I asked, that for others a death by suicide is far more difficult to bear than one by natural causes? I asked her to think how she would feel if the roles were reversed between her and her husband. She replied in an illogical way which, however, illuminated the psychological background of the whole situation. She said: "I certainly would give my husband an injection which would make him sleep forever." This was not meant as a hidden request for euthanasia, since I had spoken repeatedly of her unquestionable right to demand and expect freedom of pain and she had agreed with me that in general one does not let patients suffer in the way she had always visualized. I even had the impression that she was afraid of euthanasia; that she could accept euthanasia, so to speak, only in the form of suicide. The aforementioned remark shows, in my opinion, that her refusal pertained to the acceptance of passivity in any form. What she really said was: "Of course, I would be able and generous enough to do this to others but I could never submit myself."

This discussion was often repeated. I quickly stopped—for evident reasons—referring to her children as bearers of unfortunate consequences in case she committed suicide but reminded her how her physicians would feel. I asked her whether she ever thought what it meant to a physician when a patient dies by his own hand. She pleaded with me and claimed I could not oppose her suicide if I really liked and understood her. She wished we would not discuss this subject which excited her so much, because her knowledge that this way out was ever at hand constituted the only prop that allowed her to live and keep going. I promised I would not bring up the topic anymore and assured her I knew well that no argument I could raise would make her change her mind, but that I considered it my duty to tell her my opinion. After all, she had lived an almost perfect life, had fulfilled her duties in an exemplary way, towering far above the average in terms of her many good deeds, her constant fight for right and justice and the protection of the underdog. A suicide, it seemed to me, was not in keeping with her style of life at all, and she should not mar the splendid record she had established. But since she had made up her mind, all this was waste of breath, I added. It apparently was, since occasional remarks betrayed the perseverance of her intention.

However, on one occasion it seemed that possibly I had made a dent in her determination. She was comparing the fullness of her previous life with the senselessness of the ultimate phase. Even now, she continued, when she could not work in her profession and had to lie down for many hours a day, her life was nevertheless meaningful since her presence was important for her children and thus she fulfilled a function. But once in the hospital, knowing that there was no return home, and unable to rise from her bed, she would be reduced to a lump of useless, rotting flesh; then her life would become senseless. Although she was ready to bear unflinchingly all pains as long as there was sense in her life, why would I try to condemn her to endure suffering at a time when meaning would have vanished and life become utter futility?

Thereupon I countered that I believed she had made a gross mistake. Her life—like life in general—had been futile and without meaning even before the onset of her disease. From the beginning philosophers have vainly tried to find the meaning of life. The only difference between the two phases she had in mind was that in one she was able to attribute a meaning to life, whereas in the other she was incapable of doing this. In reality, I told her, both were bare of meaning and sense. The patient became confused, claimed not to understand me, and started to cry. It was close to the end of the hour. I expected she would come back to my argument in later meetings but she never did. It was my impression that this conversation was a turning point, that the suicidal intent was weakened from then on. As a matter of fact, the patient did not commit suicide, but acted right to the end in keeping with the standards of her past; that is to say, she lived up to the requirements of reality. However, I cannot decide whether the psychiatric treatment had any bearing upon this and whether her course would have been, in this respect, the same with or without treatment. I say this although there was evidence that with the approach of the ultimate phase, she idealized me more and more and finally even claimed that she had more trust and confidence in my treatment than in the physical treatment which she received. Furthermore, when the first signs of the final deterioration set in and repeated thoracenteses had to be performed, when she occasionally needed morphine to enable her to go to the hospital—necessities which she correctly interpreted and which she had always claimed she would not endure—she said: "I never thought I would accept this level." On that occasion she also thanked me with strong emotion in her voice, whereas until then she had done so occasionally and in a perfunctory manner. After that interview, by the way, she never again mentioned feelings of thankfulness.

I doubt whether it was the support received from psychotherapy which kept her from committing suicide. It is possible that despite her firm determination, the patient was so closely attached to life as to be quite unable to take the final step.

Yet, if it is hypothetically assumed that the aforementioned conversation actually had the effect which the clinical impression implied, then the following speculation is permissible: My statement that life, in whatever phase it is encountered and whatever forms it may take, is always senseless and meaningless must be viewed in the context of preceding interpretations. The only area into which I had carried outright interpretations concerned her conflicts about the problem of activity and passivity, the importance it must have had for her to live a life that made it comparable to that of a man in terms of success and social responsibility, her inclination to look down upon women and to appraise the male higher than his counterpart, her sensitivity to incidents of male arrogance and other factors of that kind. In other words, I tried to outline some material which passes in psychoanalysis under the name of the female castration complex and penis envy. Of course, genetic interpretations or real working through in the psychoanalytic sense was not done, nor would it have been possible or even advisable. Assistance was also given by extensive intellectualization. The corresponding problems of male development were amply discussed; around that time her little son's behavior offered the best clinical illustration one could ask for in confirmation of the psychoanalytic theory of male psychosexual development. Her overestimation of male creativity might have been temporarily diminished by the theory which I presented to her, that man's cultural contributions were greater because he had to compensate for the female privilege of creating children and that "after all no man ever created anything so wonderful as a baby." The patient seemed to accept an outlook that replaced the female penis envy by a male child-bearing envy. Thus, in those discussions a doubt was nourished as to the appropriateness of her unconscious triumph regarding her ability to compete successfully with men.

Though the theories I offered tended to alleviate the

pain which she probably had unconsciously suffered from being "only" a woman, they nevertheless might also have had a depressing effect because they seemed to question her scale of values, in whose objective validity she had believed until then. Her situation might be compared with that of the adolescent who has with great effort suppressed masturbatory impulses, only to be told suddenly that there are no valid objections to adolescent masturbation. Clinical experience shows that the effect of such information does not always coincide with the therapist's anticipation, but that the adolescent responds with a depression, since now he has been deprived of a forceful tool in his struggle against a forbidden form of sexual gratification. Comparably, after this patient had used her irrational evaluation of the sexes as a useful motive for constructive action in the community, she was told convincingly, and rather suddenly that the secret dynamic source of her unbounding energy was in reality an illusionary bias. To summarize, this bias had had apparently a twofold effect: it was a source of pain; but it was likewise the source of energetic, compensatory, and constructive action. The therapeutic interviews, while softening the pain, also cast a doubt upon those activities which had been most cherished by her.

Thus my remark about the senselessness of life in general fell on fertile soil. It may have had for her a complementary meaning to our previous discussion in the following way: not only is it senseless to compete with men since women are more creative anyway than men, but it is also senseless to be a woman, that is to say, to be passive. Since activity also is senseless—though by inference only—why refuse to accept passivity, which is blatantly senseless?

Since I was not with the patient during the ultimate phase of her sickness, I cannot quote clinical evidence for or against my assumption, but I should think that my remarks, combined with the inevitable progress of the devastating disease process, weakened her activity just enough to render her incapable of mobilizing that amount of energy which is necessary for suicide.

The patient apparently had no depression in the clinical meaning of the term. When the time of her final hospitalization came, I was told, she tried to resist first by procrastination and then by demanding release after a short period of hospitalization. The psychiatrist substituting for me advised the treating physician to take a more energetic stand at this point. The patient was told that she had to co-operate more, that she had to understand she was a patient and therefore could not impose upon the physician the course of treatment she wished to have taken. This sufficed, and after the short interlude of active resistance, she co-operated to the fullest. In the last few days she was confused—most probably because of heavy sedation—speaking about work she had to do and appointments she had to keep. She suddenly died on the twenty-fifth day of her hospitalization.

In concluding this report, I wish to point out a practical difficulty which, as far as I can see, arises only in the psychiatric treatment of the dying and which, to my regret, I had not adequately foreseen. It is known that in most specialties and particularly in psychoanalysis, the therapist's absence from town for vacation or any other reason may cause a problem. In the analysis of the neurotic this question can usually be handled with comparative ease. As has been observed by many (Alexander and French, 1946), a temporary interruption of the treatment such as that necessitated by vacation may even have a beneficial effect upon the course of treatment. Absence is much more difficult with delinquents and schizophrenics, particularly in early phases of treatment. Technical measures for preventing an untoward effect upon the patient do not need to be discussed here, though of course it is a matter of general knowledge that the treatment of a patient suffering from severe psychopathology ought not to be started unless there is enough time left, before the first interruption of treatment, to establish a workable and durable transference relationship. I am thinking particularly of one clinical example which left an indelible impression upon me. An unusually gifted and seemingly well-adjusted person sought analytic treatment for an acute problem a short time before the analyst went on a vacation. A trial analysis was started. The patient co-operated exceedingly well, and the initial period took a very promising course. Material of first importance was brought into analysis; analyst and patient parted with the understanding of a resumption of the treatment after the summer. Yet in the fall the patient refused to continue the treatment and no power of persuasion in subsequent years could make him change his mind. Moreover, his life took a course which showed increasingly that he had become the victim of a disastrous repetition compulsion which finally brought him to a tragic end. It was always my impression that the beginning of this analysis should have been postponed to a more propitious moment despite the acuteness of the conflict which was, by the way, not a dangerous one. Of course, three principal questions remain unanswered: Would his analysis have taken the same course, with the patient breaking off treatment under one pretext or another under any circumstances? Would the stimulation of the repetition compulsion have been accessible to mastery by analysis even under optimal conditions? Was he bound to become a victim of his indomitable acting out, independent of any stimulation by the treatment? Whatever the alternatives, clinical acumen should try to avoid the risk of an introductory treatment phase which can cover—for external reasons—only a short period.

In most clinical situations a substitute physician can replace the treating physician; in the psychiatric treatment of the dying, however, the assignment of a substitute should be essentially out of question. Unalterable necessities forced me to leave about four weeks before this patient's death. Several weeks before leaving I had discussed with her the necessity of my departure and demanded that she continue to see a colleague at least once a week during my absence. The patient remonstrated. I told her that I considered my departure per se unjustifiable and that I did it only under force of necessities outside my control. She remonstrated again; I continued that I was certain she would not leave town if she treated a patient who was in an equally dire exigency as she was. Here a realistic opportunity was offered for me to express my concern and my feelings about her plight in a way not offered previously in the psychotherapeutic situation. The patient seemed impressed and promised to comply—in a moment of weakness, as she said later when she wanted to be released from her promise. When I had to leave she was already in a condition where visits to a physician's office were barely possible. She was visited by a colleague in her home for a few times.* A friendly relationship developed, particularly when it turned out that patient and physician had met many years before. During the short period of the patient's active resistance to hospitalization, the physician's assistance proved invaluable. Whether my absence had an inhibiting effect upon the patient's short-lasting tendency to act out, whether she was disappointed by my absence and therefore depressed and further weakened in activity, I do not know. It is possible that my presence would have made it more difficult for the patient to accept the reality of her final hospitalization. This, of course, is only speculation

* I owe Dr. Claire Selzer immeasurable thanks for her self-sacrificing readiness to substitute for me in that emergency and to provide exemplary care for the patient.

and should not throw any doubt upon the indubitable truth that the psychiatrist who is involved in the treatment of patients who approach death must never take on commitments which might take him away from the bedside as long as the patient maintains lucid consciousness. The physician who is responsible for the physical side of therapy is replaceable, but the psychiatrist essentially is not when the moment of death is approaching.

In this moment all the functions the physician fulfills, the realistic as well as the imaginary ones of the friend, of the parental substitute, the priest, the redeemer, and the ancient medicine man—all of these fuse into an indeterminate complex in which reality and fantasy can no longer be distinguished; that is to say, it becomes senseless to measure the psychiatrist's functions in such terms, since a mind is in the process of dissolution, of losing that structure which alone makes polarities such as reality and fantasy meaningful.

In these moments the psychiatrist, who has lent himself during the terminal phase as a frame into which the patient has projected his loves and hatreds and the aggregate of all the actors who played a role on the stage of his life, becomes irreplaceable. The separation between external reality and internal reality crumbles, and the psychiatrist is no longer an object of transference; that which serves in the treatment of the living as a tool to help the patient back to life becomes here an end in itself, without a purpose beyond.

CASE THREE

Whereas in the two preceding reports attention was focused upon the psychiatric exigencies relating to the patient's death, in this report an aftermath following the patient's death, a most embarrassing one for the psychiatrist, will be an additional theme. In other words, attention will be paid to the potential dangers which the patient's death may harbor for the psychiatrist. In the instance under discussion here the psychiatric treatment had satisfactorily accomplished its goal, which had been initially to make an exceedingly sick person participate actively and adequately in the management of her rather complicated affairs and, later, to help her go through her terminal disease without becoming aware of her impending death. The patient, however, shortly before her demise had signed a will in which—without my knowledge—she had made me the heir of a considerable amount of money. This in turn was followed by the deposition of a close relative of hers, who contested the will, that I had exerted undue influence upon the patient at a time when she was incompetent.

I believe that notwithstanding its relative unusualness, this aftermath may lend itself readily to an illumination of factors which are latently present in a good many instances but which for evident reasons rarely make themselves directly noticeable within the clinical area. As can well be imagined, the incident will give occasion for a discussion regarding professional ethics which necessarily must be different and far more stringent in psychiatry than in any other professional field.

I

The patient, a thin pale woman in her early sixties, was living at the time I became acquainted with her under most difficult circumstances. Married to a successful advertising man of hypomanic temperament and bizarre character, her external condition had worsened when he became ill with a life-threatening disease which brought out his latent destructive attitudes to a degree almost unbearable to his environment.

The patient was unprepared to withstand this strain. During most of her marriage she had lived what may be called a fake existence, a kind of shadow life forced upon her by her husband, who insisted that her whole life should be devoted to the social obligations of a leisurely society woman. At the same time he firmly insisted on her being removed from all realistic contacts; she was not permitted to sign a check or handle any money matter, or even to make the arrangements for their elaborate social affairs. Whenever there might have been something for her to do in terms of practical conduct, a secretary or other help was hired in order to prevent what in his imagination must have been a besmirching contiguity. Despite occasional, weak protests, the patient had played this role well and to her husband's satisfaction. Yet the severe restrictions imposed upon her by her husband were, as she claimed, a source of great unhappiness. Her style of life had left its traces. Her movements and way of talking were deliberately calm, affected, and manneristic; her clothes were in accordance with the next fashion, and her makeup perfectly concealed signs of age. She gave the appearance of a highly sophisticated fashion doll dressed up with extremely good taste. Yet her ready references to the social influences which actually existed tended only to conceal an extensive ego defect.

Otherwise this kind of existence could never have become acceptable to her, and it may be said that the bizarre style of life her husband had imposed upon her was, to a certain extent, one of the few ways in which she could maintain contact—even if it were only a sham contact—with reality. A part of her psychopathology which was unencumbered by the direct bearing of societal influences came to the fore in the history of her childlessness. Her ardent wish to have children had been frustrated forever by surgery performed because of severe dysmenorrhea. She thought reproachfully of the gynecologist who had advised the operation, for she had since been told of the psychogenic etiology of the symptom. Here again a rationalization by the use of a reality factor was encountered, but simultaneously her masochism became visible since the operation had been forced by her excessive complaints. In order to compensate for the absence of children, she had taken a relative into her house and thought for a time of adopting her. Yet there was mutual ambivalence which constantly interfered with an affectionate relationship even half free of conflict, and thus the adoption was never carried out. Nevertheless, a kind of mother-daughter relationship was continued after the relative married and moved away to O———. It was she who asked me for help and introduced me to the patient.

The patient's ego defect manifested itself in a variety of symptoms. She was quite vulnerable to even mild signs of aggression in her environment, and became, also for this reason, easily depressed. Her extreme sensitivity led to exaggerations which looked at times like paranoid ideas. To all these symptoms was added what must be called—despite the later discovery of fatal pathology—a host of psychosomatic symptoms mainly referring to the gastrointestinal system. The patient was almost constantly preoccupied with her body and rarely spent a day without finding some reason for a physical complaint.

The diagnostic question was difficult to answer. Although some of her symptoms might have suggested schizophrenia, this diagnosis could be excluded. Besides neurotic symptoms such as anxiety, sporadic depressions, and psychosomatic complaints, she had a bizarre character with strong tendencies toward dependency and acting out. Her impulsiveness and her sensitivity made her object relations quite difficult at times. Her capacity to bear displeasure was definitely lowered; when in conversation an unpleasant topic was touched upon, she became confused or her memory went on strike. Later it was clear that she would scarcely ever be able to live completely unsupervised; but likewise it became evident that she had recovered to such an extent that this supervision could be reduced to a minimum. She needed—in view of her considerably ambivalent tendencies—a relationship which was kept free of that malignant admixture and which would permit her to review from time to time her reality situation.

In the course of the history I will have an opportunity to discuss the factors which initially made it appear inadvisable for me to take over this patient's treatment, but suffice it to say now that after a few interviews the general situation seemed less hopeless than I had thought at the beginning, and I perceived some avenues along which a rehabilitation of this patient could be attained.

Three phases which required different techniques can be distinguished in the subsequent therapeutic contacts:

Phase one lasted approximately three months and was terminated by the death of the patient's husband.

Phase two covered approximately the subsequent eight months and was terminated one month prior to the patient's moving from C—— to O—— with the intention of taking up residence there.

Phase three started after an interval of ten months which the patient spent with relatives after which she returned for treatment to C——. It was terminated fourteen weeks later by the patient's death.

The first phase of the treatment proceeded favorably. The patient gained some insight into the peculiarities of her husband's disorder, behaved more adequately toward him, and became less confused by his extravagances. I had never met her husband and therefore had to rely on second-hand information, all of which agreed on the psychopathological unusualness of his personality. There was almost no one who would have been able to get along with him for a longer period of time. Of an unquestionably tyrannical disposition, he tried to dominate, exploit, and even abuse everyone with whom he came in contact, but often he was in turn exploited precisely by those whom he had selected as potential victims of his whims. In dealing with people he was said to use a technique which unavoidably led to their devaluation. He gave them exorbitant gifts; if they were accepted, he felt entitled to claim that the recipient was corrupt and accessible to bribe. Yet if the gifts were refused, the declining party was unmasked as unrealistic and inadequate in judgment. This information was one of the reasons why I had felt averse to beginning the patient's treatment. Certainly her husband would look on me as unbidden intruder who threatened to upset the almost slavish dependency of his wife, a dependency upon which the relative equilibrium of his marriage was built, and therefore he would apply one of the many techniques apparently at his disposal in order to eliminate his wife's therapist. I had to admit to myself that the aforementioned technique of devaluation was unusually ingenious and practically insuperable. I was frank with the patient about my opinion that her husband would necessarily be the source of constant interference with the treatment—an interference which would be all the more impossible to eliminate in view of his physical disorder. However, the patient was ready to reduce the time she would spend with him and to move into town, her husband living in the country upon medical advice.

Thus the opportunity was created to induce her gradual withdrawal from playing the role of a social doll. The mild increase of inner activity also had a wholesome effect on her psychosomatic symptoms. Concomitantly with the increasing feeling of activity toward her husband and with the discovery that she could maintain internal independence even while catering to his wishes, her fears started to focus upon what would happen to her if her husband died.

The patient told me of her forebodings regarding her husband's business associates. She feared that her husband's demise would make her financially dependent on them and would leave her at their mercy. The patient's bleak outlook upon the intentions of her husband's associates sounded paranoid, but her relative had assured me that the patient was not exaggerating in that respect. During that time the patient was not accessible to reassurances regarding the ominous events she anticipated once her husband had died, which actually happened just about the time our discussion of the subject had reached a peak. This event, of course, brought on a complete change in the therapeutic task. From one day to another she was thrown out of her ivory tower and confronted with great responsibilities and grave decisions. Financial dependency or a life under strained financial circumstances would evidently have been beyond her limited adjustability, and thus the requirements of a highly acute reality situation became an important part of therapy. To the surprise of all concerned the patient proved herself to be a woman of good judgment. She developed an unexpected degree of seemingly independent activity, dismissed her husband's attorney, and engaged counsel who proved to be excellent. In psychotherapy she was willing to understand where her disorder threatened to interfere with a realistic manipulation of the complicated business situation, which at times took stormy turns and then caused her great excitement. She succeeded in keeping her neurotic whims out of the reality situation and thus got the full profit from the good business sense which until now an unfavorable social milieu had held in abeyance behind her many quirks.

Her general improvement seemed threatened again when an internist claimed he had discovered the source of her somatic complaints and strongly advised abdominal surgery. The patient responded with great anxiety to the necessity for an operation. But the favorable prospect—of which her physicians were quite certain—of being freed from her gastrointestinal symptoms made her finally agree. Despite the unavoidable fear of death, she co-operated well with her physicians before and after the operation, when, unfortunately, the gastrointestinal symptoms grew worse. A second surgical intervention became necessary. Biopsy made her physician diagnose a chronic inflammatory disease. Grave postsurgical complications set in which threatened her life, and for two days hope of her ever recovering was given up. But she rallied, and after a few weeks she was again on her feet, seemingly in fine fettle. It was really surprising how much vitality and energy this patient could show at times. Throughout the trying postoperative weeks, which could have lent themselves so well to acting out, she showed scarcely any psychopathology.

Perhaps she was one of those people who could prove their mettle only under adverse conditions when by dint of painful events their feelings of guilt have been assuaged. But it must also be considered that this patient might have had the ability, which is significant of some hysterical character types, to act in accordance with the requirements of the immediate situation as long as this is necessary for their personal advantage.

Around that time her business negotiations came at last to a successful end, and it was certain she would be able to maintain the standard to which she had become accustomed and which had become so important to her well-being. In her psychotherapy she had made progress. She became aware of her feelings of guilt toward her husband and gradually lost her fear of retaliation for his early death. Her own coming so close to death postoperatively may have meant to her a symbolic clearing off. Some of the conflicts which went through her past were discussed, such as the conflict about childlessness and the consequent ambivalence toward the relative whom she had taken into her house, and the patient seemed generally more reliable in her decisions and her comportment toward others.

When this relative suggested that the patient should move to O—— to live closer to her and her husband, I thought it might be a good idea since nothing particular seemed to hold her in C—— and these relatives were among the few people whom she liked. But the patient was not too happy about the plan. Her old conflicts about this almost adopted daughter had certainly not yet been resolved, but she would, she agreed, continue her treatment in O——. More serious was her argument that I had become indispensable to her and that she was certain no other psychiatrist could help her as I had. An analysis of her transference was out of the question. Her age alone made analysis impossible. Moreover, my many interferences in the reality situation, the frequent occasions when she had depended on my direct advice, had of course mixed up the transference situation and led to one of real assistance and dependency. In this situation, I knew, no argument would help. Therefore I resorted to telling the patient that I accepted her reasoning, but that it should be checked first in order to find out whether it was based on fact. I suggested that she should be treated for a month by another psychiatrist and find out for herself whether her claim was valid. The patient agreed and after a month's time she had to concede that I had been right. She had received equally good service from the other psychiatrist. Now there was no obstacle to her moving to O——.

Shortly before her departure I met her again. Her condition seemed excellent; she felt reassured that she had gained an adequate independence from me and was looking forward to moving to her new environment.

Thus everything might have been set for her spending the rest of her life peacefully and pleasurably in following up her hobbies and enjoying all the amenities which are accessible to a member of the leisure class. I, however, had learned not to maintain prematurely that a patient was untreatable by psychotherapy, as I had done at the beginning of this case.

For ten months I heard scarcely anything of the patient; then I was suddenly notified that she had left O—— and wanted to see me.

When I met her, her physical appearance alarmed me. She was paler than usual, underweight, and short of breath. She coughed from time to time but was sure that her physical symptoms as well as the nightly attacks of anxiety which had started a few weeks earlier were psychogenic. She had been carefully examined in O—— as well as upon her arrival in C——, but no physical pathology responsible for the cough had been detected. She spoke with great anger of her relative, reporting a few incidents which had made her stay in O—— unbearable and reproached me for ever having let her go to O——. She was determined to stay in C——, never to return to O——, and to stand on her own feet from then on. She felt independent and was certain that she could now manage her affairs successfully, because she had left O—— against her family's advice, had prepared the move alone, and had traveled alone, something of which she had previously been afraid. She was disturbed only by the reappearance of anxiety at night and by the cough. She begged me to help her in getting rid of these symptoms so that this time nothing would stand in the way of her fulfilling the great wish which she had had since early youth, namely to live an independent life. A brief exploration revealed that shortly before the onset of her nervous cough and anxiety, a person who had played an important role in her life had died. This suggested a connection between the nervous cough, the return of anxiety, and a feeling of guilt which she habitually tended to develop after the death of a person close to her.

Yet despite this seemingly indubitable psychogenic connection and the claim of two specialists that she was free of organic pathology, I told her, for reasons to be discussed later, that I had to insist on a renewed physical examination and continuance of her treatment by a physician familiar with psychiatric techniques but who knew more about internal medicine than I did. The patient was disappointed but amenable to my suggestion, and an appointment was made with a specialist. To my horror, I was subsequently informed of the diagnosis of an inoperable malignancy. I could do nothing but deplore that death would prematurely stop the patient who had, against heavy odds, rallied all her resources in order to realize finally some of the potentialities which seemed to have been dormant in her.

It was obvious that the patient ought not to be apprised of the fatal nature of her disease. The consultant agreed and was ready to take over the physical and psychiatric treatment. The patient was told that the physical nature of her disease had been discovered, that it concerned a benign disease which would require protracted treatment and later, possibly, hospitalization. She thanked me profusely for having saved her life because I had insisted on a further physical workup and asked to be permitted to call on me if she should later desire to do so. I protested her belief and promised to fulfill her request.

When the necessity for hospitalization arose, and later again on the occasion of his vacation, the internist asked me to help him out. I found the patient mildly depressed, complaining about nurses, and discouraged by the persistence of her symptoms. In view of her complaints it was decided that I should take up treatment again, since the strong attachment she had formed to me might give me a better chance to carry her through the final phase of her fatal disease than the physician with whom she had become acquainted only recently. Thus her treatment was divided between the internist and me.

The clinical task was unusual. A patient who was determined to turn energetically toward life was fatally sick but unaware of the hopelessness of her condition. Therefore she should be kept ignorant of the gravity of her state, encouraged to maintain her optimism and her morale, and prevented from falling into a depression. It was clear that there was no alternative to concealing from the patient the true nature of her disease since any other procedure would have precipitated severe psychopathology.

However, there was one factor which deserved special attention. Shortly after her return from O—— the patient had told me that if she knew she were dying, she would change her will instantly and distribute part of the money which had been allocated in a previous will to her quasi-adopted daughter to other relatives, who were in need of financial assistance. But since she was assured that her sickness was benign, she did not see any reason to proceed in a hurry. Pointedly—and evidently in order to test me—she added that she was certain that I, since I had never let her down, would tell her to make a will now if her life were in danger. A decision to make myself instrumental in the preservation of the patient's illusion of approaching recovery thus might have had detrimental consequences for some of her relatives, inasmuch as they would obtain less of her estate if she died prior to executing a new will. However, I decided that the patient's mental and emotional welfare had to be my paramount goal even though, if all circumstances were known to the members of her family, I would be liable to the justified complaints of those who might be injured by the patient's premature death. I am fully aware that I might be censured by some members of the medical and juridical professions for such an opinion, but I do not see how a different decision can be made if the patient's welfare is made the physician's uppermost goal, which, after all, it should be.

However, after some time—it was two weeks before her demise—she did decide to change her will and seemed relieved after she had accomplished this. From a previous experience I knew that she was the victim of superstitions with regard to the making of a will, and that she had to go through a struggle before she found enough resolution to do anything active in testamentary matters.

The working plan I had made my own for the final phase of the treatment was the following: I would make use of the strong affectionate tie which the patient had formed and of the feeling of omnipotence she had projected upon me. Again, a technique had to be evolved which was contrary to the usual technique applied in the treatment of neurotics, when the growth of transference beyond the physiological optimum must be immediately reduced to combat the patient's illusionary belief in the therapist's omnipotence.

This last phase of her illness was, of course, over-shadowed by the gruesome effect of her fatal disease. The rapid progress of her body's destruction was appalling. My main fear was that the illusion of her recovery might be destroyed by the irrefutable signs of her appearance, proving the opposite of what I wanted her to believe. The narcissistic gratification derived from her attractiveness was an important, perhaps even the main, source of her stamina. Hospitals, so well equipped for the physical care of those approaching death, do not always consider the mental qualms of this final process. A dresser with a huge mirror had been posted at her bedside, as if she should constantly be reminded of the vanity of her worldly existence; arrangements were quickly made to have flowers before the mirror.

The outbreaks of anger against her relative softened, and when she expressed the feeling that she seemed able now to forgive her, she seemed well on the way to achieving internal peace. She died in her sleep, without ever having consciously doubted that she was on the way to recovery, and to the end she believed that I had saved her life by sending her to an internist and that she would soon embark upon an active life in the pursuit of long-cherished ambitions.

II

Whereas I could feel contented with having succeeded in protecting the patient from a depression and thus having made it possible for her to pass away without emotional agony, I was most painfully surprised by the information that the patient had left me a considerable legacy and had made me the executor of her will. It was evident that the acceptance of any benefit derived from a patient's will would be unethical and I informed the attorney that my legacy had to be distributed among the other legatees or given to charitable institutions, whatever might be the proper procedure. About the acceptance of the executorship I was in doubt. When I was informed that if I did not accept it there was the possibility of an outbreak of family quarrels, I agreed to accept under the condition that the same reservations I had stipulated regarding the legacy would be valid for my functioning as an executor. Shortly thereafter, however, Mr. X., the husband of the patient's aforementioned relative, wrote me a letter informing me of a depression he suffered from because of severe doubts about my honesty. A few letters were exchanged in which I stated my previous determination not to accept the legacy. At first he seemed reassured by this answer but later he claimed he had received information from some acquaintances of his who had visited the patient; they maintained that she was definitely confused at the time she had signed the will. He was, he wrote, compelled to take legal steps.

A short time later he submitted in court objections to the probation of the patient's will, alleging under oath that the patient was not competent to make a will at the time and that the will was obtained by me—who was made the executor and one of the principal beneficiaries of the will—through undue influence. The matter was settled later and Mr. X. withdrew his objections.

III

The foregoing report requires examination from two separate viewpoints. A few psychiatric problems related to the peculiarities of this patient, but of general psychiatric interest, have not yet been discussed. Also, there is a series of problems related to the contest of the patient's will and to the grave accusation raised against the treating psychiatrist. I will start with some of the psychiatric problems.

A certain factor which is with relative rarity brought into psychiatric discussions is the difficulty caused by a patient's wealth, a factor which had made me skeptical regarding the prognosis of this patient's treatment. More frequently than not we become aware of the damaging effect of poverty and destitution. But the opposite economic factor also presents its pitfalls for psychotherapy. It seems to be quite generally true that extremes of any kind cause their particular difficulties in any kind of psychotherapy.

The economic environment from which, as I believe, patients with the most favorable psychotherapeutic prognosis come, is the upper middle class. This would be in conformity with the general contribution which the upper middle class makes to the welfare of this country. The wealthy, notwithstanding many exceptions, have an outlook upon life which can be characterized by the implicit belief that everything desirable can be bought for money. At certain historical times this has led to the belief that even eternal bliss is purchasable.

In psychotherapy and in psychoanalysis the patient is subjected to severe frustrations since the bulk of the patient's wishes aroused in and by the transference situation must not be gratified. Automatically—almost like a reflex—the wealthy patient then tries to make the psychiatrist abandon the relatively firm and distant therapeutic attitude by the offer of gifts, that is to say, by bribery. When the psychiatrist proves himself inaccessible to bribery, this may amount to an unbearable frustration and the patient may quit the treatment using one or the other excuse. This problem can be handled in psychoanalysis with less difficulty than in psychotherapy, the latter requiring greater personal closeness than the former.

This patient, whose positive transference set in rapidly with the first interview, pursued at times a similar technique by the offer of smaller and larger gifts. Yet she graciously assented to the repeated explanation as to why the acceptance of gifts would lead to a detrimental psychotherapeutic situation and did not react with unfriendliness or hostility to the feeling of rejection which unavoidably occurs when a gift is refused.

Another taxing complication was the patient's physical condition. Her history may serve as a paradigmatic warning to all those who believe that the physical or psychogenic etiology of a disease can be determined by the patient's history. Notwithstanding the many instances in which such determination seems to have been successful, it always amounts to a grave risk for reasons which can easily be derived from Freud's writings. In *The Interpretation of Dreams,* Freud (1900) has clarified the relationship that exists between physical factors and psychic dream mechanisms. A physical factor such as an ungratified physical need or an urge or an irritation caused by external stimulation will set in motion the same psychic mechanisms which are activated in the dream work of those dreams which are caused exclusively by the demand of unfulfilled psychic stimuli. That is to say, images, recollections—briefly, the whole array of psychic material—will attach themselves to the physical factor and intrude into the dream, using its power to overcome those forces which would otherwise keep them away from consciousness. Such a process, in which one impulse borrows strength from another, is quite frequent. If one has the occasion to analyze acts of self-defense, in which a person has committed justified acts of aggression—for all outward appearance necessitated by reality for the sake of survival—he may be greatly astounded to find that the most archaic and the most deeply repressed impulses were gratified in those actions which seemed to serve exclusively the rational purpose of self-preservation. Likewise, one discovers in those dreams which occur under the impact of a strong physical urge the most archaic material. If one examines physical disease under this aspect, he finds the same experience in many patients. In most physical diseases the psychic apparatus is subjected to a more or less constant irritation. This physical irritation is not necessarily perceived as such but may become the carrier of deeply repressed material which now may have an opportunity, by means of the detour offered by the physical disorder, to enter, though still highly disguised, the area of consciousness. Therefore it happens that in taking a history of a patient's physical symptoms, one often gets with surprising quickness a history of a patient's neurosis (Felix Deutsch, 1949), which fact then is often and erroneously interpreted as proving the psychogenic origin of the respective symptom.

However, two entirely different clinical situations must here be differentiated. In prolonged and deep psychoanalysis one learns that physical sickness regularly affects the unconscious; that is to say, a psychoanalytic exploration of psychic processes which occur before, during, and after physical disease proves that in the unconscious and repressed part of the personality psychic material regularly becomes attached to the irritation which issues from physical disorder, but this does not mean that this unconscious material which is firmly attached to the physical stimulus regularly enters the area of consciousness, or as one would say nowadays, of the ego. A healthy ego will keep this unconscious material from its borders despite its reinforcement by physical disease.

However, everyone knows that in the initial stages of a physical disease even the best adapted ego may be deceived and respond to physical irritation as if it were a psychic stimulus. Yet as soon as this stimulation transgresses a certain intensity, the ego automatically responds in correspondence with the true nature of the stimulus, and the psychic content is again separated from its physical carrier. Patients whose egos have preserved an infantile relationship to the body fail in this act of differentiation. They react in almost the same way as does the infantile ego, in which no psychological differentiation between physical and psychogenic symptoms is possible or, perhaps, even necessary.

The infant who is physically sick is also emotionally sick, in the literal meaning of the word, and likewise an emotional disorder always affects physiological functions. Thus in the infant a physical disease of any consequence becomes a psychic trauma.

This patient's ego undoubtedly had not achieved in its structural relationship to the body that degree of explicitness which is necessary if the stimulus originating in the body in the form of pathological irritation is to become differentiated from the flow of id stimuli (including the repressed part of the personality). It can be said that the structure of the psychic representation of this patient's organic diseases was similar to the structure of the dream which is formed under the impact of a strong physical stimulus.

From the beginning of my treatment I had to hear that the bulk of her physical complaints was "psychosomatic" until an organic disease was diagnosed. When symptoms persisted after her discharge from the hospital, they were again imputed to her neurosis until new X-ray findings made a second operation advisable. She was dismissed from the hospital with the erroneous diagnosis of a benign intestinal disorder. Before her return from O—— she was examined by an internist who diagnosed her complaints as psychogenic, as did a specialist upon her arrival in C——.

Subsequently, in my first interview, I obtained a perfect psychogenic history of her symptoms, but by this time I had learned my lesson and insisted on a renewed physical check-up. I think that this case permits the conclusion that it is just those patients who suffer from physical symptoms —but from whom a psychogenic history is obtained with particular ease—who should be suspected of having a physical disorder if the aforementioned archaic amalgamation of psychic apparatus and body representation is extant.

In a patient suffering from true hysteria, the psychogenic history of a physical symptom usually cannot be obtained with such ease, since the ego is more differentiated in patients suffering from true hysteria than in the other type of patient.

In discussing the peculiar way in which this patient deceived experienced internists by giving the appearance of suffering exclusively from a neurosis when she was actually laboring under a severe physical disease, one must not forget to mention the deep masochistic trend which was gratified by such deception. In view of the seat of the malignant growth, a correct diagnosis made at an earlier time would not have had an essential bearing upon the course of the disease, but in a case in which the growth was accessible to surgery, such masochism as this may actually be the indirect cause of a patient's death.

IV

The aforementioned aftermath regarding the contest of the patient's will should now be discussed. The effect which a patient's will has upon the community or upon the patient's close environment is a structural part of his death. By means of a will a person extends his effect upon the world beyond the grave, and the realization of this effect is guaranteed by law. Therefore, an essential matter regarding a will is part and parcel of the sociopsychology of death. As I mentioned before, a relative of the patient contested her will mainly on two allegations; namely, that she was not competent to make a will at the time she made it, and that this will was not a free expression of her intentions since she was under the undue influence of the psychiatrist, whom she made the executor of her estate and who was also the beneficiary of a considerable sum of money. I will divide the following discussion into three parts and must apologize beforehand for occasional digressions into the dry and often tedious field of legal matters, but the particular attraction of the problem lies in a comparison of the legal aspect with the psychological one, a comparison which, to the detriment of the community and of the continued evolving of the law, is rarely made. The first part will be devoted chiefly to a legal discussion of the problem, the second to the way the same problem appears in the light of modern depth psychology, and the third one to a few concluding remarks regarding some allied topics.

V

Although the medicolegal situation is comparatively simple in this instance, I want to discuss the legal aspect first in order to show by contrast the variety of problems introduced into ethics and law by the theories and discoveries of twentieth-century depth psychology. Not being a jurist, I will discuss the forensic question in terms of two recent texts (Davidson, 1952; Guttmacher and Weihofen, 1952) which were written for psychiatrists as guides in just such matters.

One part of the statement made by Mr. X claimed that the patient was lacking in testamentary capacity. Davidson cites three criteria of that faculty: (1) the person must know that he is making a will; (2) he must know the nature and extent of his property; and (3) he must know the natural objects of his bounty.

The first criterion was well satisfied. The patient was seen by four or five physicians on the day she made her will or shortly thereafter. No signs of disorientation were noticed by any one of them, and no doubt regarding her competence was ever stated at that time or afterwards, until she went into the final coma. She recognized the attorney she had called although she had not seen him for many years, and she had told the nurse that she did not want to be disturbed by anyone during the time he was present. The following day, when she signed the will, a stranger who was visiting the hospital functioned as a third witness. The will was read to the patient in the witness' presence, and the patient had an extensive, rational conversation with her about all kinds of matters.

The fulfillment of the second criterion regarding the nature and extent of her property is documented by the will itself. In the will, items of property were correctly enumerated, and the total amount of the money she distributed among the inheritors coincided fairly well with the value of the estate. This was no easy matter because the patient's funds consisted of a variety of items—stocks, bonds, debentures, etc.—and she could not refer to the assistance of any other person since the attorney had no knowledge of her estate.

Also the third criterion is evidenced by the will itself, which contained a long list of almost all of her relatives, coinciding fairly accurately with the names she had mentioned in a will made before her first operation, many months earlier. The only points which need further comment are the inclusion of the psychiatrist in her will and the reduction of the share of Mrs. X (the wife of the contesting party) as compared with a previous will—both of which will be discussed later. The law is quite explicit upon one of these points. It does not require the bequest of any property to the natural objects of the testator's bounty; the law insists only that the testator knows who these natural objects are or understands "his obligations towards those who are related to him or who have legal or moral claims on him" (Guttmacher and Weihofen, 1952).

In regard to the second part of the sworn statement, namely that the patient had acted under my undue influence, the following may be said: I did not know of the patient's intention or action. When, in the presence of witnesses, I was informed of it, I expressed my determination not to accept the legacy. Previously, when notified of the patient's fatal sickness, I had transferred the patient to another physician and had resumed treatment only upon the request of the patient and her physician. Since one prerequisite of undue influence—for evident reasons—must be in the intent of the perpetrator to induce the victim to act in accordance with his wishes, the foregoing factors may suffice to show that the patient was not acting under undue influence when making or signing the will.

In turning now toward an inquiry of the same subject from the point of view of modern depth psychology, it is fascinating to notice that a simple and clear-cut forensic situation may become quite complicated, thus demonstrating how little true psychology has yet touched upon legal institutions.

VI

The modern psychiatrist will rightly say that, granted my actions were free of indices necessary for the assumption of undue influence in terms of the law, the patient nevertheless has acted under my influence and may have been psychologically as unfree as the person who is under undue influence in terms of the law. In a letter, Mr. X, the contestant, had actually expressed himself in that sense. He wrote that he did not mean to charge the therapist with using his influence to obtain money, rather, he thought of an unconscious utilization of a transference or of unconscious opportunism.

The unconscious utilization of a transference and unconscious opportunism are possible and—I am certain—occasionally do occur. Yet, interestingly enough, the law does not acknowledge the effect which an influence unconsciously exerted has upon the subject. Legally, undue influence is present only when a will "was obtained by the deception, threat or persistent suggestion of a domineering relative or confidant knowingly taking advantage of a weak-willed person" (Guttmacher and Weihofen, 1952).

Recent research abounds in observations proving the sometimes uncanny influence of one person's unconscious upon that of another. I remember well one of the earliest instances when I got substantial clinical evidence of the extent to which this may take place, and it may be worth while to describe briefly the incident.

A mother asked me, during my Army service, to help her little daughter of four who suffered from a severe phobia which made it impossible for her to tolerate solitude as soon as darkness had set in. Since I was stationed in a small community devoid of a child psychiatrist and did not know how to manage such a little child, I suggested that the mother have weekly interviews with me. When I took the mother's history, she denied the recollection of any gross neurotic symptoms having existed during her own childhood. Then, after seven or eight interviews, the mother suddenly recalled suffering at the age of four from a neurosis identical with that from which her child was suffering now. As soon as this memory had been recovered, the girl's manifest symptom disappeared. Since I had not given the mother any therapeutic advice as to how to treat the girl or behave toward her, I concluded that the girl's symptom was correlated to a repressed memory of the mother and consequently the symptom could dissolve as soon as the mother's unconscious had ejected the memory.

In order to avoid an untoward influence of the therapist's unconscious upon that of the patient, the psychiatrist should be acquainted with his own unconscious by means of his personal analysis. But even if a psychiatrist has followed Freud's golden rule that analysts should undergo a personal analysis every five years (Freud, 1937), he nevertheless could not be certain beyond all doubt about all the contents of his unconscious. We must accept the fact that the unconscious is a formidable power. Despite the knowledge acquired in the last three decades about the variety of techniques with which the ego deals, often successfully, with the unconscious, it nevertheless must be still appraised as quite as formidable as it appeared at the time of Freud's initial discoveries. It may penetrate in some way or another all ego functions, and often it has its deepest hold upon the ego just at the time when the ego believes it is securing its own, reality-adequate, goals. This ever-present possibility of the ego's being tricked by the unconscious is a potential pitfall of greatest importance, particularly in psychotherapy.

Of course this statement must be qualified: one may rightly expect that under proper conditions a psychiatrist or psychoanalyst would not utilize a transference even unconsciously or be opportunistic in the way the contestant suspected; this is rather a matter of character and not of the unconscious, the way the term is used here. The contestant did not really present the problem in its full gravity. The question is whether some wish, quite unconscious in the therapist, may nevertheless be perceived by the patient—probably also unconsciously—and then be reacted upon by the patient out of an intensive transference relationship. The stronger the transference the more astutely would the patient's unconscious respond to the therapist's unconscious wishes.

Thus it is quite feasible that a therapist, even when motivated by irreproachably honest *conscious* motives, inadvertently creates in a patient the disposition toward giving him a gift. I do not need to construct all the possibilities of how this may happen. The question of interest here is: how can one ascertain that unconscious strivings colored the physician's behavior in such a way as to create a disposition of that kind in a patient? Evidently the therapist's assertion that he did not behave in a reproachable way is not decisive since the behavior concerns his unconscious and he therefore must be ignorant of it, in case such a striving should become operative. The therapist is here in a difficult situation. He is accused of unethical conduct of which he is supposed to be unconscious; he has no witnesses since psychotherapy does not accept the presence of a third party; and the victim of his allegedly unethical conduct cannot be questioned because she is dead. Yet, I believe that the nature of a therapist's unconscious strivings will show up in a plurality of situations and will not remain restricted to an isolated instance. The fact that I continued to insist upon a change of therapist when it became clear that the patient was fatally sick and that I refused acceptance of the legacy (both of which were brought to the complainant's attention) had been two focal points in which one might rightly expect the appearance of unconscious strivings.

A strong conviction of the therapist's unconsciously influencing a patient could, if carried to extremes, take on ludicrous forms as would happen in the following hypothetical instance: Let us assume that a patient commits suicide during psychoanalytic or psychiatric treatment. The therapist is sued for malpractice. He testifies of all the measures he has taken and the treatment he has instituted.

"That is quite right," says the complainant, "but how about your unconscious death wishes against the patient? After all, the patient disturbed your night's rest and did not show any signs of improvement. Also, we read in modern textbooks of psychiatry how difficult it is to withstand the patient's suppressed aggression, which comes to the fore in a depression and to which the patient's environment reacts with regularity. How did you react? Can you swear that you never dreamed of this patient's death or never wished his death in your unconscious? Did not the patient perhaps notice from your mien or a gesture that you regretted ever having taken him into treatment? And did not this message which you sent unconsciously into the patient's unconscious add a burden which at last sent him to his death?"

What analyst could really swear that he had never had an unconscious death wish against a patient who later committed suicide?

We notice that the problem is not formulated precisely enough. It cannot be a question of whether this or that occurred in the therapist's unconscious but only of how the therapist's ego reacted to a stimulation by the unconscious—in case such stimulation occurred at all. The mere fact that a patient bequeathes a legacy to a therapist suggests alternatives of the following kind: (1) the patient acted out the transference which is part and parcel of the treatment; (2) the therapist abused—(a) purposely or (b) inadvertently—a therapeutic situation. The first alternative may be an unavoidable incident in an adequately conducted treatment or the consequence of a technical mistake unrelated to the therapist's personality; (2a) would be a misdemeanor, and (2b) would be a sign of professional incompetence. If no other facts are known, the interpretation of a patient's bequest depends on factors in the interpreting person. Depending on the bent of his imagination he will choose one of these three alternatives.

But another and even more important aspect imposes itself. This patient undoubtedly acted under the influence of a strong transference. Since transference per se, and a strong transference even more, is comparable under certain circumstances to hypnotic states, the question may be raised whether the mere acting out of the transference is tantamount to acting under the impact of undue influence.

At this point a few remarks regarding the handling of the transference in psychotherapy, which is still a moot question (Leo Stone, 1951), cannot be avoided. Some therapists base their psychotherapy mainly on transference interpretations. However, I am in the habit of using a technique which keeps the discussion of the transference at a minimum. I believe I have observed that once the clinical situation necessitates a direct interpretation of transference, psychotherapy has a poor prognosis. Transference interpretations require follow-ups and the infrequency of interviews in psychotherapy militates against the use of this tool in psychotherapy, although it is the most important one in psychoanalysis. This rule is not meant literally. In this patient's treatment, transference interpretation became necessary at one point during the second phase of her treatment when she had a dream, the transference character of which was visible in the manifest content.

Transference, however, whether interpreted or not, is the essential lever of psychotherapy, as it is of psychoanalysis. In psychotherapy I prefer to use transference as much as possible through the everyday channels of interpersonal communication. The whole inventory of stimuli with which one person acts on the other stands here at the therapist's disposal. It depends on his knowledge and skill whether, on the one hand, these stimuli are used in such a way as to reduce the patient's anxiety or the other emotions which block his access to reality-adjusted action, or, whether, on the other hand, they are used to facilitate the patient's access to the sources of pleasure and enjoyment at his disposal. The intensity of the transference which is necessary to accomplish these two goals varies from patient to patient. It was evident in this patient, who had suffered for many years from a serious disorder, that the optimum of transference was a very high one. Only if she felt reliably protected would she dare to develop that degree of activity which the particular circumstances of her life situation required.

The question which is of interest here concerns the extent to which a therapist must or may make himself the protector of the patient. I believe that in such instances as the one under discussion, when the patient had gone through a long series of highly traumatizing disappointments, there was scarcely an upper limit if the patient's confidence in the world and in herself was to be restored.

I want to quote an extreme example. When the patient's negotiations with her husband's business partners had broken down and court action, which would have meant a financial and psychic catastrophe for this sensitive patient, seemed unavoidable, I drafted a letter for the patient. The letter had a beneficial effect. The two parties got together again, and the disagreement was peacefully carried to a compromise. Of course, I had taken a great risk. I had never met the person to whom the letter was sent, but from various reports which I had received I had formed a certain image of him. If that image had been wrong, and the letter had led to a worsening of the situation, the patient's relationship to me would have suffered a severe blow and might have ended the whole therapy. Such risks are unavoidable in any case of a serious disorder. Usually such a technique is considered ill-advised in view of the danger of causing strong dependency reactions in the patient. However, if the situation is properly handled, the dependence of the patient does not become unmanageable, as I could see again in this patient. The liquidation of the transference was not too difficult at the end of the second treatment phase. It was only necessary to demonstrate by concrete action that the patient had overrated my indispensability. In this particular instance the one month she spent with the other psychiatrist served as an equivalent to the transference interpretations which would have been given in a bona fide psychoanalysis.

I believe that those psychotherapists who warn against the establishment of a positive tie by dint of concrete wish fulfillments might have suffered bad experiences with the technique because it was used in situations where the wish fulfillments were enforced by the patient or concerned areas in which the patient could have functioned adequately by his own effort. The wish fulfillments I have in mind concern those which are given without the patient's anticipation or asking, and in my limited experience they have a stimulating effect upon the patient's desire and capacity for independent action. During the terminal phase, of course, the necessity for maintaining a maximum positive transference—if it still can be called transference—was evident, and any consideration of the problem of the patient's dependency would have become incongruous in the exigencies of the clinical situation. I trust it is not necessary to emphasize that these opinions concern exclusively the technique of psychotherapy and even within this area only exceedingly sick patients and emergency situations. To raise this question regarding the psychoanalytic technique proper would betray a misunderstanding and lack of comprehension of the basic fundament and the goal of that technique.

Thus it is quite evident that the patient had a very

strong transference relation to me, and therefore it must be affirmed, from the psychoanalytic point of view, the patient did not act as a free agent when she included me in her will; she was under an undue influence, yet this was not a result of the psychiatrist's conscious or unconscious scheming and plotting but occurred by virtue of a situation which is medically unavoidable because it is necessary to the patient's welfare. The effect of this situation can be channeled into proper directions under average conditions, but the extremity of the clinical situation as encountered in the management of a patient who approaches death greatly reduces or perhaps even nullifies the possibilities of organizing the transference relationship in the way this is done under less tragic circumstances.

However, the patient's not having acted as a free agent should not be equated with the general causal determination of psychic processes. When Freud (1915c) wrote: "The transference-love has perhaps a degree less of freedom than the love which appears in ordinary life and is called normal," he indirectly referred to this problem though in a different context. Transference reactions are outside the scope of the ego's will power. The ego is victimized here by impulses which are beyond the strength of its regulative apparatuses. The patient had evolved a very strong transference; I was the only person in her environment whom she trusted and by whom she felt protected, and the seeming—seeming only as we shall see later—generosity of looking at me as an "object of her bounty" does not require the assumption of any foul play on the side of the psychiatrist, but rather it becomes explainable by considering well-known clinical facts.

The particular and unique prominence which the transference acquires in mental treatment in turn requires particular and unique professional ethics for the worker in the field. Since only in mental treatment does the

handling of the transference coincide with essential professional activity, the psychiatrist (and all the more, of
course, the psychoanalyst) must take a different attitude
toward the result of the positive transference than is necessary in any other profession. If the patient's attorney or
surgeon had helped her to the extent I had done, and she
had left a legacy to either of them, there would have been
no objection to their accepting the bequest, although positive feelings of the transference nature might have been as
much at work as they were in the patient's relationship to
me. But in surgery and law practice "positive transference"
is taken for granted as an unknown and undetermined
factor for which the person who becomes the subject of the
patient's or the client's "transference" does not carry responsibility in the way in which the psychotherapist does.
If surgeons and lawyers do not intuitively handle transference correctly, they will soon be out of business, though
they may be excellent surgeons or lawyers. If a psychotherapist or psychoanalyst does not handle transference
in a therapeutically correct way, he may nevertheless increase his clientele, but he will not cure his patients, and
therefore he must be considered a poor therapist despite
the success he may have in his social group. The austerity
which the therapist must impose on the patient must be
equally valid for himself, and he cannot enjoy some of the
benefits which other professions are permitted to enjoy.
Therefore, I made a mistake when I initially thought my
bequest could be used for charitable purposes. Even if
this could be done in strict anonymity, without any benefit to the therapist's prestige, it still would have been
against a self-evident and therefore unwritten basic principle.

Theoretically the psychiatrist ought not to receive anything from the patient beyond the previously fixed compensation for the time during which he is engaged in his

therapeutic work. However, there are exceptions—not to be discussed here in detail—to this rule. For example, in psychotherapy the refusal of a gift might end the transference; then the acceptance of the gift is put into the therapeutic process and has become necessitated by therapeutic requirements, but this must be viewed as a therapeutically enforced deviation from a rule not allowing otherwise any exception. Likewise it was my mistake to accept executorship even with the understanding that I would not be compensated for the service. The moment the patient died there was nothing else for me to do but to discontinue any practical connection with her affairs. Once a psychotherapeutic relationship has been initiated, every action must be organized exclusively by therapeutic deliberations or else oblique and indeterminate situations arise. When death has ended the relationship, the psychotherapist ought to refuse the acceptance of continued function, although the law and prevailing customs do permit this.

VII

The clinical situation in the instance of this patient and its consequences for the psychiatrist are particularly challenging and instructive because the consequences were brought on by the successful achievement of the goal of treatment. Here was a situation where a maximum of transference was necessary from the psychiatric viewpoint. Had I been more intuitive and foreseen the patient's action, or had she even told me of her intention, this probably would not have altered very much. In the latter case I would have mildly remonstrated and tried to change her mind, but certainly would have avoided under all circumstances the danger of creating a conflict, since my main function at that time was to eliminate the seed of conflict.

Had the patient told me of her intention I would have been in a situation comparable to the following which occurred in a treatment conducted by a colleague in accordance with the rules of classical psychoanalysis. A patient tending toward severe acting out put the analyst's name into her will two days before undergoing a dangerous operation. The analyst could prevent her from going to extremes, but there was no time to analyze the transference situation. An outright prohibition of mentioning the analyst's name would have caused a panic in the patient, who was extremely afraid of the impending operation. The analyst had to condone temporarily a mild acting out and could correct the situation only after the patient resumed psychoanalysis subsequent to surgical treatment.

We encounter here even within the framework of classical analysis a situation which comes close to the one under discussion; that is to say, even under therapeutic conditions which, in terms of present-day knowledge, are the best fitted to pursue and control the patient's transference, by a freakish combination of circumstances a patient may succeed in getting the analyst into a situation which might appear contrary to a basic principle of professional ethics.

Let us return to the original problem. Transference, particularly in psychotherapy, may rise to an inordinate intensity. All the latent strivings of a positive nature, desires of giving and of expressing affection might become mobilized and focus upon the therapist. The intensity of these strivings in its relationship to the strength of the ego can be compared to a hypnotic state. Without any stimulation from the outside in the form of the therapist's unconscious acting out or in the form of the therapist's unconscious wishes, the patient's transference wish still may find a symbolic and factual gratification in giving the therapist a gift. In the situation of the dying this may easily lead to the psychiatrist's inclusion in the will of the patient who looks at him as an object of his bounty. The question arises whether from the point of view of modern psychology this makes the will invalid, notwithstanding the laws admitting the physician as a natural object of the patient's bounty. I believe this question must be answered in the negative. A will does not become invalid merely by the fact that a patient acts out the transference in the form of making the treating psychiatrist a beneficiary. It would actually lead to an infringement upon the patient's freedom if he could make a valid will only by excluding his psychiatrist. But from the point of view of modern psychology, the psychiatrist is not permitted to *accept* the inheritance. In this moment of refusal the "undue influence" under which the patient stood—if the constellation is viewed in terms of modern psychology—is canceled out; the psychiatrist returns the inheritance to the estate and the consequences of his treatment, which had left a trace in the patient's will, have been eliminated. If a patient left his whole estate to the psychiatrist, it would become incumbent upon the court to decide its further disposition.

Yet the contestant raised still another question for which it is equally important to find a solution. He contended that the patient had paranoid feelings about his wife and that I overlooked this, thus implying a neglect of my duty. The function a psychiatrist has to fulfill in such a situation is unique, as I will presently show, and I believe the contestant was mistaken when he felt disappointed in me. While it is beside the point, I will briefly mention that—oddly enough—the patient's will per se almost proves that she did not suffer from any delusions, at least none regarding her relative. Whereas in a previous will she had made Mrs. X the principal heir, in her last will she had divided the bulk of her estate in equal shares among a number of close relatives (including Mrs. X) and me. By leaving Mrs. X a substantial amount of money it is proved that she knew her to be a natural object of her bounty, and by not reducing her share to a nominal sum she demonstrated freedom from a schizophrenic reaction since an acute schizophrenic conflict always leads to an extreme decision. The all-or-none reaction type is, though not a proof, a prerequisite for the diagnosis of that disorder. Certainly the patient did not indulge in this type of action when she set up her last will. A more stable and less sensitive person than the patient might have forgiven or overlooked the renewed disappointments which she had suffered; the relative restraint which the patient had shown may demonstrate the growth she had made since the time when she felt incapable of forgiving an offense.

Let us return to the contestant's important implication that the psychiatrist carries responsibility for the way a patient disposes of property in a will.

A comparison of psychotherapy with classical psychoanalysis again appears necessary at this point.

Let us assume that in a classical analysis the question of the content of the patient's will comes up. The psychoanalyst is principally concerned with that area of the ego's organization where it comes to grips with superego, the id, and reality. If a patient tries to solve a conscious or unconscious conflict by the way in which he sets up his will, the analyst will interpret this action and bring to the patient's attention the unconscious motives and aims, the defense mechanisms at work, and the connection with the genetic material so far brought to the surface. The patient may or may not respond to these interpretations, and the particular subject will be handled in the same way as any other subject coming up in the treatment, with one exception only. It is feasible that a patient's resistance may take the course of embarrassing the analyst by deciding to bequeath a legacy to him. If the patient's resistance is not amenable to interpretation and the patient insists upon his decision, the analyst might easily be compelled to take the ultimate step of demanding compliance if the patient wants to continue his analysis. With this one exception, I believe, there is no problem involved in that area when classical analysis is concerned.

In psychotherapy the problem is possibly different. The therapist's activity is much greater here, since he is interested more in the patient's conduct and comfort than in changes of personality structure. The scope of the therapist's direct responsibility is concomitantly larger. In psychoanalysis the patient is the sole and exclusive object of the analyst's concern. This is one reason why fewer patients are eligible for psychoanalysis than for psychotherapy. All those in whom the organization of the ego is not firm enough to bear the relative freedom acquired in the course of a psychoanalytic treatment without abusing it for asocial gratifications are not proper candidates for that therapy—at least in so far as the classical technique is applied. The psychotherapist, with his freedom to tell the patient what or what not to do, if such necessities should arise, is in a far more advantageous position in this instance than the classical psychoanalyst. He can arrogate to himself a function which ought to be discharged by the patient's superego. Other functions, too, which rightly belong to the patient's personality organization, may be temporarily delegated to the psychotherapist. The rationale of the procedure is, of course, the expectation that in the meantime the injured function will be restored and the patient enabled to take upon himself the responsibilities for which he has been temporarily incapacitated. Yet despite the large area of the therapist's responsibility, in the particular instance of the patient setting up his will, the psychotherapist's scope of activity is a limited one. The will should be a free expression of the testator's desires with regard to the disposal of his estate. The maximum activity permissible for the psychotherapist would be a discussion of the testator's motives for making one decision or the other.

In this particular situation, the purpose of the law would be vitiated if a therapist actually were to tell a patient what, in his opinion, the content of the will ought to be. A Probate Court does not want to be informed of what a just and equitable will should be under the testator's circumstances but what the testator's desires were at the moment of his signing his will.

In general it is not too difficult for the therapist to gain an objective view of a patient's duties and responsibilities. Although this is an area where personal convictions might lead a therapist astray, a study of the conflicts aroused by the patient's ambivalence leads in the majority of instances to a realistic frame of reference adequate within the society of the patient and the therapist. The content of a will, however, is one of the few situations where concepts of "justice" and "equity" cannot be adequately discussed in terms of the American community. Should the will be correlated to the likes and dislikes of the testator? Should it consider the needs of the prospective inheritors? Or the needs of the community? All three eventualities are considered as equally equitable in the American community, and the law leaves it up to the testator to choose any one or to compromise between them. But since in this instance three entirely different frames of reference can be equitably applied to the same social act, I must consider this circumstance as an additional reason why a therapist, even when he assumes maximum responsibility for his patients, should not let a patient know what his opinions are with regard to the patient's last will, except for the eventuality of the patient's wanting to provide the psychotherapist directly or indirectly with a benefit.

From the point of view of depth psychology, any advice in that matter would amount to undue influence since the psychiatrist's word counts so much with the patient when he is in the state of positive transference.

In my browsing through some of the legal literature I found a passage (*American Jurisprudence, 57*:355) which seems to cover this very situation:

> An influence which overcomes the testator's freedom of action is an undue influence which invalidates the will, notwithstanding the person who exerted the influence may have had no evil design but, on the contrary, acted for the purpose of thwarting the testator's design to make a will contrary to his duty. In other words undue influence invalidates a will even though the person who employs it believes that he is acting thereby in a worthy cause.

It is important to note that here the law seems to delineate an area upon which a therapist must not take action, even if the patient should indulge in acting out.

VIII

An adequate presentation of the problems involved in this case is greatly impeded by my having little knowledge of what the psychic processes were in the contestant. Only such knowledge would permit an exhaustive exploration and explanation. After the matter was settled legally, of course, I was most eager to find out in what possible way I could have given cause for such a grave accusation as undue influence upon an incompetent person—and for the sake of material gain!—and I therefore wanted to arrange a meeting with the contestant. Mr. X was a professional man of impeccable reputation and comfortable means; he had been a social acquaintance of mine, with whom I had maintained friendly relations. Yet he refused such a meeting and gave a reason which ostensibly was an excuse. I drew the conclusion that he had not acted in good faith.

Be this as it may, the clinician will want to know whether such incidents can be avoided. Could I have prevented the accusation of the party who felt damaged by the patient's last will? As far as I can see, the only step I had possibly neglected might have been the following. Upon notification of the patient's last will I could have informed the prospective contestant of my ignorance of the patient's action and of my decision not to benefit from it. Yet I doubt that this information would have had a greater effect on the contestant's behavior than the identical one which he obtained subsequently.

One must admit that here, conceivably, is a situation in which even a perfect technique would not necessarily avert consequences of greatest embarrassment to the psychiatrist. If he treats a dying patient adequately, the patient will form a very strong transference which may easily lead to the psychiatrist's being included in the patient's last will. Since psychiatric treatment necessitates the psychiatrist's spending much time alone with the patient, he exposes himself to suspicion. Even when the psychiatrist is astute enough to foresee the patient's intention of making him a beneficiary, he has no other means to counteract this but a mild protest since the patient's critical situation does not permit any move that would possibly result in an emotional aggravation. The psychiatrist must face the possibility that under such conditions he may become the victim of the acting out of the patient's relatives or of deliberate action aimed at exploiting the possibilities of present legal institutions.

In the particular instance I am reporting here, I was relatively fortunate. The contestant's aim, evidently, was to obtain money; when he was informed that in my refusal of the legacy I did not insist that it be returned to the patient's estate nor did I object to its being given to him or his wife, he withdrew his objections to the will. I admit, however, that if the contestant had aimed at higher stakes, such as my professional standing or my reputation—about which luckily he did not care—I would have faced a desperate situation. Perhaps one must accept the possibility of such incidents as specific professional risks comparable to the risks which the epidemiologist runs when treating infectious disorders. I once heard it said of a psychiatrist—evidently of unusual stature—that he never contradicted a member of the family who accused him of negligence after a patient of his had died. He was fully aware of the feelings of guilt the mourning family must harbor, and he was willing to do the last great service for them by letting them shift their self-reproaches onto him. Such an attitude, I believe, is at the peak of humaneness, and the most outstanding expression of the sense of medical duty. It goes without saying that only a few exceptional people can possess that degree of idealism. I thought often of this man in the course of this affair of the legacy because his way of thinking and acting proffered a possibility of reconciliation with the almost unbearable consequences which evidently may arise when we venture into the as-yet-unexplored territory of dealing psychiatrically with those who are approaching death.

The release of feelings of guilt after the demise of a person to whom one was close occurs fairly regularly, and in many instances the preferred defense is projection. In this instance monetary interests had evidently played a considerable role in the relationship which the contestant and his wife had maintained with their relative, and this may have been one of the reasons why their accusation against the physician revolved around the conviction that he was consciously or unconsciously motivated by greed for money. This, however, would be valid only in the event that Mr. X's reaction was of a neurotic nature.

The psychiatrist as well as the psychoanalyst is relatively well trained in countering hostile actions which are the derivatives of neurotic or even psychotic attitudes in a patient's relatives. Less is known about the techniques necessary for the management of actions which are based on the deliberate or purposeful intent to harm the therapist. Here, there is no opportunity for undoing rationalizations or interpreting the unconscious, since the ego consciously becomes a partisan of a wish, the immoral nature of which is well known and which it does not want to curb.

IX

There remains a remark regarding therapeutic ambition. It is well known that such ambition is the archenemy of psychoanalysis, but even in psychotherapy one does not evolve inordinate therapeutic ambitions without punishment. Without some therapeutic ambition I certainly would not have been able to help this patient, who not only suffered from a relatively rare and severe sickness but who also had to face most unusual reality situations. I fear, however, that I was inordinately ambitious in her instance. No hurdle was too high for me to take; when the patient was in a calamity I always was at hand to help her out. I encountered no reproaches from her except the one for having let her move to O——. There scarcely ever occurred those misunderstandings which so often are arranged by patients in order to channel their ambivalent feelings. The patient was indeed a surprisingly co-operative patient, although she was a very ambivalent person. Where were her ambivalent feelings toward me? I must admit that throughout the treatment I never asked myself this question but took for granted that she was exceedingly satisfied with my services. When she made me one of her heirs, she managed to make real what I had unwittingly forced her to suppress or to hide. To be sure, I do not know what course the treatment would have taken had I tried to plumb her ambivalence.

I have observed patients in psychotherapy whose positive transference has broken down as soon as even a slight degree of negative transference entered the therapeutic relationship. The treatment of such patients is prognostically more than dubious. Whether or not this patient belonged to this group I do not know, for I had never given her an opportunity to express negative feelings about me, and it is an important fact that I never asked myself where the patient's ambivalence toward me was hiding. While it may sound strange to attribute an act of seeming generosity to a hostile impulse, it must still be considered that this patient, notwithstanding her grave emotional disorder, had a firm sense of reality. She was quite intuitive, and despite her complaints she had achieved her goals more frequently than not. She had spent her life in luxury and wealth and had played to perfection the role which her husband had devised. Inasmuch as under no other condition could this marriage have endured, much that looked like psychopathology was a perfectly structured device in her bitter struggle for social survival. Furthermore she was a woman of the world, quite aware of the ill repute in which some people hold psychiatry and psychoanalysis precisely because of the allegation that monetary interests play a prominent role in these specialties. Not only must she have known that I would never accept her legacy, but she must also have been aware of the danger and suspicion to which she exposed me. With particular finesse, under the guise of a special favor, she made me the victim of an ambivalence which must have dated far back in our relationship.

Had she, consciously or unconsciously, also calculated a plan to perpetuate her vengeance upon her relatives by seemingly showering me with her beneficence? No doubt the patient had succeeded beyond the grave in gratifying her ambivalence toward me; whether she was equally successful with her relatives I never had an opportunity to find out.

PART THREE

Concluding Remarks

In the Introduction I have tried to outline various aspects of the problem of death, and in the three case histories I have tried to illustrate the psychiatric work with patients who were approaching death. In neither instance have I contributed anything essentially new—aside, perhaps, from some suggestions regarding a psychiatric technique which may be helpful in dealing with the clinical situation. However, if these technical suggestions were to be interpreted as amounting merely to the advice that one must be kind and helpful in caring for the dying patient, I would object, although I might have given cause for this misunderstanding.

Furthermore, I fear that my presentation may not have an encouraging effect in terms of a more intensive concern with the problem. The reader may easily draw the conclusion that therapeutic work with the dying patient is after all too unpromising and strenuous and dangerous. Psychiatric and psychoanalytic work has its danger spots in general, and, I must admit, the dangers are greater in this area than in most others. Also I must admit that the personal strain is greater here than in most other clinical situations. Although I have made some remarks regarding this factor, I have held back more that could have been said, for obvious reasons. It is almost impossible at this point to decide what portion of this strain has to be ascribed to an objectively justified reaction provoked by the clinical situation and what portion to subjective factors. Since we know so little about death, and therefore even a partially objective frame of reference is still lacking, it is hardly possible to separate at this point the reality-adequate response from the effect of unconscious imagery. There are many for whom death does not seem to be a particular problem; they act and feel about their own deaths and those of others with relative unconcern. This is not necessarily the effect of denial as it is in the hero type described by Freud (1915a). It looks as if for them this part of nature had not acquired too great importance. Possibly this unconcern is always a sign of a lack of differentiation of the personality since the problem of death is a perennial one and appears in all cultures, even though with varying intensity.

Although I do not know whether the following difficulty is a personal or an objectively justified one, I nevertheless do not want to let it go by. The subjective strain was particularly intensive in Case Two which was, no doubt, the most tragic one. The technical difficulty centered, as can easily be understood, in the fact that the patient knew of her impending death, a situation which was aggravated by her medical knowledge and her inability to form illusions. In this situation the difference of outlook and general emotional climate between the person who—rightly or wrongly—believes he will live for some time and the patient who knows his lifetime is measured in terms of days, weeks, or at best, months was felt most painfully. If I may say so, it was embarrassing—at least it so affected me—to talk to the patient with confidence and/or encouragement or even to give an interpretation which would make sense only by its implication vis-à-vis the future, when the patient knew her lifetime was limited and my own was not threatened by any known impending disaster.

It would be extremely tactless to treat with psychotherapy or psychoanalysis a chronically hungry or generally destitute person. The discrepancy between such a person's actual state and that which psychotherapy offers is too great to satisfy the patient, and such a patient would, if treated, very easily counter the therapist's interpretations, or any comment which was not of a direct consequence to his hunger or destitution, with the reproach "You just do not know what it means to be hungry and therefore it is easy for you to use big words and be so reasonable." As a matter of fact, a well-known writer who was living as a student under very strained conditions sought therapeutic advice from Freud; he reports (Bruno Goetz, 1952) that after the therapeutic interview was over, Freud handed him an envelope which contained a large amount of money. Aside from the expression of generosity and charity there was also, possibly, an acknowledgment of embarrassment in that gesture by means of which the annoying emotion was temporarily abolished. The question may arise for the psychiatrist who faces a hopelessly sick patient: which is really harder, to die or to witness death? To some this question may sound cynical and hypocritical; nevertheless, it has its justification when the contact with the dying is an intimate one.

I have scarcely discussed the clinical situation of easy dying so ably described by Felix Deutsch (1936). The pain involved in such an instance appears to be very small. Some persons when witnessing a patient gradually succumbing to death may suffer greater pain than the patient to whom the beneficence of a painless death is granted. Yet it is misleading to compare the experience of physician and patient in this situation. Instances of easy dying are—with certain exceptions—based upon the extensive use of denial, usually also involving repression and regression. Therefore, the comparison has to be made between the pain evoked by the conscious knowledge of one's impending death and that of witnessing it in a patient. Then it becomes clear that despite all pain suffered by empathy or by identification with another person, this pain does not measure up to the anguish suffered in connection with the approach of one's own death unless there is extensive denial at his disposition. This generalization, however, is probably not valid when parents, particularly a mother, lose a child. The loss of a child is for many mothers absolutely inacceptable and the loss of her own life would, without using any mechanisms leading to denial, be more acceptable. However, the psychology of this relationship is unique and—granted a maximum of charity in the relationship between physician and patient, even when it follows closely the pattern of a mother's love for a child— the physician's compassion cannot approximate the intensity of that feeling which a mother suffers in the equivalent situation. Thus we must conclude that the physician will always be more afraid of his own death than of that of a patient. However, there was no doubt that in Case Two it would have helped if I could have told the patient that I, too, was suffering from a disease bringing me slowly closer to death. In this moment a community of spirit would have been established which would have permitted an identification on her side.

The patient's strong, and highly narcissistic, identification with the therapist is a prerequisite necessary in the treatment of some disorders such as the delinquencies and schizophrenias. It is unnecessary, even detrimental and therefore avoided, in the therapeutic work with neurotics. But in the two aforementioned groups, the identification is indispensable at least in the initial treatment phase in order to render therapeutic moves effective at all. A delinquent usually does not listen favorably to advice as long as he has the feeling that the person who addresses him is not part of the world in which he is living. Yet the wall which separates those who expect to live from those who feel themselves to be close to death is probably even higher than that which separates the delinquent from the allegedly law-abiding and honest sectors of society.

Whereas we know the technical means necessary to tear down the barrier between the delinquent and the therapist, whom he initially takes as a part of honest society and therefore distrusts, similar means are not known regarding the therapeutic contact with those who are marked by death. The priest or the minister is in a more favorable position since he is a representative of the power beyond, before which the faithful who is dying believes he will soon appear; the basis for a narcissistic relation is thus implicitly given. Since the psychiatrist does not have this advantage, he must first establish the platform which the man of God finds ready made in each instance in which he is called for consolation to the bedside of a dying person.

This particular problem became acute only in the clinical work with Case Two. The most decisive interview—at least in my opinion—was that in which I tried to convince the patient that life in whatever form or phase is meaningless. This, however, was also the interview in which I felt most strikingly the embarrassment previously mentioned. Although I was farily well convinced of the correctness of my opinion, nevertheless I felt that it was easier for a healthy person to indulge in the quasi luxury of such a philosophy—sad as it may be—than for a fatally sick patient to accept it and to be expected, in addition, to adjust her emotions to it. The patient, however, did not respond on this level, but apparently let the thought have its effect upon her outlook. She had previously told me the following dream: "You were in a blue Navy uniform with two stripes, a lieutenant junior grade, which is impossible, since the lowest grade for a specialist is captain. My children are close to you; you are leaving, and in the process of liquidation." She quickly added that Navy officers have a good life in peacetime. She told me of an acquaintance of hers who had cancer and who believed herself to be indestructible. The dream—according to my interpretation, which I did not communicate to her—pictures me in the state of happily dying. I was marked by the uniform as she was by death, and I was in the process of liquidation as she was. The dream has still other meanings, such as a strong ambivalence expressed by the exaggerated status she thought was due me and that which I actually held in the dream. Yet this ambivalence was evidently well compensated for and did not lead to an interference with a positive object relationship, as the quick addition following the dream report indicates. I am reporting this dream—it was the only one which she communicated—to show that in her unconscious I had become one of the crowd of those who are in the process of dying, an interpretation which I think is confirmed by her telling me in the same hour that she had given up hope, was ready to accept any advice and no longer felt frightened when discovering new glands diseased with cancer. Thus I, too, was dying but in a peaceful and stoic way like the captain who goes down with his ship. Because she had unconsciously drawn me into the orbit of her personal world, she could respond to my philosophy as if one dying person gave advice to another. How it had happened that she had accepted me as such I do not know. With the delinquent, a special and rather difficult technique must be applied, the theory of which has been worked out by Aichhorn (1925). I cannot—to my regret—present the corresponding theory regarding the treatment of those who know of their impending death, but can only guess that the patient perhaps had responded to that process which I have tried to describe earlier as the partial death of the psychiatrist. Unsatisfactory and enigmatic as this description may be, it possibly pertains to an essential prerequisite for a constructive therapy in such instances. If the psychiatrist succeeds in identifying part of his personality with the dying patient; that is to say, if he succeeds in experiencing the approach of the patient's death as if it were his own, he might induce the patient to welcome him as an acceptable companion on the last leg of his sad journey.

The role of the therapist's identification with the patient in the therapeutic process is not yet solved. Is empathy possible without identification? Should the psychiatrist identify with the patient (Reich, 1951)? Can a uniform answer be given here, or does it not depend on the individuality of the psychiatrist as happens also in artistic creation (Worringer, 1906) and in the experience of art (Müller-Freienfels, 1920), where different types—each of which has its own validity—are encountered? I can imagine that strong identifications with the patient could be used for the patient's welfare by one type of psychiatrist whereas a different type would rely on a different mechanism and would be greatly impeded by identification. Also it must not be forgotten that there are different types of identification (Freud, 1917c, 1921; Fliess, 1953); nonetheless, the question of the personality type of the psychiatrist or psychoanalyst has its own validity.

Yet in the treatment of the patient who approaches death this might be different. The required technique is possibly characterized by the necessity of the therapist's partial identification with the patient. A therapist whose personality does not permit a free use of identification would possibly not be able to give such a patient the help he needs. The treatment would differ further from other clinical procedures because this identification must not be a superficial one, but a deep one and must go so far that the patient actually feels its existence. In the treatment of the delinquent it is essentially immaterial whether the therapist really identifies with the patient or not as long as he talks and acts in a way which induces the patient to identify with him. Furthermore, if the therapist were a delinquent or if the patient thought the therapist were really a delinquent, the therapy would never lead to success. The difficulty in treating this disorder is partly caused by the necessity of creating for the delinquent an appearance with which he can identify without going so far as to create a state of real identity. In the treatment of the dying this extreme identification would not impede the therapeutic process but favor it. Even the identity based on the reality factor—the patient and the physician alike suffering from fatal diseases—would be, in contrast to the treatment of the delinquent, a therapeutically favorable factor. However, the psychiatrist's identification with the patient must not be a total one and must not lead to the evolvement of anxiety in the therapist. A part of the therapist's ego must remain free of identification. As has been remarked earlier, even the belief in immortality must be activated. If the therapist's own fear of death is considerable, he will either recoil from even a partial identification or become anxious, if not depressed. In both instances he is bound to harm the patient. The calm with which he bears the experience of a partial death becomes a source of succor to the patient, but the main function of the identification is, as has been said before, to make it possible for the patient to establish a therapeutic relationship which is at all usable. It will depend on the depth and sincerity of this identification whether the therapist can talk with the patient without embarrassment about the latter's impending death.

REMARKS ON DEATH AND THE BIOLOGICAL SCIENCES

Not only the specialty of psychiatry but also the whole field of medicine has neglected the problem of death. Such appeals as that by Roswell Park (1912), who coined the term thanatology, have remained by and large unheeded. Reluctant as the psychiatrist may be to enter, in practice as well as in theory, the field of thanatology, one day he will be expected to master the problem of the dying patient as he has mastered so many other problems which had previously been considered alien to the field but which have become part and parcel of psychiatry. Yet in order to contribute his best to thanatology the psychiatrist will have to make the great sacrifice of divorcing himself almost completely from his biological knowledge. One of the greatest barriers to a full grasp of the problem of death seems to me to be the inner compulsion by which we are forced to think of death in terms of impaired physiological functions or of destroyed physical structures. It must be stated that even if biology had said everything that this specialty can say about death, much would still remain to be added by the mental scientist. Death is also a problem of the mind; it may even be *principally* a problem of the mind and is possibly the *foremost* problem of the mind; but our thinking about death has been warped by biology, which must be called narrow at this point when compared with the vastness of psychology. This should not be interpreted as an antibiological approach. As with so many other problems, psychology has to borrow from biology in investigating the problem of death. (Freud has shown at what points biology may contribute to a psychology of death.) But once this step has been taken, psychology must come into its own rights and must proceed in accordance with its own methods and precepts.

It is questionable whether a person who has gone through our present medical schools, where his mind has been clamped for years and years in the narrowness of the biological sciences, can still fathom the vastness and depth of the problem, despite the heavy sprinkling of so-called psychosomatic medicine often juxtaposed nowadays to the other medical disciplines. It is most remarkable to study case histories of patients who have died in a hospital. As

far as I have had an opportunity of perusing them, they
have not contained any information regarding the patient's *dying* aside from the biological data which referred
to the patient's terminal disease. Zilboorg (1943a) believes
that "there is one special aspect of being a physician which
cannot be acquired anywhere but in medical training. The
medical student . . . is thrown into close contact with
patients—with people who are ill, who suffer a great deal,
and who frequently die under his own eyes." He praises
the "calm concern dictated by the constant need to do
something to control the illness . . ., to combat it, to
destroy it."

I do not share Zilboorg's belief in the humanizing effect
of medical training. While his idea is beautiful and appeals to our common sense, the hard facts of reality offer a
different picture. Moreover, the spirit of doing, con-
trolling, combatting, and destroying diseases is probably a
great impediment to the understanding and study of death.
Therefore it is not surprising that medicine has contributed so little. In view of death there is nothing to do,
to control, to combat, or to destroy, and I believe that
most of those who were trained in medical schools feel
out of place when they face the approach of death in their
patients. If the process of the patient's dying is not adequately described in medical case histories, there is an
intrinsic reason. The man of medicine knows well how to
describe a sickness, its symptoms, its course, its causes, and
its termination, but death is for him something negative, a
deficit, the absence of something. How should he then
describe a nothingness unless it were in terms of the signs
which a corpse shows subsequent to life's departure? These
signs, I believe, are really the only characteristics of death
which are taught in medical schools. They are the most
insignificant I could think of regarding the problem.

Although the medical man seems to be particularly unfitted for the understanding of death, there is no one else in our present society who knows more about the basic concepts of a thanatology and therefore would be better equipped to undertake such an inquiry. Perhaps one day psychiatry, despite all internal and external barriers, will make a meaningful contribution to thanatology. The psychiatrist after all, could study the problem in its most individual implications.

What we call death in speaking of the human species covers an immense area. If one compares the various forms and the circumstances under which the phenomenon takes place, he encounters a confusing variety. The human mind is fascinated by the one factor which this variety has in common. Thus, because of the almost hypnotic effect which the end stage has on the human mind, the individual forms are barely recognizable.

If we compare extremes, such as the death of a newborn baby who has taken a few short breaths with the death of an old person who dies in his sleep after a life of toil and labor, or if we compare the death of the patient whom I have reported in the second history, with its tragic personal implications, with Lincoln's death, which left an indelible mark on the history of his country, we may well ask what they really have in common aside from a few biological factors which are the proximate causes of the cessation of the organism. Thus the phenomenon of death must be comprehended first in each instance as an individually formed process. It is formed as individually as each single action had been formed in the pathway which led finally to death. The last moment of life, is, of course, the end product of the total preceding history of the dying person and probably also of that of his ancestors. But the problem of death is infinitely more complicated, as can be demonstrated by a biological fact which Freud used as a paradigm when discussing the interlacing of ontogenetic and phylogenetic factors in the passing of the oedipus complex. Then he wrote (1924a):

> Even at birth, indeed, the whole organism is destined to die, and an indication of what will eventually cause its death may possibly already be contained in its organic disposition. Yet after all, it is of interest to follow up the way in which the innate schedule is worked out, the way in which accidental noxiae exploit the disposition.

From the biological point of view, the biological future of the organism may be already determined at the moment of birth. It may be biologically preordained at this time from which dysfunction this particular organism will die if it constantly lives under optimal conditions, and also against which accidental noxiae this particular organism has a large or a decreased resistance, that is to say, which external factors will postpone or accelerate its death. Yet the two extremes, which I want to outline presently, will show a different facet of the problem. There are instances where the whole course of an individual life is bound, so to speak, to an organic malformation or dysfunction, and the development and structurization of the ego is dominated by this. Then again, there is the case of Franz Rosenzweig (1953), who died from an amyotrophic lateral sclerosis; his ego had obtained an unbelievably firm, if not unconquerable, structure before the "organic disposition" took on the devastating form of a paralysis which lasted seven years and was almost complete for four. During these seven years the ego continued to work, think, organize, create, and all this with far greater intensity, concentration, and effect upon the community than is ever expected by the vast majority of those who are in full command of their bodies. The view that the biological cause of the individual's death is imprinted upon the biological matrix, possibly already at the time of birth, is in all probability correct in this case also. But this particular clinical instance shows the limitations of an exclusively biological viewpoint, since here a structure had been evolved which resisted with astounding vigor the biological inroads, thus proving most impressively the independence of mind and its essential autonomy, of which Sir Arthur Tansley (1952) writes. In this instance we probably would not use the term amyotrophic lateral sclerosis if we were able to think in concepts of true individualism. Rosenzweig's sickness was really different from all those instances in which the patients showed the same physical symptoms from which he suffered. Consequently, it may be said that his death was also an event different from the other deaths caused by lateral sclerosis.

The biological preordination of death probably has its equivalent in a psychological preordination. In view of present-day knowledge, one is led to assume that with the resolution of the oedipus complex, or at puberty at the latest, the psychological preordination may be accomplished. Here of course one would like to know what the relationship between the biological and psychological preordination is. It could well be that both grow out of the same matrix and therefore follow identical laws.

However, it may be that the psychological factor per se has either a life-prolonging or a life-shortening effect. Freud (1938) wrote: "Thus it may in general be suspected that the individual dies of his internal conflicts but that the species dies of its unsuccessful struggle against the external world. . . ." In this passage the life-shortening effect is brought forth. Man cannot convert the optimal amount of death instinct into aggression; in addition he must also internalize part of that aggression; thus he falls prey to his own drives, a theory which is the equivalent of the biological view of the organism's dying because of its inability to remove products of its metabolism (Montgomery, 1906; Lipschütz, 1915).

Yet another aspect must be mentioned. The psyche, that is to say, the human personality, may possibly serve the function of prolonging the biological existence (Bernfeld and Feitelberg, 1930). This problem has at least two aspects. Man's ingenuity has elaborated methods to compensate for noxiae brought on by culture and those caused by nature. Thus man's knowledge, if properly used, may effect a prolongation of life. But the psyche may have inherently the function of postponing death.

In discussing this possibility it is necessary to say a few words about the relationship between the capacity to grow and the necessity of dying. Biologists have emphasized that an organism is doomed to die when it is deprived of the capacity to grow (Pütter, 1911). Mühlmann's (1910) objection, that growth in turn may lead to impeding the provision of organs with nourishment, is probably not warranted. Yet the general statement that a cell which loses the faculty of division is unconditionally bound to perish even if the cell is otherwise constantly kept under optimal conditions is indubitably correct. In other words, there is a relationship between growth and death. If organisms were able to grow eternally, some of them perhaps could live eternally if protected by optimal conditions.

The intimate relationship which exists between growth and death, in so far as an organism is not doomed to die for internal reasons as long as it grows, opens a new vista upon the psychology of the ego. Does the ego preserve the faculty of growth when the organism or important parts of it have lost this faculty? The ego, of course, has its biological matrix (Heinz Hartmann, 1950) and the cortex is one of its most important parts. Yet it is feasible that the organic substructure yields its inherent growth potential to the psychic structure which it supports and that the ego in this way is provided with its seemingly infinite potentiality of growth. Thus, by prolonging the phase of growth, one might speculate, the psyche has a life-prolonging effect upon the organism. When Ullmann (1926) writes that "man's life substance is used up [*abgenützt*] much more slowly" than that of other homoiothermal animals, and when he calls man "a much more perfect machine" than encountered otherwise, one feels inclined to raise the question whether such, and allied, physiological peculiarities specific of the human species should not be viewed in conjunction with the psychical potential which is inherent in the organic structure.

I have tried—for ostensible reasons—to reduce to a minimum a discussion of problems pertaining to the biology of death, but I cannot avoid adding a few general remarks regarding the relationship of growth and death, since Szasz (1952) used this very relationship as an argument against the biological fundament of Freud's theory of the death instinct. The difficulty of such a discussion lies in the nature of the arguments, which do not concern facts *in sensu strictiori* but their interpretation, and refers to the old disagreement between the views of Goette (1883) and Weismann (1884). In discussing the biology of death, Freud (1920a), of course, raised the question regarding the point in time at which death appears in organic development, and he brought into focus the strange fact that unicellular organisms can divide indefinitely under optimal conditions, thus seeming to be endowed with potential immortality. Weismann (1884) therefore thought death a relatively late acquisition of organisms, whereas growth and propagation are primary properties of organic substance. Goette (1883), on the other hand, assumed the appearance of death at the earliest beginning of organic development. If Weismann's view is correct, Freud's theory of the death instinct loses its biological fundament and can be regarded as disproven. A death instinct which forces organisms to a return to an inorganic condition but which is acquired only at a relatively high level of organic development would, of course, be an absurdity. Weismann's theory has not encountered a uniform response. Some authors like Max Hartmann (1906) or Jankélévitch (1910) objected; others like Doflein (1919) or Kammerer (1923) agreed with Weismann and denied a tendency to die which was inherent to organisms. The list could, of course, be enlarged. Those biologists, however, who claimed the potential immortality of organic substance seemed greatly supported in their views by the experimental finding that well-nigh every cell can grow indefinitely by division when kept under very special, that is to say, optimal conditions. This was particularly surprising for the ganglion cells and the cells of the heart muscle, since brain and heart are the first organs in the human organism to stop growing and perhaps are for this reason the usual sources of man's natural death (Mühlmann, 1914; Nothnagel, 1900).

Szasz (1952) bases one of his main arguments against Freud's theory on the very fact that biology has proved the potential immortality of any kind of tissue cell. For him there is only one instinct, a life instinct, which if opposed in its gratification by frustration leads to differentiation and subsequently to death. "If all interferences with the life instinct were eliminated, living systems would be immortal" and "death is the price we pay for development"— thus Szasz returns to Weismann's early theory. However, Doflein (1919) had pointed out that differentiation per se cannot be considered a cause of death since the germ cells are highly differentiated yet preserve their potential immortality.

I want to follow in my argument a different line of reasoning, which Max Hartmann (1906) has initiated. He interpreted the life of unicellular organisms in a different way. For him the division of these organisms, by which mechanism they can maintain their seeming immortality, coincides with their deaths. And he may be right. Does the protozoon really still exist once it has undergone division? To be sure, its organic substance still exists in the two cells which resulted from the division of the parent cell, but the original organism has ceased to exist in its former individuality. About the unicellular organism one may say that it cheats death like a debtor who eschews punishment by quickly arranging a settlement with his creditors before the judge can pass a sentence. If the unicellular organism did not divide or had no opportunity to divide—that is to say, give up its individual existence—it would die as multicellular organisms do. The unicellular organism also dies, so to speak, when dividing, but the organic matter of which it is made up does not reach the inorganic state, because prior to this event it is intercepted in the form of two daughter cells. Yet the individual protozoon is as little immortal as the multicellular organism. If man's propagation followed the law of unicellular propagation, we would describe this process also as death. We need only to imagine an old person suddenly falling apart into two babies. In figurative language one could say: since the unicellular organism is particularly prone to be destroyed by the death instinct, the life instinct has to tear it apart before the former has reached its goal; thus the life instinct acquires a new lease on life. In artificial tissue cultures, this very process is repeated over and over again. The single cell is forced, so to speak, to give up its individual existence in favor of the two daughter cells. The multicellular organism consists of masses of bricks which singly have preserved a property which is manifest in the protozoon, or in other words, the metazoa consist of masses of protozoa. To a certain extent the result of tissue cultures could have been predicted on theoretical grounds. The whole problem is, to my mind, somewhat obscured by the ambiguity of the term *growth*. When it is spoken of as the growth of a differentiated organism, the term refers to the increase in the total number of the cells of which it consists, of the enlargement of single cells and usually also of the simultaneous death or atrophy of other cells in the same organism. But this process of growth preserves the individuality of the organism in which growth takes place. Nothing of that kind takes place in tissue cultures: under optimal conditions one generation of individual unicellular organisms dies and is replaced by a generation consisting of the double number of organisms.

Freud's theory of the death instinct might be disproved if optimal conditions were discovered which would provide a differentiated organism with potential immortality. The coincidence of death and propagation in the unicellular organism conceals the existence of death, and Freud's reasoning, I believe, was quite correct when he wrote (Freud, 1920a) :

> The primitive organization of these forms of life [protozoa] may conceal from us important conditions which are present in them too, but can be recognized only among the higher animals where they have achieved for themselves a morphological expression. . . . The instinctive forces which endeavor to conduct life to death might be active in them too from the beginning and yet their effect might be so obscured by that of the forces tending to preserve life that any direct evidence of their existence becomes hard to establish.

This reasoning, however, is also applicable to tissue cultures which, after all, consist of an aggregate of unicellular organisms.

Yet in this context the counter question may be raised;

namely, what forms of propagation in the protozoa would permit the assumption of a death instinct or, in other words, what conditions in nature would have to exist in order that the opponents of Freud's theory of the death instinct would feel convinced of its correctness?

According to Freud's theory the organic development started through the operation of stimuli upon the inorganic. These—and all subsequent—developmental steps were enforced against the tendency of the organic to return to the inorganic; that is to say, the organic was wrested from the inorganic against a strong resistance. We therefore may expect to find at the beginning of life the simplest structural relations which are indispensable for the continuation of life as such.

The unicellular organism is the simplest biological, viable unit in which this question can be studied, and I wish to discuss what possibilities of propagation are conceivable in this unit. The organism could expel part of its protoplasm which in turn could develop into a full-grown protozoon. The parent organism could then die after it had fulfilled its propagative function. This manner of propagation would come closer to the way multicellular organisms propagate; it also would result in the existence of a corpse. But—assuming this form of propagation really existed—it quickly becomes evident that life would have perished soon since no state would ever have been reached where more than one cell existed; thus, with the annihilation of this one cell, all existing life would have vanished. This form of propagation would not have led to an extensive evolvement of life. Therefore the minimum requirement would have to be that the parent cell would repeat the process of expelling protoplasm repeatedly and then die. This of course would have resulted in a particularly luxurious form of propagation because one unit of a generation would have been replaced by a plurality. Again the existence of a corpse would have seemingly satisfied the requirements of Freud's theory, since from the beginning of life each unit would have died in a way similar to that encountered in multicellular organisms. Yet this form of propagation would by no means fulfill the demand for minimum requirements. One may expect, perhaps, that the expulsion of protoplasma should occur only twice, although it is not understandable why such an important function should be activated only twice. Yet even by a reduction of propagative processes to two, this form would be more luxurious than the one actually observed in protozoa, because at one point in time three units (two daughter cells and one parent cell) would exist simultaneously instead of the original cell.

Thus we see that the actual division of one parent cell into two daughter cells is the scantiest way of propagation. Any different way would either have been incompatible with the preservation of life or would have caused a multiplication far beyond the bare minimum. Forms which excel the bare minimum are actually observed in multicellular organisms. Man, for example, produces germ plasma which under favorable conditions could replace two parent units by a huge number of units; the protozoon is the only organism which can replace, potentially and *de facto,* a parent unit by only two units. The reduction of the earliest propagative form to the bare minimum which is still compatible with the continuation of life as such warrants the assumption that the earliest forms of organic life had already been evolved against an intensive resistance. Death was by no means a price that had to be paid for sexual propagation and individual existence, but sexual propagation abolished the coincidence of death and propagation as it is observed in unicellular organisms, and thus sexual propagation made individual existence possible.

DEATH AS A PSYCHIC EVENT

The idea—often expressed by philosophers and well supported by the psychoanalytic conception of the personality —that the whole preceding lifetime is reflected in the terminal phase of a human being seems to be correct. In Case Two this could be seen at least approximately. Histories of patients consistently subjected to psychoanalytic observation would prove this in greater detail and more convincingly than it can be expected in reports based on psychotherapy.

In dying, man consummates his whole previous life, but the possible stimulation of new structural processes through the terminal phase should not be overlooked. Consummation of the past, evolvement of new structures, and destruction of already existing ones would be concepts which might be useful as operative tools in that part of a psychology of death which is concerned with the psychic processes of the terminal phase. However, the conspicuous features of the terminal phase which usually attract the observer's main attention derive from the inroad of disturbed physiological functions upon the personality. When we observe the dying person we believe we perceive the disturbed biological apparatus (Schilder, 1921); the psychic phenomenon is then reduced to a medium through which we observe one or several biological processes. The closer a person comes to death the less we are able to describe the observed phenomena in terms of the dying person's personality, that is to say, in terms of the vicissitudes of the psychic apparatus; rather, they are described in terms of the disturbed biological function which has its effect upon the psyche. The psychic apparatus and the biological substructure almost coincide again as in the newborn. This is the way the dying person appears to the eye of the contemporary observer. But are we right in experiencing the terminal phase in this way? In earlier times when man witnessed the parting of a human being, he perceived death struggling with angels or gods with demons and many another phantasmagoria.

In *Faust,* second part, Faust dies shortly after the third of the four grey hags, Want, Guilt, Care, and Necessity, breathes upon him. It was not an arbitrary choice by Goethe that Care was selected as the one of these four scourges of mankind which finds access to Faust's palace and prepares him for his final consummation (Türck, 1899). (Note the leading role which the conception of Care [Sorge] plays in Heidegger's thanatology.) Thus Goethe presented a psychogenic death as the end of Faust's earthly days; and yet *Faust* is the play of man's destiny meant to be written in generally valid symbols. In reading these few concluding scenes of the tragedy, in which man's dying is presented in an indescribably moving way, each event is understood without further reflection. Of course Faust must be blinded when struck by Care's breath and this must be the first direct step toward death; and Faust must sink down dead when he reaches the moment described by him as being so beautiful that it should never pass. But as soon as we stand at the patient's bedside and witness his death, it is the embolism, it is the ruptured heart muscle, it is the fibrosis of the brain because of which this human being is dying. No longer can we experience this individual death as the end result of a fate or of a destiny, unless it is the destiny of cells. But who is right? When we follow Faust's vicissitudes, do we relive animistic projections or do we experience an area of psychological reality? I will not try to answer this question but only suggest that in a future thanatology the terminal pathway will have to be described in terms of the individual's destiny, a task which cannot yet be fulfilled because of certain limitations inherent in the emotional as well as intellectual spheres of our times. The extent of this limitation and narrowness can be well documented—to take one of many examples—by the notes which a great man like Hermann Nothnagel wrote a few hours before dying when observing in himself the signs of the approach of death. In his lecture upon dying (Nothnagel, 1900), he had discussed the problem with unusual breadth and understanding, transgressing by far the scope of internal medicine, yet in the hour of his own dying, he clung to the manifestations of the weakening of the heart muscle as if these signs were the all-embracing clues to an understanding of his terminal phase.

DEATH AND TIME

A psychology of death will need as a prerequisite a psychology of time. Death and time are indelibly connected in our subjective experience. If man could not experience time, he could never fathom death, which would then be as meaningless to him as it is to the animal. One of the greatest drawbacks encountered in an attempt at a psychology of death seems to me to be our relative ignorance in matters which concern the psychology of time. This is not the place to review the literature and the relative progress made in our century concerning the subject (Merlan, 1947). Yet while refined analyses of the inner experience of time such as that by Husserl (1905-1910) can barely be outdone, nevertheless one puts his essay away in the mood of Augustine who said: "What then is time? If no one asks me, I know; if I want to explain it to a questioner, I do not know."

Time, I believe, is one of those problems not accessible to our era; the successful investigation of it will be the prerogative of a later epoch. It is barely possible to know what the limitations to an inquiry into this problem really are. If we knew their nature, perhaps this would enable us to overcome them. Perhaps we are forced to think of time in terms of physical movement or of psychic movement or of a physical, objective entity. However great the contributions of physics (Reichenbach, 1951) have been and will still be to the problem of time, I do not think that decisive steps toward a psychology of time will come from this quarter. Time is constantly in us and around us; nevertheless, we cannot grasp it. Probably there is a fundamental resistance in us to understanding it, a resistance which goes far deeper and is far more basic than that which is encountered in the ego when it fights off a content in the repressed part of the personality. It is conceivable that this ego would be seized by fright when facing the true issue of what time really is. And again one can well understand when Augustine breaks out in the essentially blasphemous words: "O, my Lord, my Light, shall not here, too, Thy truth mock at man?" The primary experience of time, I would think, is entirely bound to the course of inner processes and occurs much earlier than perception of time. Perception of time is a function of a relatively high organization and is a later product, gradually formed out of an archaic time experience. The latter seems to be indelibly attached to the psyche; even if the individual has never experienced an external perception there still would be an experience of time. This basic experience is, of course, to a great extent fashioned and molded by the infinite series of external perceptions, of actions, and by the activation of practically each psychic function, but the effect of these functions is bound to an experience which is more archaic than the phase in which single functions are differentiated. The experience of time—this is probably a redundancy and one should only speak of time—is bound to the earliest emotions, to the earliest instinctual processes. When time becomes an explicit content—possibly a catastrophic experience in the development of the personality—the whole aspect of the problem takes on a different appearance. In that moment, death also becomes an explicit content, for there arises the question of what will happen when time stands still or there is no time to be lived. It is possible that the type of person whom I have mentioned before, who appears oblivious of death, owes this relative immunity to a lack of differentiation of time experience.

However, the concept of fear of death ought to be kept apart from that of fear of annihilation. The latter is ubiquitous: in order to experience it, no particular differentiation within the ego is required. It is not always easy to distinguish these two fears, one of which easily slides into the other. I would tentatively say that the fear of annihilation pertains primarily to the fear of the body's destruction but does not necessarily include the destruction of the psyche, soul, ego, or personality, or whatever still must be added in order to convert fear of annihilation into fear of death. The early fears of the infant and of the child probably are fears of annihilation, the fear lest something dreadful will occur. The destructive nature of the impending event will be strongly represented, but the exact nature of the event aside from its extremely displeasurable quality will be left vague. Likewise, it is questionable whether what is commonly called the fear of death in primitive peoples is really such, since in their belief the annihilation of the body is immediately followed by the continuation of existence in the shape of spirits (Kelsen, 1943). Whether the belief in these spirits is a defense against the idea of death, I do not know. The historically later belief in the immortality of the soul is unquestionably a denial of the knowledge of death. Such a conviction, purified of the element of denial and doubt, would automatically eliminate the affect of sadness or grief after the death of a beloved one. A person as psychologically astute and sensitive as Augustine rightly asks forgiveness for having wept at the occasion of his mother's death.

Those religions which teach belief in the immortality of the soul apparently try to reduce death to the mere annihilation of the body, but the affective response of those who mourn for the passing of a person they have loved proves that the knowledge which should be denied by the believer's faith returns and unfolds its full effect. The difference between the fear of annihilation and the fear of death can be clearly seen in the detail of senile dementia, which I have mentioned earlier. The demented person fears the annihilation possibly brought about by an operation but is fearless of death. Since the image of annihilation refers to the present or the near future, still included in the biological present which is also the earliest time category consciously experienced by the child (Spielrein, 1923), the senile patient is therefore still capable of fearing annihilation.

Thus one may say that the psychology of death has a footing in the psychology of time. To be sure, the problem of death can never be dissolved into the problem of time. If anything, the opposite might be conceivable, since beings endowed with eternal existence possibly would not experience time. In this way at least I believe we must understand what Augustine means when he says of God:

> Your years neither go nor come; but our years come and go, that all may come. Your years abide all in one act of abiding: for they abide and the years that go are not thrust out by those that come, for none pass. ... Your years are as a single day; and Your day comes not daily but is today, a today which does not yield place to any tomorrow or follow upon any yesterday. In your today is eternity.

Rightly Augustine postulates as one quality of the Godship that it be outside of time. When one listens to Augustine's despair as he tries to penetrate into what time really is, one seems to perceive envy of an existence which can escape that which was evidently for him a painful burden. So he writes:

> For when a man is singing a song he knows, or hearing a song he knows, his impressions vary and his senses are divided between the expectation of sounds to come and the memory of sounds already uttered. No such thing happens to You, the immutable and eternal.

Strangely, but possibly quite rightly, Augustine claims here that the unfolding of time into three dimensions creates a basic division in consciousness which is present even in the simple act of perceiving. Husserl (1905-1910), in his analysis of time consciousness, also accounted for these facts, describing them as retention and protention, which are indispensable when experiences unfold themselves in the stream of time (Merlan, 1947).

Here we enter the phenomenology of the experience of the present from which inquiries into the psychology of time usually start. I want to make here only one remark about this topic. I believe that a pure experience of the present is rather rare, at least in the adult. The present is taken here, not in the sense of physics, as a pinpoint in time, but as the psychological present which also has duration. I believe that Augustine is right in saying that man's present is divided between the memory of things past and the expectation of things to come. The interference of the two other time dimensions with the experience of pure present occurs in manifold ways quite aside from retention and protention. The experiences of the past force the mind to experience the present in conformity with them. The world can no longer be experienced by the adult as an aggregate of color blots, but *things* are perceived. Pure sensation has become converted into indices of external reality. The essential change which the world of perception undergoes in the course of development is one of the most fundamental ways in which the past is indelibly attached to the present, even on the purely perceptive level. The single perceptive act is also the end product and result of the past of the perceiving person (Brunswik, 1929, 1934), and even with effort this factor cannot be excluded (Brunswik, 1947). The past is objectively attached to each function.

But this objective disturbance of the experience of pure present has its counterpart also in the realm of the subjective experience. It is only because the interference of past and future has become an indelible quality of almost every experience that this interference is usually not noticed explicitly. Inasmuch as the ego has the ability to synthesize these interferences into one act, they remain subliminal.

Yet this is true not only of the experience of the present. The experience of pure past or of pure future is likewise absent. When Augustine says, "There are three times, a present of things past, a present of things present, a present of things future," he points out how the experience of present interferes with the experience of past and future. He is well aware that he describes here three different functions: "The present of things past is memory, the present of things present is sight [contuitus], the present of things future is expectation." But is memory possible without sight and expectation? Sight without memory and expectation, the latter without sight and memory? The relative inability of the psychic apparatus to experience single time dimensions in their purity is perhaps part of the general inability to experience untainted sensations, such as complete silence, complete darkness or pure colors, all of which can be experienced only in dreams, if at all.

Although the experiences of pure present, pure past, or pure future are never accessible under ordinary conditions, I wonder whether there are not states whose uniqueness is partly based upon the experience of pure time dimensions. I believe that in an adequate orgastic experience pure present is experienced. The experience of pure present in the course of an orgasm is even an indication of whether the orgastic experience was adequate or not. During coitus there is no perception of time (Bergler and Róheim, 1946), but the experience of time is not abolished. Indeed, whenever a pure time dimension is experienced, perception of time must be abolished. During the orgasm the ego span is reduced and completely filled out by a complex of sensations which objectively follow each other in succession, that is to say, objectively take place in time. The factor of objective succession, however, plays an essentially different role here than in the succession of perceptions like those which lead to the hearing of a tune or to the sight of movement. The evolvement of such configurations requires, and is only possible within, a constant experience (and perception) of time; that is to say, the past and the future must be represented in the present. In the experience of orgasm, however, there is a continuous present at least when the acme is reached; past and future are abolished; the present becomes an eternity. When Augustine defined eternity as standing and not passing and having in itself no past or future, he gave the indices of time experience during orgasm. (The discussion of the time problem in Goethe's *Faust* would confirm my thesis, but I must forego this digression.) The reduction of time to eternal present in orgasm is possible because the ego is submerged into pure sensations which are unrelated to any indices of external reality. The fusion of body, ego, and world into one complex, indivisible experience inaccessible to further analysis makes it possible for time to become pure present. In the early phases of psychic development all psychic contents probably abide by a similar kind of time experience. Strangely enough, certain artistic experiences also seem to bear the quality of pure present. It would not militate against the foregoing if pure present were also encountered in ecstatic experiences.

Is there a state in which the ego experiences pure past? I want to repeat that with pure past I mean a state which is beyond that which Augustine called "the present of things past." If a subject relives in hypnosis a past condition as if it were present, he comes close to an experience of pure past, yet this past still presents itself with all the earmarks of present, even if this present is completely filled out by a past and long-forgotten state. The formal quality of this state which presents itself as if it were the present obviates the full experience of pure past. It seems that the requirements of an experience of pure past are fulfilled in deep, dreamless sleep. The personality then regresses to a former state. Ego and body delve into an archaic condition. This submersion into the past is a complete one and includes the perceptive functions. In re-experiencing the past, as might happen in hypnotic states, the perceptive systems also regress, as is evidenced by their not fulfilling the primary task of conveying the indices of present reality; instead they submit to a temporary dissolution of the comprehensive ego organization which becomes submissive to an ego-alien force, the hypnotist. In deep, dreamless sleep the perceptive systems follow an even deeper regression and discontinue any kind of contact with any sector of external reality. The perceptive systems are drawn into the general retreat and do not disturb the regression by converting past into present as happens when the state of deep sleep is temporarily interrupted by a dream.

It is necessary to digress here. Husserl (1913), in discussing time in his "General Introduction," describes the stream of experiences as an infinite chain of *now*-points (impressions), each of them surrounded, so to speak, by a retention (a now-point just passed) and a protention (an expectation of a now-point which is still in the future but which will become a now-point in the present). As Merlan (1947) following Husserl convincingly demonstrates, no impression is possible without either a retention or a protention. Consequently Husserl's claim (1913) that "the stream of experiences cannot start or end" seems to be well justified. This of course is not meant objectively but subjectively (Merlan, 1947). As a matter of fact, no one can remember the moment of birth; that is to say, a first impression not preceded by a retention; nor can anyone experience his own death; that is to say, the last impression, not followed by a protention. Merlan, who drew important conclusions particularly from the first part of this thesis, writes: "There can be no such thing as a perception of a first temporal event, and no such thing as a perception of a last temporal event."

Convincing as such reasoning is, it is not quite correct within the reality of psychic processes. The situation of being suddenly awakened from deep sleep by external irritation actually provides the experience of a first impression. In accordance with Husserl's research, this first impression is not experienced as a temporal event since it is bare of an adjacent retention; thus this circumstance may be used as a proof that here is actually a true first impression. Also it may happen in states of fever that the world of perceptions falls apart and no longer conveys temporal events but an aggregate of first impressions. This is definitely part of psychopathology, whereas the former example can be regarded as belonging to normal psychology. Grotjahn (1942) speaks of the rebirth of the ego, and Silberer (1911), in analyzing an example of hypnopompic dreams, compares awakening with dying. The subjective experience of sudden awakening from deep sleep induced by external stimulation is very difficult to describe. It is not uniform, but varies and often contains complete disorientation in time and even in place. The first impression (in the sense of Husserl) is sometimes strangely reminiscent of modes of experience occasionally described by paranoid patients with regard to delusionary impressions. Yet the first impression at the occasion of sudden awakening proves that during deep sleep no new retentions are formed; in other words, the present is completely abolished. I do believe, however, that this is true only of deep sleep. The experiments of the Borings (1917) and of Brush (1930) did not convince me of the contrary, since their experimental conditions did not assure deep sleep.

Yet time is not discontinued during sleep. The objective period of time through which a person sleeps is definitely not experienced as a gap or a hole; the ego as a continuum is preserved during sleep. This, I believe, is not always the case during a fainting spell or unconsciousness caused by a head trauma. Periods of unconsciousness enforced by anemia or other pathology sometimes temporarily abolish the ego in its existence; that is to say, the objective time period which is covered by this kind of unconsciousness is often viewed retrospectively as a gap, a period of nothingness, so to speak, which the person, thus traumatized, tries to fill with something which might re-establish the feeling of a continuum. Sleep never affects the ego like a trauma. The awakened sleeper does not look back at the recent past of unconsciousness as if it had been a gap. The two recollections are different in quality. Evidently no new impressions or new retentions are formed during deep, dreamless sleep; nevertheless the state of sleep must also be considered a temporal event in the subjective meaning of the term, because the ego retrospectively acknowledges the past period of unconsciousness as a part of the past through

which it has lived and by no means sees it as something
alien.

After a deep, dreamless sleep a person awakens with the
feeling of being rejuvenated, and actually he is biologically
younger than he was at the time when he fell asleep. If
each of the factors enumerated is considered—the retro-
spective aspect of lived duration, the rejuvenation, the
experience of a first impression when suddenly awakened,
the total regression, the absence of the formation of new
retentions—one may draw the conclusion that the subjective experience of duration during sleep, the experience of
sleep as a subjective temporal event, is possible by the
experience of pure past. At least this is, as far as I can see,
the only mode of time experience which would be compatible with the aforementioned five factors.

We have now to deal with the far more difficult question, namely whether the experience of pure future is
possible at all and—if the question should be answered
positively—under what circumstances this might take
place. From the discussion of the experience of pure past
it becomes clear that this experience also can take place
only outside a conscious state, since the *donnée* of consciousness forces the quality of a present upon all of its
contents. In the religious hallucinatory vision of the faithful who see themselves seated at the right of God's throne,
this experience of an anticipated future is still presented
in the form of the present. It would be the equivalent of
the hypnotic state in which the subject experiences the
past.

The following remark belongs to metaphysics: One
may describe the state of being dead as one in which pure
future is experienced. The fact that death is the end of
life would not be an adequate argument against this construction. If death is that state of the future toward which
life converges—and all life processes seem to work toward

this end state—then man reaches in death his final goal, a state which will be his permanent future and beyond which no contents which are new or subjected to variation are to be expected.

In other words, if it is true that death is not an accidental occurrence but the necessary, the logical and sense-adequate result of all life processes, then by dying man reaches that stage which is destined to fill out his whole future. The difference between present and future would be abolished; the experience of the present would be eliminated as in sleep—not by regression, this time, but by a continuous thrust forward beyond the present moment. The state of being dead would be the counterpart of sleep. Both are beyond the present; but in sleep the future is excluded by the tie to the past and by the corresponding paralysis of those structures which organize the dimension of future time; in death the past is excluded by the destruction of all memory-forming apparatuses. From this point of view it is, of course, immaterial what the state of death is *realiter,* since the question as raised here concerns itself only with the manner in which the state of death can be described exclusively in terms of an event in time. In a hypothetical form it could also be said that a being who could live constantly ahead of the present without experiencing this future in the form of the present—who lived truly in the future—would be unable really to live at all; that is to say, such a state would be incompatible with life.

The acceptance or rejection of such a speculation is immaterial in an empirical psychology of death, yet its possible value might become apparent if it were considered as a starting point for a critical discussion of existential philosophy. From the viewpoint of an empirical psychology it can be said that the psychic apparatus is incapable of the experience of pure future but approxi-

mates it in the state of terror induced by the real or assumed certainty of immediately impending death.

In analyzing the time dimensions in the state of terror
induced by the certainty of immediate death, I want to
outline briefly one difference between anxiety and terror.
As far as one can ascertain clinically, even at the height of
anxiety experienced by the adult in the state of wakeful-
ness, the anxious person envisages the dreaded event as
uncertain; this degree of uncertainty may shrink to a
minimum and the ego may consider its occurrence as almost certain, but some uncertainty is present as long as
anxiety persists.

With the complete abolishment of uncertainty, anxiety
regularly changes into another emotion. Sometimes the
ego may greatly fear an event, yet the moment of its actual
occurrence may be followed by peaceful calm, even relief;
or the occurrence may just as well be followed by sadness,
grief, or despair. When, however, a dreaded event of the
future is envisaged as a certainty and there is no doubt
at all regarding its occurrence, then anxiety changes to
terror. Terror requires a factor of certainty, whether this
factor refers to the future—an expected event—or to a
past event. Anxiety, on the other hand, always refers to
the future and always to an uncertain event.

I refer to essentially the same situation when I say that
anxiety stops when the representation of alternatives has
been abolished and replaced by the certainty of a dreaded
future event. It is puzzling that this emotion, which is one
of the most painful, can occur only in reference to an
uncertain future. Why should the ego regularly bear such
an intensive displeasure only about those events the certainty of which has not yet been ascertained?

In the acute terror of death the ego experiences itself
as having reached the point when time comes to a standstill and the whole future has been reduced to the pinpoint

of the last moment of life. This last moment is visualized as being deprived of duration (biological present). Here a paradox is encountered. The envisaged tribulations of the last moment would become more easily acceptable to the ego if they could be repeated. In other words, a person would possibly reconcile himself to death if death were an infinite aggregate of last moments, a situation where seemingly an increase of pain results in a lessening of pain.

When the terror of death reaches its peak, the individual is in the state of despair. The inescapability of the shrinkage of the future to the pinpoint of a single moment is experienced as a reality. The ego feels as if the whole possible future were experienced in this one short moment; the free flow of time is stopped; future is not converted into present and the latter into past. The personality no longer grows in time but reaches a deathly standstill. It is possible that in the terror of death, when death becomes an inescapable immediate reality, the ego comes close to the experience of pure future. It is very remarkable that, when suddenly and under circumstances quite unforeseen by a person, external circumstances enforce the certainty of impending death, mechanisms of denial automatically set in and a regression into the past is enforced (Pfister, 1930), as I mentioned in the Introduction. Strangely enough, this temporary solution, so very pleasing and so really useful for the ego in terms of the pleasure-unpleasure economy, is usually not accessible when death by internal reasons is threatening or when the danger of death has covered a longer period of time.

Anxiety vis-à-vis death, however, is significant because it refers to an event which objectively will take place with certainty. When the ego is ridden by anxiety of death, the question does not concern the "whether-or-not" of the event—as in most other instances of anxiety—but the "when" of its taking place (Georg Simmel, 1918; Heidegger, 1927). To be sure, there is also anxiety over other events about which there is certainty, such as aging. But this anxiety also is only a forerunner of the anxiety of death.

Freud tried to dissolve the anxiety of death into other components such as castration fear. The clinical investigation of patients whose fears center around death supports this view. Almost regularly the analysis of a preoccupation with, or intensive fears of, death leads to the uncovering of intensive castration fears. However, one also finds quite often in such patients fantasies of wanting to be castrated in order to bring about the preservation of life by virtue of this sacrifice. The conscious and readily verbalized fear of death seems to serve, then, the denial of a castration wish, and I wonder whether the psychology of the fear of death can be adequately studied in such patients. Also the theory of the death instinct may require—on theoretical grounds—a revision of Freud's theory of the fear of death.

The investigation of patients whose ego has accepted the concreteness of death and no longer indulges in the belief that eternal life can be bought for some price may throw a new light on the psychology of the fear of death. The question whether an ego can actually lift itself to a vantage point at which one's own death can be viewed as a part of reality will be taken up later in a different context.

A remark regarding existential philosophy is also necessary here. A constructive discussion between ontology and an empirical science such as psychoanalysis will have to start, in my opinion, with an exact description of the differences regarding the conception of anxiety. There are difficulties which are unavoidable in discussions between a scientist and a philosopher when they use the same term without their referents being the same (such as when the psychoanalyst and the phenomenologist use the term ego), or when a conception holds a prominent place in one discipline without having an equivalent in the other (as is the case with the conception of existence). All these difficulties should be eliminated when the discussion turns toward an entity which is as well-defined, well-circumscribed, and concrete as anxiety. However, the ontologist may start out by setting forth his views upon the fear of death, about which the analyst can speak only in the negative.

And yet one may rightly expect that anxiety with regard to death will hold its proper place in psychology. It is the only anxiety which refers to an absolutely certain event of the future and the only one which—as far as I know—disappears when the ego succeeds in maintaining an unbroken representation of the future, as I will try to show later.

I have mentioned earlier states in which, presumably, pure time dimensions are experienced. These states are also significant by their relation to particular experiences of the pleasure-unpleasure series.

I mention the possible relationship between the structure of the time experience and the pleasure-unpleasure experiences, since it may be precisely the structure of the time experience which may make certain experiences of pleasure-unpleasure explainable. Freud (1905a) devised a simplified model of pleasure-unpleasure experiences in which every increase of excitation was earmarked with unpleasure and every decrease with pleasure. This model, though probably adequate for organisms of relatively simple structure, will definitely not suffice for structures as complicated and highly differentiated as the human personality (Jacobson, 1953). Freud himself laid the foundation for a revision of the simplified model by introducing time in the form of gradient (Freud, 1920a) and rhythm

(Freud, 1924b) as additional factors bearing upon the pleasure-unpleasure quality of an energic process.

The disappearance of unpleasure when a pure time dimension is experienced, as in orgasm and sleep, cannot be a coincidence. Actually the experience of a pure time dimension implies a negation of preconscious and conscious time experience. The constant changes of the future into the present and of the present into the past are stopped. Then the self is not carried within that constant stream of inner growth which makes it different from moment to moment despite its remaining an identity. The abolishment per se of this aspect of the experience of self may become a source of pleasure. Boas (1950) has succinctly shown the traces of an intrinsic aversion against the acceptance of time even in logical thinking.

The experience of time depends on manifold factors. The biological state gives constant coloring to it. In a state of fever, hunger, or thirst, time is experienced differently. The experience of time also depends on age. The frightening speed of time as one grows older as contrasted with the almost eternal distance from one Christmas to another in childhood is well known. All these variations of time experience, I believe, are possible because all the enumerated factors have a fundamental bearing upon emotions. The interplay of emotions, their speed, their gradients, the ego's acceptance, rejection, or denial of them, and many more factors which are involved in the appearance and disappearance of emotions, appear to leave their imprint upon the way time is experienced. Contrary to the usual opinion that the external changes within perceptive contents are the *fons* and *origo* of time experience, I want to stress primarily the inner changes within the psychic apparatus, which I would esteem as the indispensable sources of time experience—without underestimating, however, the effect of external factors. One of these will be discussed more closely. It is one of the indisputable merits of Spengler (1918)—however correct his critics might have been—that he brought to general attention the fact that the experience of time and its meaning as well are correlated with the historical period and vary in accordance with the period. Just how the historical climate achieves this fundamental effect upon a configuration as basic and as deeply rooted in the unconscious of the person is, I believe, unknown. It is more easily understandable that the respective historical period has its impact on the prevailing forms of instinctual gratification, since the mode of gratification is made part of law, custom, and child rearing. But nowhere, I surmise, has time experience per se been made the discursive content of society's contact with the individual. Of course, society bears upon the individual's way of organizing time, but the mode of time experience establishes itself automatically, and a person cannot exercise conscious influence upon it. I believe that society by its impact upon the emotional sphere, upon a person's attitude toward his body, upon the concept of death, and in many more ways, leaves a characteristic imprint upon time experience.

The genesis of the individual time experience is no matter of concern at this particular juncture. Suffice it to say that individuals who live, create, and act under identical historical circumstances have something in common with regard to their time experience. This does not, of course, permit the conclusion that the time concept is identical in members of the same civilization. Townsend (1946) very succinctly presents the considerable differences in time concept of Plato and Aristotle. But these conceptual differences do not disprove the existence of a background in terms of a subjective time experience identical for almost all members of the elite actively engaged in cultural processes. The concept and meaning which death holds in a society will, of course, show with particular succinctness certain characteristics which are significant of the respective time experience. In turn the recoil upon the mode and structure of time experience will be particularly great if a change occurs within any sphere connected with the representation of death. As can be expected, it may take a long time until this recoil has its organizing effect on the time experience which prevails within the entire cultural community. The Christian concept of death amounted to an incisive break with the meaning of the corresponding concept in Graeco-Roman society. Yet, although the new meaning of death was quickly integrated upon the conceptual level, it took a much longer period of time until it affected the mode of time experience in such a way as to modify art, architecture, or sculpture.

EUTHANASIA VERSUS ORTHOTHANASIA

In view of the penetrating effect which the feeling about death, the teaching regarding it, and the intellectual as well as artistic representation of it have, it is particularly noteworthy that throughout almost the entire development of Occidental culture the practical thinking of philosophers and laymen occupied with death has centered upon euthanasia. Dying in happiness or with ease or in harmony, or at least without remorse or fear or trepidation, has been the cherished goal throughout the ages, and a philosopher who could prove that adherence to his particular system would by necessity obviate a painful death could count on a general agreement that his philosophy must be the true one.

However, this general striving for the extension of the pleasure principle to the situation of dying ought not to be taken for granted. At first sight, man's craving for a death bare of suffering appears self-evident and in no need of further justification. But it may be easily overlooked that this seemingly self-evident craving implies a certain appraisal or, better, contempt of death. The underlying ideology seems to be that death is under all circumstances a nuisance, a kind of *summum malum* which, since it is unavoidable and imposed upon us by a superior force against our will, should at least take place with a minimum of discomfort—in much the same way one tries to sweeten an unpalatable medicine. However, since death is part, and a very important part, of reality, we are justified in trying to extricate the outlook on death from the scope of the pleasure principle, which is implied by the concept of euthanasia, and to extend the reality principle to this necessity which dominates human existence. Therefore the concept of *euthanasia* requires a counterpart in the form of *orthothanasia,* which would signify dying in a manner adequate to the reality of death.

I would like to discuss one of the many systems which were evolved ostensibly with the purpose of taking the sting out of the bitterness of death. A type of reasoning, quite characteristic in its own way, is that of Socrates after his condemnation to death. One step in reducing the effect of terror brought on by the prospect of close death is to declare it a small calamity when compared with others. This reasoning, one might expect, ought to be particularly consoling when it concerns a calamity through which we have often gone and which it is easy to reproduce. "The difficulty," Socrates says in the *Apology,* "is not to avoid death, but to avoid unrighteousness." In so saying, death is declared an evil lesser than unrighteousness, and since no man can rightly claim never to have been unrighteous, death, it follows, cannot have upon man an effect more painful than what he has experienced quite often—such as the pangs of conscience and the humiliation he is bound to suffer when being unrighteous. Further, Socrates devises the famous dichotomy of death as either a dreamless sleep or a migration to a place which is preferable to any other place because of the illustrious company encountered there. He expresses the hope that death is a good, whereas before the supreme sentence had been passed, he had declared that man was ignorant about whether death was the greatest good or the greatest evil. On the day which Socrates knows to be his last one, he goes a step further, this step is an ultimate one which, if one accepts his way of reasoning at all, cannot be excelled. He says, in *Phaedo:* "And now . . . I desire to prove to you that the real philosopher has reason to be of good cheer when he is about to die, and that after death he may hope to obtain the greatest good in the other world." All doubt is gone; what was first unknown to man and then a hope becomes at last a certitude provable beyond doubt, by unassailable ratiocination. The true philosopher, reasons Socrates in a confessing way, "is always pursuing death and dying." The great distractions which endanger the true philosopher's search for truth and knowledge are bodily pleasures, the body in general, and the sense organs in particular. Therefore the disseverance of the soul from the body must be the utmost and constant goal of the philosopher, a goal which is accomplished in the act of dying. A man's repining at the approach of death is "sufficient proof that he is not a lover of wisdom, but a lover of the body, and probably at the same time a lover of either money or power, or both." Here it seems as if a basic pattern of orthothanasia had been evolved, at least for one type of man, namely the true lover of wisdom. What Socrates seems to say is that if someone really wants to be a true philosopher he necessarily must rejoice at the approach of death. But the emphasis of the argument is still put upon euthanasia, and the fact that Socrates' reasoning leads to euthanasia is taken as a proof that it also must be orthothanasia. How could an argument, so the listener must feel, which makes the dying person foolproof against agony be wrong since man cannot aspire to anything beyond a painless or even a joyful death? Thus the effect of the pleasure principle becomes unmistakably evident in Socrates' reasoning. However, if orthothanasia should succeed in eliminating the pleasure principle it may become clear that an entirely different kind of response would be far more adequate than that which Socrates holds as the only correct one for the lover of wisdom.

Socrates based his system of euthanasia on two premises which will not necessarily appear succinct to the present-day investigator: first, that the body and the pleasures which it provides are an impediment to the search for truth and knowledge, and second, that the soul is immortal. The first premise might have been correct in view of man's attitude toward his body in ancient Greece, but it has lost its validity since then. The second premise will also militate at present against a generally acceptable orthothanasia. The belief in the immortality of the soul—though it grew out of the basic structure of the human mind and though it probably is still unavoidable, quite independently of its acceptance or refusal on the intellectual level—serves, of course, the purpose of denying what is precisely the essential feature of death, namely that death is irrevocable and ultimate and irreconcilable with any further existence in any form, shape, or manner.

Man's belief in the immortality of the soul is, indeed, a most noteworthy phenomenon. It seems scarcely possible for him to overcome it, for a long array of psychological reasons which I do not want to venture to discuss here. A short remark, however, may be permitted regarding the difference in man's outlook upon his past and on his future. Notwithstanding the still unsolved problem of how and when man obtained insight into the facts of procreation (Jones, 1924), it is reasonable to assume that there was a period—probably of a vast duration—when he was ignorant of the biological sequences leading to pregnancy and birth. By and large, however, despite a strong internal desire to deny the fact by fantasy or to escape its full truth by additional hypotheses about the origin of the soul, biological procreation and the beginning of individual existence at a certain time-moment have been accepted by mankind. Recognition of these facts must have been a great trauma and a profound blow to man's narcissism. Both effects can also be observed nowadays when the child discovers the truth about his origin, but the child learns to accept this truth—as primordial man did—at least within the scope of his conscious and reality-adjusted thinking. This relative reasonableness toward the past, that is to say, man's final bow to the reality principle regarding his individual origin, did not find its counterpart in an equivalent acceptance of the reality principle regarding his future. Although man in general does not claim the eternal existence of well-nigh anything which he sees, hears, smells, touches, tastes, or—quite generally—meets in his personal universe, nevertheless he stubbornly insists that the most vulnerable and the latest developed entity, namely his mind or part of it, his soul, is actually endowed with the capacity for eternal existence. The ease with which he deviates here from the reality principle is facilitated by some characteristics of the time dimension of the future. The past, of course, lends itself as a screen upon which to project illusions, the individual past as well as that of the group or of mankind. The fantastic ideas—sometimes with the full feeling of their correctness—which neurotics evolve about their past (Freud, 1909b) illustrate the projection of individual illusions, and the myths regarding the national past or the origin of mankind illustrate the projection of group illusions. Yet there is no doubt that difficult as it may be to overcome such illusions, it is far more difficult to purify one's outlook on the future from them; for example, while an anthropologist hardened by the effect which his learning and research have had upon him may have buried his former belief in the Biblical tale of the origin of mankind, he may, nevertheless, accept the dogma which refers to man's future. This readiness regarding the formation of illusions about the future is partly due to the character of the future as a potential field of action. The feeling that proper action might give the future a shape conforming with man's desires seems to result in an irresistable temptation to anticipate as certain a future which is identical with such wishes. The past which has obtained a definite, irreversible form by its character of being a deposit of accomplished actions compels man with greater force to submit to the reality principle than do the potentialities of an as-yet-unformed future. When Weininger (1904) calls the lie the will for power over the past, he refers to this problem.

A short digression about man's feeling with regard to the past may be interpolated here. I quoted Mead's (1932) elaboration upon this topic. The past is actually not irreversible but constantly changes. The feeling that the past cannot be undone stems possibly from the verdict of the superego that an evil action cannot escape punishment, or revenge, respectively. The belief in the irreversibility of the past finds its equivalent in the seemingly irrefutable statement—basic to any true psychology of the human personality—that every moment in the life of every human being is unique and impossible to repeat. However, man is here, also, possibly deceived by an illusion. Nietzsche (1881/82) raises the question of how man would react if the demon told him:

This life as you are living it now and have been living it, you will have to live once more and still innumerable times; and there will be nothing new in it, but every pain and every pleasure and sigh and all unspeakably small and great [things] of your life have to come again and everything in the same sequence and succession. . . . The eternal hour-glass of existence is always again turned around—you, atom from dust, with it. [See also Appendix, viii.]

It is my impression that if some basic tenets of science are taken seriously, the present conviction of the uniqueness of each life moment can be disputed. It may be assumed that if in any other sector of the universe a cosmic constellation should occur which was, is, or will be identical with any one which has been present in our planetary system, then all events which have taken place in the world of our planet must be repeated. In other words, if in any other sector of the universe the identical chemical and physical combinations of elements should occur as they existed when our planet was formed, the same development of organic life would have to occur. In view of the vastness of the universe and the lengths of time involved, such repetitions are conceivable. As far as I can see, there is no objection to assuming that possibly in this very moment an undetermined number of persons identical with me are writing the same words as I do or that in the past this same event has taken place or will take place in the future for an undetermined number of instances. However, if once upon a time the human mind had penetrated into all sectors of the universe, its repetitive nature would become questionable, because then the number of past, present or future repetitions would be known and this factor would obviate the repetition of identical events. Thus the structure of the human mind may eventually preclude the possibility of identical repetitions.

Since our present field of operation does not transgress the human world of this planet, the possible truth that individual existence may repeat itself has no bearing on our present research and therefore this remark has no practical consequences. It only serves the purpose of outlining an area where the human mind may be deceived by an illusion stemming from man's narcissism, which plays such an eminent role regarding his feeling of certitude about the assumed course of the future.

A scientific orthothanasia will also have to drop illusions which extend into the future if it wants to exclude the reduction, by denial or by any other mechanism, of the gravity of the problem of death.

Taking these few factors into account, it is not probable that orthothanasia will generally coincide with euthanasia. Despite our ignorance about death (and consequently also about orthothanasia) a situation is known in which the conditions of orthothanasia are easily definable and, strangely enough, they coincide in this particular instance with euthanasia. I am referring to the dying of the martyr. For whatever cause he may sacrifice his life, an identical constellation is encountered. The death of any martyr is characterized by two conditions: First the cause for which the martyr dies is more important to him than his life; and second, the way he will face his extinction might well have a significant effect upon the future of the cause for which he is ready to die. The point of gravity of narcissism has shifted in the martyr away from his own self into an extraneous structure. Thus even when he dies, that which is most loved, wanted, and cherished by the martyr does not perish but continues its existence. In the case of the martyr, the psychological future is not discontinued by the ending of his existence. The only thing which appears to him to be of any importance, his cause, will not only continue but by his very extinction will resurge in victory and beauty. Quite rightly the martyr responds to the belief that the brave and unflinching attitude of a person when facing death must have the social effect of proving, or of coming close to proving, the truth of the conviction for which he is dying. Of course, this belief is irrational, and regardless of how a man responds when he knows that he will be forcefully deprived of his very life, this does not prove an iota for or against the correctness of his conviction. But the social effect of his way of dying may be decisive. Archaic beliefs regarding the ordeal (Zilboorg, 1943b) are here at work. His fortitude in the face of death is taken as God's judgment that he must be right. As a matter of fact, grandiose empires have been shaken by the terrible effect which the fearless death of the wretched yields. Rightly, those in power tremble when the persecuted dies in a way which gives him the aura of martyrdom.

For the many examples regarding the psychology of the martyr which I could quote, one may suffice. This is Walter Husemann's farewell letter to his father shortly before his execution by the Nazis (Poelchau, 1949):

> Be strong! I die as what I have lived: as a fighter for the working class! It is easy to call oneself a communist as long as one does not have to bleed for it. Whether or not one really was one, he proves only when the hour of the supreme test has arrived. I am one, father. I do not suffer, father, believe me. . . . To depart honorably from life is the last task which I have set myself. Prove yourself worthy of your son. . . . I am dying easily, because I know why I have to die. Those who kill me will suffer in not too long a time a more difficult death. That is my conviction. Remain hard, father! Hard! Don't give in! Think in every hour of weakness of this last demand of your son Walter. [See also Appendix, ix.]

Here the martyr's becoming the embodiment of the superego in close proximity with death is movingly expressed.

For the martyr it is, one is inclined to say, easy to brave
death because by virtue of the shift of his narcissism death
does not result in the discontinuance of the future so much
feared by the ego. In this exceptional situation death can
achieve more than life, and therefore—granted supreme
devotion and loyalty to a conviction—death under proper
circumstances becomes a reality-adequate goal for man's
striving. In the instance of the martyr one can observe that
the psychological problem of death really focuses around
the preservation of a flow of time toward the future. A
political martyr may be an atheist and may be convinced of
the finality of death—as much as man may be capable of
evolving such convictions—and despite the lack of denial
regarding death, he may nevertheless die without anxiety
in the full vigor of his strength and with the full longing
for earthly pleasure in his heart solely because this specific
constellation permits the full maintenance of time-directed
representations despite the conviction of the impending
total annihilation of his own person. I do not account in
this context for the contribution of aggression. The martyr
dies in the belief that his death will achieve the destruction
of an adversary, who could not be conquered by the aggression at the disposal of the living. Thus the martyr finds—
without further deliberation—all the specifications of an
orthothanasia which, however, coincides with euthanasia,
since any deviation from orthothanasia would result in
grief and self-reproaches in the moment of death whereas
his living up to the standards of orthothanasia must yield
a unique bliss which can scarcely be achieved otherwise.
However, our relatively good knowledge of orthothanasia
in the case of the martyr and the coincidence of orthothanasia with euthanasia in this instance, are possible because the martyr's dying is a matter of *savoir vivre* and

not of *savoir mourir*. For the onlooker the martyr succumbs to a frightful death; he himself, however, has the
feeling of generating new life in that very moment.

Behavior in the face of death is regulated for the martyr
by a code of ethics which is valid for almost all of his life
situations, and therefore the moment of death does not
introduce any new principle that would require a special
solution.

This strange consequence, that *savoir mourir* is only a
particular aspect of *savoir vivre,* is also valid for the dying
of the true Christian, particularly of the devout Catholic.
Since dying is for him only the passage to a new and more
desirable form of life, orthothanasia does not involve more
than the riddance of the effect of past sins, a task which he
has regularly lived up to throughout his adult lifetime.

Little can be said yet regarding a scientifically acceptable
orthothanasia. The topic has been badly neglected by
science, perhaps for the reasons which I have tried to outline in the Introduction. Rightly, the topic ought to have
been granted special consideration since it would meet one
of man's greatest needs. The comparatively rare verbalization of this need should not deceive us about its presence
and urgency. The spirit of the present times, particularly
within the American scene, is characterized by a supreme
effort at the denial of death and the concomitant preponderance of—not to say, addiction to—the present. This
insistence upon the exclusive importance of the task to be
done now and here, the reluctance to submit to the exigencies of a far-away future, and the refusal to consider
in the present the anticipation of that future, may have
been caused by, or may have resulted in, the denial of
death. The question arises whether the evolvement of
orthothanasia and its teachings might have an influence
upon the time experience now so dangerously restricted
to the present. Can the time experience of a historical

period be changed by deliberate effort at all? The usual channels of enlightenment and education must come to naught in trying to fulfill this task, since they would affect the intellectual sphere only, hardly penetrating to that depth of the psychobiological unit in which the basic structure of the time experience originates. Attitudes toward death, however, by their unavoidable effect upon the emotional sphere have had historically a profound bearing on time experience, and orthothanasia may be the detour by virtue of which science may also affect this, perhaps deepest, layer of the personality. Not much can be expected here from the churches. An attempt at reviving the medieval imagery and fear of death will only enhance existing mechanisms of denial. The idea and the necessity of death might be integrated by the living, once science has provided knowledge and understanding of what death really is and has simultaneously outlined a generally valid orthothanasia based upon this knowledge. This orthothanasia will have to fit the newly gained understanding of death into the framework of the human personality. It will have to consider the variability of individuality and the consequent multiplicity of responses possible to the one objective entity of death. Thus science ought to guide man in his adaptation to death. As in most other instances, science will not exhaust the whole matter but will leave enough room for the individual to imprint his own personal stamp upon the terminal pathway. Orthothanasia will serve as a rational guide in a matter which possibly will always remain partly irrational to the human mind. It will protect man against the inroads of superstitions and irrational fears, on the one hand, and, on the other, against the superficiality of a cheap denial of one of the gravest issues in human existence. It will help man in finding his own individual way in coping with this issue without trying to coerce him into accepting a more or less arbitrary doctrine about the soul and its future existence. With such support, the individual of our society may gain courage to brave the impact of the problem of death in its full vastness and terribleness. When this has happened, then the thinking about death and the preparation for its occurrence will have become an integrated part of personal culture; it may also happen that the narrow outlook limited to the present may broaden and man will include in his responsibilities and in the area of deliberate action the future as far as it can be foreseen. Thus the greatest danger which possibly can threaten a society may be banished, and the ancient terrible prophecy that the iniquity of the fathers will be visited unto the third and fourth generations will become —let us hope on just grounds—converted into the more hopeful outlook that each succeeding generation may obtain a blessing from that which has preceded it.

AGGRESSION AND THE BELIEF IN THE IMMORTALITY OF THE SOUL

It is a well-known and proved fact that among the large array of factors on which a person's capacity to love others depends, the fullness and concreteness of the representation of his self is one of no minor importance. Schilder (1935), to quote only one instance, showed that a lack of integration of a person's body image is correlated with aggressive behavior, of a kind which aims at the disseverance of the bodily unit of others. Many other examples could be adduced illustrating the parallel between a disturbance in the relationship to the You and that to the Me. In studying the representation of the self one will notice that, quite generally, it is not represented as one which— though endowed with duration and extending into the future—is destined to die and therefore to lose its existence. This lack in the representation of the self as a structure limited in time possibly has a profound bearing upon man's relations to his fellow man.

The incompleteness of the representation of the past has been adequately studied. The consequent limitation of the adult's relationship with the child has been described by Bornstein (1948) and Olden (1953). Something prevents the adult from experiencing the child on his own terms, mainly because the adult's development is not represented in its full extension toward the past. However, the adult is particularly drawn toward the infant's early phases of narcissism which are experienced as static (Freud, 1914), because the representation of the adult's self still carries a property of this early narcissism, namely the belief in its eternal durability. The representation of the self as an entity without time limit is greatly favored by the religious teaching of the immortality of the soul. Possibly one has to search here in order to find one of the reasons for the comparatively little effect which the Gospel has had on the taming of the destructive instincts of Occidental man, a fact which has been noticed more readily by outsiders, for example, the Indian Chief Hatuey who "when urged at the stake to embrace Christianity, that his soul might find admission into heaven," inquired if the white men would go there. On being answered in the affirmative, he exclaimed, " 'Then I will not be a Christian; for I would not go again to a place where I must find men so cruel!' " (Prescott, 1843). This fact was also noticed by some enlightened members of the Occidental elite such as Goethe, who said: "I a pagan? Now, I have let Gretchen be executed and Ottilie starve to death! Is this not Christian enough for people? What do they want more Christian?" (Varnhagen von Ense, 1843). It sounds like a paradox that the belief in the immortality of the soul— a belief usually upheld with particular pride and considered a sign of particular ethical greatness—should have a detrimental effect upon man's ethics. The topic is a rather comprehensive one and its adequate discussion would transgress by far the scope of this study; therefore I want to limit myself at this point to an incidental observation which I made in myself. Once in a distressing situation when I had to cause some harm—which I hope was not severe—to a person whom I would have preferred to help, I suddenly had the flash—contrary to my opinion that man in his totality is most mortal—that God would compensate him after his death for the suffering he had to endure because of me. To what extent this irrational thought, evolved on the spur of a distressing moment, contained a typical pattern I do not know, but it is conceivable that a self represented as unlimited in time shows less mercy to others than one which knows—and here the word "knows'" is meant to extend also to the unconscious parts of the personality—that human existence is restrained in all of its aspects to a well-defined and circumscribed finiteness.

Orthothanasia might evolve man's representation of self as one which is limited in time, which in turn might make him concede this finiteness to others and thus make him less liberal in dispatching his fellow men to where they can partake of the alleged immortality of their souls.

INDIVIDUALITY AND PHYSIOLOGICAL FUNCTIONS

Of the many antinomies between which human existence takes place, I want to mention one which may appear to be of less importance. Man's many functions extend from the extremes of the gratification of biological needs to the highly differentiated one of creating new, original, and individual values, whether these pertain to art, religion or to any other cultural area. Whereas the former group is significant by its monotony, the latter

appears even confusing by its well-nigh excessive variability. For example, eating has been the same for thousands of years, and despite whatever meaning man might
have attributed to it, it has always consisted of the monot-
onous repetition of the same physiological acts: biting,
chewing, mastication—that is to say, preparation for
swallowing—and swallowing itself. Yet whenever man succeeds in lifting himself above the biological sector of his
existence, an infinity of acts of individualization can be
seen which would make an observer almost believe that the
variety of these cultural products could not stem from the
activity of the same species, unless he takes cognizance of
the replacement of biological evolution by cultural development.

Yet what concerns the first part of the thesis—the seeming monotony of the physiological function—reveals on
closer observation that the physiological function also (and
this, in my estimation, is one of the most surprising discoveries of Freud) is subject to the law of individualization.
Whereas for the geneticist, biologist, and physiologist the
uncounted number of human generations since man has
existed are linked by the repetition of identical acts of the
copulation of the two sexes, for the psychoanalyst this chain
of events appears rather as an aggregate of highly in-
dividualized acts. In the psychological scrutiny of subjects
one finds the biological functions (though almost monot-
onously identical in their behavioristic aspect) individually
structured. This is meant not only in terms of the objects
which a person selects in order to gratify his needs, or of
the meaning which a biological function acquires for a
particular person, or of the rituals and customs which
grow around biological gratifications, but rather in terms
of the biological function per se.

There seems to be a derivative of the view regarding the
identity of biological processes in Georg Simmel's soci-

ological remarks (1908) about sex and marriage. Although, as he says, copulation is the only factor which is common to all known forms of marriage, it is just this biological factor which is the least significant of the marital institution inasmuch as the sexual relation is *not* marriage. "Whatever," Simmel continues, "marriage may be, it is always and everywhere more than sexual intercourse; divergent as the directions might be in which marriage transgresses [intercourse]—only the fact that marriage transgresses it makes marriage what it is." However pertinent these remarks might be, I wonder whether one would not raise nowadays the question of whether and in what respect the psychology of marital intercourse is different from that of extramarital sexual gratification.

I have gone into these details in order to outline the new vista which has been gained from the aspect of Freud's psychology of biological processes, and I want to add that in them even the most individual facet of a personality can be encountered. The biological process per se is the area where man is the most unfree. With an iron hand nature imposes upon man the invariable and unchangeable biological form of gratifications and man has to bow to this biological imprint, but simultaneously in accordance with the law of individualization these immutable forms are varied or modified by individuation. The fact that individuality is here subjected to a seemingly unmodifiable impact, or, in other words, that individuality is here exposed to a force strongly endowed with the capacity of extinguishing it, makes the situation of biological gratifications one in which the most individual facet of an individuality becomes observable. Individuality works here, so to speak, against the strongest possible resistance.

If we return now to the very opposite group of functions, that group which pertains to the creation of values when man seems to indulge in the highest possible degree of freedom, one makes—in my estimation—an observation which is at least as surprising as the one just mentioned. If, namely, the contents of these creations are abstracted, and the creative function per se is studied—at least in its most sublime form—one notices that almost nothing individual can be said about it. As a paradigm, such different artists as Goethe and Rilke may be compared, each in the moment of creating one of his sublime poems.

Goethe reported that he often awoke from his sleep with a completed poem on his mind. The only difficulty he encountered in preserving it referred to the finding of a technique which would permit its being written down without fully awaking him.

Rilke revealed a comparable process to a friend (von Salis, 1936). Habitually he preserved in a notebook what came to his mind whether or not it made sense or showed a meaning. Such morsels got "into unexpected contexts." He quotes the instance when he wanted to write a poem for a certain occasion. He browsed in his notebook, picked out a French word that seemed to fit the occasion and wrote a German poem using the word as a central theme. Yet the precipitating word had been French and he felt the urge to rewrite the poem in that language. He abandoned himself to his inspirations and promptings, "as it was his way to construct nothing with purpose but to be obediently present when verses formed themselves in his imagination and under his pen." He was taken by surprise, when the new French poem went in a different direction than the former German poem.

I know that there are other ways in which poems originate, but it strikes me as quite far-reaching that Goethe as well as Rilke cannot say anything but "it occurred" about the moment of highest inspiration when each was capable of creating something which made him essentially different for all eternity from any person who has lived or will live. Indeed, the process of inspiration is so much de-individualized that A. E. Housman compares it with human or animal secretion (Kris, 1939). The antinomy of the biological functions as the medium of most poignant individuation in contradistinction to highly differentiated ego functions, which per se are almost bare of individuation but lead to contents of highest individualization, has also its bearing upon the psychology of death. So much are we accustomed to seek the individually significant in areas of relative freedom that death as the result of the strongest biological force has become concomitantly completely devoid of individuation. Yet Rilke (1903), in what may be called a twentieth century prayer, wrote:

> Oh Lord give everyone his own death,
> the Dying which goes out of that life
> in which he had love, sense and plight—
> for we are nothing but the shell and the blade—
> the great Death which everyone has in himself,
> that is the fruit around which everything revolves.

> * * * * *

> Lord we are poorer than the poor animals
> who die in their own way though blind,
> for all of us are still *un*died.

> * * * * *

> For this makes dying strange and difficult
> that it is not our death; it is one which
> takes us at last only because we have not matured
> our own.
> Therefore a storm goes in order to brush all of us
> away.
> [See also Appendix, x.]

In these verses much is expressed poetically that belongs to orthothanasia. There is a biological direction, a law, a necessity, or whatever we want to call it, which makes death inescapable. But as little as other biological forces remain without individuation, as little can (or should one say *ought*) death remain untouched by the individuality which will succumb to it. To a certain extent one could say: we do not need to pray to God to let us die our own deaths since we cannot but die our own deaths; yet Rilke is right, inasmuch as the deaths we die are not envisaged as events which we have "grown ripe" or "brought to maturity"—or, as Rilke says, in another poem, an event to which we give birth—but as an event "which takes us away."

It would be wrong to interpret Rilke—and this view would be also alien to a scientific orthothanasia—as if he expressed a particular longing for death. An event may be recognized as meaningful and necessary and nevertheless the ego may turn against it with full force and strive for its postponement. Of course, in Rilke's verses one feels the great anxiety which he suffers over death. As a matter of fact, as soon as he felt marked by death—far earlier than the fatal diagnosis had been made by his physician— he stopped talking or writing of death (von Salis, 1936).

A similar receding even from the word *death* in any context has been shown also in the life of Goethe (Simon, 1949; for a discussion of the problem in a broad context, see Susman, 1954) and is by no means unusual, perhaps is even the most frequent, external response to the awareness of an acute change in man's relationship to death. When Rilke wrote the aforementioned verses, death was for him still an abstraction—despite his submersion into death imagery at that time. When it dawns upon man that the first stroke of that disease which irrevocably will destroy his material structure has hit him, death acquires an essentially new quality of concreteness. It would be one of the tasks of orthothanasia to strengthen man so that this receding, which apparently was particularly prominent in Goethe, would not occur when death becomes concrete reality. The way suggested in Heidegger's ontology, to be "free for death," is one of the many possibilities but not the only one.

Apparently Rilke's personal motive for writing the verses was the striving to convert the imagery of death into an ego-syntonic one. Death as a purely biological event is "cold and heavy," but a man who dies his personal death has integrated what otherwise remains alien: to die a personal death becomes a personal task as Rilke (1903/10) so delicately implied in "The Notebooks of Malte Laurids Brigge."

> This excellent hôtel [writes Rilke of Paris' oldest hospital] is very ancient. Even in King Clovis' time people died in it in a number of beds. Now they are dying there in 559 beds. Factory-like, of course. Where production is so enormous an individual death is not so nicely carried out; but then that doesn't matter. It is quantity that counts. Who cares today for a finely-finished death? No one. Even the rich, who could after all afford this luxury of dying in full detail, are beginning to be careless and indifferent, the wish to have a death of one's own is growing even rarer. . . . One dies just as it comes, one dies the death that belongs to the disease one has (for since one has come to know all diseases, one knows, too, that the different lethal terminations belong to the diseases and not to the people, and the sick person has, so to speak, nothing to do).

Here the ignominious death is contrasted with noble death. To die as an appendage to a sickness, to die as one in the crowd in an institution like the Hôtel-Dieu at Paris —a factory producing death—without perhaps even knowing of the approach of death is apparently ignominious. But to die in the way Malte's grandfather died—as Rilke described on subsequent pages, when the old *Kammerherr* Brigge kept a community trembling for two months, so long did it take him to die—then death loses its ignominy.

Rilke's imagery about death as a castration is very conspicuous, and the symbolism of his poetry betrays an excessive fear of castration. The unconscious equation behind the prayer for an individual death probably was: "If I have to be castrated I want it to be done on my own terms, in my personal fashion," an equation not infrequently found in neurotics who are particularly sensitive to that kind of fear. Death in battle or after heroic defense, then, becomes a cherished imagery compensating for the ignominy of castration, an imagery which has social validity to the degree that death on the battlefield automatically makes the soldier a hero. This recoil of external circumstances upon the phenomenology of death is noteworthy. To a certain extent it is the opposite of Rilke's aspect. For independently of the personal and subjective form which death has taken in a specific instance, an assemblage of factors essentially alien to death as such is arbitrarily earmarked as an assemblage of traits characteristic of a particular instance of death. Nevertheless this spilling of the peripheral into the essential is perhaps a preliminary step toward the individuation of death. The idea of the individual death has had its bearing on the imagery with which public imagination and fantasy sometimes surround the deaths of outstanding personages. The last words falsely imputed to Goethe actually reverberate the structure of his past, and if Goethe had had to choose—for this occasion—two words which would be pregnant with symbolic meaning and would conclude his life in the most dramatically possible way, he could not have succeeded better than the ornamentors of his legend. This ornamentation indirectly expresses the idea of, and the longing for, an individually structured death.

At this point I want to interpolate an observation which impresses me as a particularly apt illustration of the idea of individuate death. A sensitive and intuitive scholar in

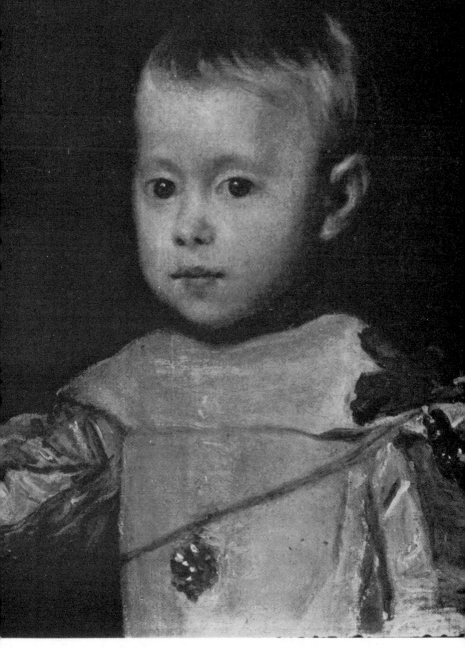

Kunsthistorisches Museum, Vienna

INFANTE PHILIPP PROSPER, *by Velazquez*

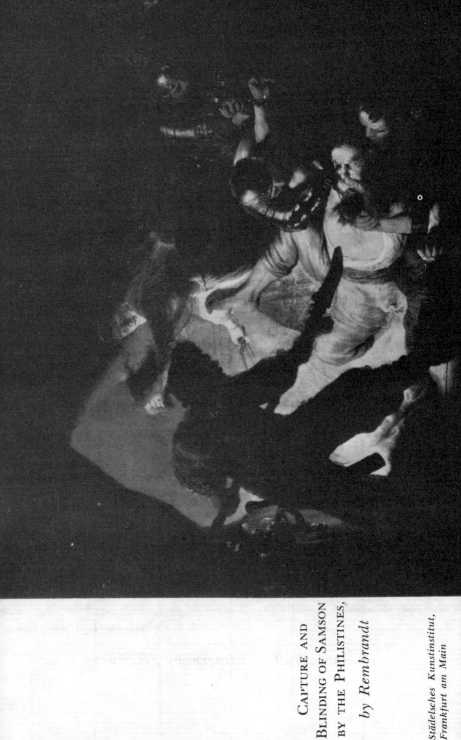

CAPTURE AND
BLINDING OF SAMSON
BY THE PHILISTINES,
by Rembrandt

*Städelsches Kunstinstitut,
Frankfurt am Main*

the field of the history of art, Fr. G. Grossmann, was impressed over and over again, when viewing a certain portrait by Velasquez, by the idea that the subject, a child, was destined to die soon after the time his portrait was made. Such was the impression—the source of which cannot be verbalized—which Grossmann obtained from the facial expression. The child, the Infante Philipp Prosper, is pictured in the manner in which Velazquez frequently painted the members of the imperial family, particularly its children. He is standing upright, quietly and officially, resting his right arm with dignity on the back of a chair. It is a typical pose and a typical appearance. The face is pale and the eyes melancholic. As a matter of fact, the child was two years old when he was portrayed and died at the age of four (Justi, 1888). The artist himself died the year following the child's portrayal. Was he himself sensitized to the soft forewarnings of death in the faces even of the young ones? But what a marvel that the head of a child can be painted in such a way that three hundred years later an intuitive mind can read from the eyes: "This child will die soon."

ON BASIC PRINCIPLES OF ORTHOTHANASIA

A consistent pursuit of the consequences which follow the idea of an individuate death may lead far afield. In a 1914 letter, Rilke wrote a passage about thoughts he had while standing before Rembrandt's painting of the capture and blinding of Samson. The painting was made in 1636, when the artist was thirty years old and had reached a critical juncture in his life. It is worth while to consider for a moment some features of the painting in order to understand better Rilke's reaction to it.

The event is presented in its full, naked brutality with an incredible realism of physical and psychological detail.

Samson is overpowered by five soldiers. He is chained and held down; his beard is torn while he is being blinded at the same time. Each of the five soldiers participating in the capture seems to carry out his own sadistic impulse; nevertheless, the whole group becomes a unit in what may be described as strength being overpowered by the knavish and weak. Delilah hurries toward the entrance of the tent; she turns her head back to see, once more, Samson defeated. In her left hand she holds Samson's hair and in her right the treacherous scissors. Her face shows triumph, horror, and erotic excitement in a mixture which only Rembrandt could express in a human face. Her eyes are peering and the mouth half open. Lying on the floor and tightly held by a soldier below him, Samson writhes in pain. The right arm, lifted in order to strike a blow, is stopped by the Philistine who chains him. His right eye is scooped by the dagger of another who also tears at his beard. The toes of the right foot, which holds almost exactly the center of the painting, are curled in pain. He is a strong husky man, but he has passed the pinnacle of his manhood. He must be over fifty. His face has something uncouth which is enhanced by the expression of acute pain. Delilah looks young and charming. The motives of female sexual ambivalence, of attraction and repulsion and resulting revengefulness as well as of male sexual arrogance defeated by female cunning form the psychological background.

The subject of castration has scarcely ever been represented with such intrusion, made visual to the very limit that is still compatible with the laws of aesthetics. The beard, the eyes, the hair, all of them are well-known symbols. The picture shows the castration of a father substitute, first by a seductive, young mother substitute, and then by five sons—all of this in one. As a matter of fact, Rembrandt had three older brothers and an older sister

(Hofstede de Groot, 1906). His younger sister had actually been his model for the Delilah of a previous painting (Brown, 1907). Yet despite the brutality, if not to say the crudeness of the uncompromising realism of detail, the painting is at no time in danger of affecting the onlooker like a horror show; it is always sublimely beautiful.

Let us return after this introduction to Rilke and what he had to say about the painting. He wrote (1914):

> Recently it made me think how the most extreme art renders innocent the most cruel. Look only at this stream of the happiest light which intrudes in order to push the most insane violence to the clearest day: he who would present a martyr in this way would have on his side the most sublime mind—but here occurs a crime and the painting does not revolt against it; the painting embraces it like nature and the blissful colors behind the unbearably painful foot do not cease to be blissful.
>
> What is that? Is there in life something similar? Are there relations of the heart which include the most cruel for the sake of completeness because the world is yet world when *everything* occurs in it? I was able to imagine God always only as Him, who permits *everything*, who continuously faces the whole inexhaustible world in all its modifications. He who would know this entirely, how undaunted would he be. [See also Appendix, xi.]

Starting out from the artistic cosmos, Rilke draws a conclusion regarding the real world. An action which is out and out crime may become a source of beauty even when the artist does not omit one single detail of the horrible event. The color of beautiful light—and indeed Rembrandt drowned the gruesome scene in marvelous grey-blue—may undo the evil, and when one's mind is encompassed by the beauty of the painting, evil becomes an acceptable part of the human world. The same brutal details illustrating the death of a martyr would pose no problem at all. But evil should engender evil and not beauty. Here is asked the equivalent question which has puzzled the greatest thinkers of the Christian era: "How can the irrefutable existence of evil be reconciled with the idea of an almighty and infinitely kind God?" Rilke makes a grandiose turn and says that everything that happens in the world makes the world what it is, belongs to the world, is part and parcel of the world, for the whole world is God's creation and therefore nothing, even the evil, is to be separated from it. The good one who fights the evil with all the power at his command and the evil that regenerates itself over and over again and is just as strong as it was millenia before, both are necessary parts of the world wanted and acceded to by God. Though such an idea may be easily abused by the moral opportunist, such philosophy is actually far from opportunism.

This is a courageous attempt—following many of a similar kind—to heal a dehiscence which goes through Judaeo-Christian mythology and imagery of the history of man. An elaborate and appealing vision—of what man is, of his virtues and weaknesses, of his origin and his destiny, of the limiting he must suffer by virtue of his finiteness, and of the height he may reach because he was created in the image of God—has been handed down from generation to generation within the Occidental orbit as a rational system and as a historical account embellished by legend and folklore.

Every problem of human nature seems to find its place in this comprehensive justification and explanation of man's function and of his standing in the universe, and the faithful feel grateful that they can be submerged in this vast edifice of concepts, theories, illustrations, and descriptions, all of which appear synthesized into a unit by their beauty and all of which appeal to human imagination as well as to the desire to find guidance and peace. Yet this pageantry of man rests on one great tragic event which brought on a turn incomparable to anything that followed, namely the fall of man, whose state and fate were essentially different before and after.

Before the fall, man was immune from death, ignorant, and free of frustration; afterward, he became mortal, knowing, and frustrated. Yet this tragic turn, from which time on—so we are taught—the misery and suffering of man had their origin, was followed by much more than misery. Not only did evil spread in the shape of envy and destructiveness, causing that ocean of suffering of which history records only a small part, the greater part of which went by unrecorded and unrevenged, but man became also a being capable of love and charity and of a sense of beauty. Here Occidental man faces the great Christian dehiscence. Are we to believe that the cathedrals and verses and music and the innumerable acts of unselfishness, charity, and self-sacrifice, as well as man's delight in trees and flowers and the sky and his passionate longing for his mate—are we to believe that all these blessings are also the work of Adam's fall and that without his sinfulness man would still stroll in the Garden of Eden? Doing what?—meditating upon whether or not he should eat from the tree of the knowledge of good and evil? For nothing else was left him by the Lord unless he was to become entangled in sin. If all the evil is the consequence of the fall of man, then, too, is all the good we love, for in paradise man was beyond both; yet then—it must be concluded—any reasonable being would prefer the state after the fall of man to that before, despite the terrible consequences mythology imputes to Adam's act of choice, a thought which is so beautifully expressed in one of the verses of Young's *Night Thoughts*: "Death gives us more than was in Eden lost."

Thus Adam appears as the one who was greater than his

creator; Prometheus becomes visible behind the tattered rags of the repentant sinner. Such consequences were intolerable to the sensitive, God-loving poet, who put God right back where he belonged, into the place of the creator of the whole world and consequently also of death.

The myth of the fall of man is so important here because, according to the Christian belief, the conclusion is unavoidable that "Adam's immortality . . . . was something that would have been given him if he had observed the conditions accompanying God's promise" (Smith, 1949), or as Paul wrote: "It is just like the way in which, through one man, sin came into the world, and death followed sin, and so death spread to all men, because all men sinned." This identification of death with sin destroys man's deepest link with nature. It suggests that although all living substance has to perish by virtue of the will of a divine power, man has been destined to be the only exception to a law that is a basic prerequisite of life as such. If death were really the consequence of evildoing, then man would stand isolated in nature and would not be the end product of a long development which has led to a structure endowed with faculties incomparable to any others. He would be only an ostracized culprit who never was a part of nature, but became such by an act of dishonor. As a compensation for this stigma, Christianity offers man, if he adheres to the divine precept, the prospect of a future state which is almost like that prior to the fall of man.

Just as it is unacceptable that a superior power could ever have created man in His image and banished him into a Garden of Eden, so it is engaging that man, once upon his future, will be in a state of eternal blissfulness. What could be more wished for than that man after his toil and struggle and conflict and disappointment would receive his just reward in the form of an ultimate and eternal synthesis providing the bliss of which he receives so little during his earthly days. Yet here again one would expect the divine power to be kind and wise enough to embrace all mankind in that synthesis and not to imitate anew the human compulsiveness of classifying each and every thing into good and evil.

Orthothanasia, though it has to destroy the comforting illusion of eternal life, restores death to a place which is free of evil and good. Death becomes a natural event which, though it cannot be integrated by the unconscious part of the personality, can be integrated by reason.

Like most sciences orthothanasia will ease man's life in some respects and make it more difficult in others. Its primary purpose cannot be to provide consolation but only to assist in recognizing reality. Reality is always—and in this instance particularly—complicated, serious, and heavy to bear.

What the teachings of orthothanasia will be cannot be predicted. Possibly it will bring the terror of death to fuller awareness than any doctrine has before, or perhaps the outcome will be quite different. In view of the past findings of psychology, the most probable outcome is that death, despite is monotony in terms of physical consequences, will be found to be one of those biological forms which is highly accessible to individuation. Because it is carried by the strongest biological power which exists in the human universe and since the ego is consequently most powerless when encountering it, it is also the greatest challenge and therefore possibly the one great event where individuality can rise in its most differentiated form. To ask whether the latter is horror or a vision of harmony or indifference means to raise a wrong question.

Orthothanasia will guide the individual in finding his individual way toward the end of all ends. This way will be a synthesis first of all of the individual's past and of the objective meaning of death. As Jaspers (1919) says: "Death is a universal situation of the world and simultaneously a specifically individual one." A generally valid model of orthathanasia will derive its frame of reference from a variety of sources. It will have to consider the dying person's personality, his past history, his biological state, his sense of the future, the culture by which he is surrounded, and the responsibilities toward his contemporaries and posterity. Within all these variations, there will remain, nevertheless, something which is common to all.

Orthothanasia will try to prevent the individual from entering the event in a state of illusions, whether the latter be the result of historical tradition or individual acquisition. Man has so often bravely faced the truth, and the truth about death might be the most difficult to bear. Yet truth, bitter as it is, may enlarge man's self—as it has so often done in the past—and man, having shed one more denial, may enjoy the state of enlarged inner freedom despite the recognition of how merciless that reality is of which he is a part.

The ancient Greek myth that man was created from the blood of the Titans (Guthrie, 1935) may have come closer to psychological truth than that of his having been made of dust.

APPENDIX

i

FRANZ ROSENZWEIG, *Der Stern der Erlösung*

Vom Tode, von der Furcht des Todes, hebt alles Erkennen des All an. Die Angst des Irdischen abzuwerfen, dem Tod seinen Giftstachel, dem Hades seinen Pesthauch zu nehmen, des vermisst sich die Philosophie. Alles Sterbliche lebt in dieser Angst des Todes, jede neue Geburt mehrt die Angst um einen neuen Grund, denn sie mehrt das Sterbliche. Ohne Aufhören gebiert Neues der Schoss der unermüdlichen Erde, und ein jedes ist dem Tode verfallen, jedes wartet mit Furcht und Zittern auf den Tag seiner Fahrt ins Dunkel.

ii

GEORG SIMMEL, *Lebensanschauung*, p. 100

An den grossen tragischen Gestalten Shakespeares spüren wir fast von ihren ersten Worten an die Unentrinnbarkeit ihres Endes, nicht aber als eine Unlösbarkeit verwickelter Schicksalsfäden oder als ein drohendes Fatum, sondern als eine tiefe Notwendigkeit, ich möchte lieber sagen: Beschaffenheit ihrer ganzen inneren Lebensbreite, die in dem dramatischen, schliesslich tötlichen Geschehen nur kanalisiert ist, nur eine auch logisch begreifliche, auch dem Weltlauf gemässe Ausgestaltung gewinnt. Der Tod gehört zu den apriorischen Bestimmungen ihres Lebens und des mit diesem gesetzten Weltverhältnisses. Dagegen, Nebenfiguren in diesen Tragödien sterben, wie es der äussere Geschehensverlauf gerade mit sich bringt; sie werden nur irgendwie umgebracht, gleichgültig gegen das Wann und gegen das Ob überhaupt. Nur jene haben es dazu, von innen her zu sterben; das Reifwerden ihres

313

Schicksals als Lebensausdruckes ist an sich selbst das Reifwerden ihres Todes.

iii

FRIEDRICH NIETZSCHE, *Die fröhliche Wissenschaft,* Book I

Aus der Bewusstheit stammen unzählige Fehlgriffe,
welche machen, dass ein Thier, ein Mensch zu Grunde
geht, früher als es nötig wäre—. . . Wäre nicht der erhal-
tende Verband der Instinkte so überaus viel mächtiger,
diente er nicht im Ganzen als Regulator: an ihren ver-
kehrten Urtheilen und Phantasiren mit offenen Augen,
an ihrer Ungründlichkeit und Leichtgläubigkeit, kurz
eben an ihrer Bewusstheit müsste die Menschheit zu
Grunde gehen. . .

iv

LESSING *to J. J. Eschenburg on the 31 December, 1777*

Ich ergreife den Augenblick, da meine Frau ganz ohne
Besonnenheit liegt, um Ihnen für Ihren gütigen Anteil zu
danken. Meine Freude war nur kurz. Und ich verlor ihn
so ungern, diesen Sohn! Denn er hatte so viel Verstand! so
viel Verstand!—Glauben Sie nicht, dass die wenigen Stunden meiner Vaterschaft mich schon zu so einem Affen von
Vater gemacht haben! Ich weiss, was ich sage. War es nicht
Verstand, dass man ihn mit eisernen Zangen auf die Welt
ziehen musste? dass er so bald Unrat merkte?—War es
nicht Verstand, dass er die erste Gelegenheit ergriff sich
wieder davon zu machen?—Freilich zerrt mir der kleine
Ruschelkopf auch die Mutter mit fort!—Denn noch ist
wenig Hoffnung, dass ich sie behalten werde. Ich wollte
es auch einmal so gut haben wie andere Menschen. Aber
es ist mir schlecht bekommen.

v

GEORG SIMMEL, *Lebensanschauung,* p. 110

Die Unzulänglichkeit, die zwischen unseren Trieben
und Vermögen einerseits und den realen Erfüllungen,

inneren und äusseren, andererseits besteht, muss zu den
Motiven für die Bildung des kontinuierlichen Ich ge-
hören. Wenn unsere Wünsche sich immer restlos erfüllten,
so würde mit dieser Erfüllung der Willensakt sterben und
ein neuer, mit neuem Inhalte, würde beginnen, der innere
Vorgang wäre mit seinem Verhältnis zur Wirklichkeit
völlig erschöpft, das Ich würde sich aus dieser Verflech-
tung mit der Wirklichkeit, die es auf Schritt und Tritt
begleitete, nicht herausheben. Dies aber geschieht, wenn
der Wille seine Berührung mit der Wirklichkeit übersteht,
weil sie ihn nicht stillt, wenn das wollende Ich noch da
ist, wo die Wirklichkeit nicht mehr ist. Ein harmonisches,
durchgängig befriedigtes Verhältnis zwischen Wille und
Wirklichkeit würde das Ichbewusstsein viel mehr in sich
einsaugen, würde das Ich in seinem Eigenlauf viel weni-
ger erkennbar machen. Das Nein und das Zuwenig der
Aussenwelt gegenüber unserem Willen lässt ihn über die
Berührung mit ihr so hinauswirken, dass das Ich sich
daran seiner Unabhängigkeit, vor allem aber der nur aus
seinen eigenen Impulsen quellenden Kontinuität bewusst
wird.

vi

HAROLD POELCHAU, *Die Letzten Stunden*, p. 78

Ist nicht dieser Lebensabschluss doch vielleicht der rich-
tige, vom Unbewussten gewollte und gemeinte, ich der ich
schon mit fünfzehn Jahren von Giordano Brunos Schicksal
und Sterben schwer beeindruckt wurde? Auch mein Leben
war ein Ringen um Erkenntnis, Sinn und um eine Idee, in
erster Linie, . . .

vii

GOTTFRIED KELLER, *Der Landvogt von Greifensee*

Als einst das 10-jährige Söhnlein eines Nachbars in
unheilbarem Siechtum darniederlag und weder das Zu-
reden des Pfarrers, noch dasjenige der Eltern das Kind in
seinen Schmerzen und seiner Furcht vor dem Tode zu
trösten vermöchte, da es so gerne gelebt hätte, so setzte sich

Landolt ruhig seine Pfeife rauchend, an das Bett und sprach zu ihm in so einfachen und treffenden Worten von der Hoffnungslosigkeit seiner Lage, von der Notwendigkeit sich zu fassen und eine kleine Zeit zu leiden, aber auch von der sanften Erlösung durch den Tod und der seligen wechsellosen Ruhe die ihm als einem geduldigen und frommen Knäblein beschieden sei, von der Liebe und Teilnahme, die er als ein fremder Mann zu ihm hege, dass das Kind sich von Stund an änderte, mit heiterer Geduld seine Leiden ertrug, bis es vom Tode wiklich erlöst wurde.

viii

FRIEDRICH NIETZSCHE, *Die fröhliche Wissenschaft,* Book IV

Dieses Leben, wie du es jetzt lebst und gelebt hast, wirst du noch ein Mal und noch unzählige Male leben müssen; und es wird nichts Neues daran sein, sondern jeder Schmerz und jede Lust und jeder Gedanke und Seufzer und alles unsäglich Kleine und Grosse deines Lebens muss dir wiederkommen, und Alles in derselben Reihe und Folge—. . . Die ewige Sanduhr des Daseins wird immer wieder umgedreht—und du mit ihr, Stäubchen vom Staube.

ix

HAROLD POELCHAU, *Letzte Stunden,* pp. 75-76

Sei stark! Ich sterbe, als was ich gelebt habe: als Klassenkämpfer!

Es ist leicht, sich Kommunist zu nennen, solange man nicht dafür zu bluten hat. Ob man wirklich einer war, beweist man erst, wenn die Stunde der Bewahrung gekommen ist. Ich bin es, Vater. Ich leide nicht, Vater, glaube mir das! . . . Anständig aus dem Leben zu gehen, das ist die letzte Aufgabe, die ich mir gestellt habe. Erweise Dich Deines Sohnes würdig. . . . Ich sterbe leicht weil ich weiss, warum ich sterben muss. Die mich töten, werden in nicht so langer Zeit einen schwereren Tod haben. Das ist meine Überzeugung. Hart bleiben, Vater! Hart! Nicht nachgeben! Denke in jeder schwachen Stunde an diese letzte Forderung Deines Sohnes Walter.

x

RAINER MARIA RILKE, *Das Stunden Buch*

Oh Herr, gib jedem seinen eigenen Tod,
das Sterben, das aus jenem Leben geht,
darin er Liebe hatte, Sinn und Not.
Denn wir sind nur die Schale und das Blatt.
Der grosse Tod, den jeder in sich hat,
das ist die Frucht, um die sich alles dreht.

— — — — — — — — — — — — — —

HERR: wir sind ärmer, denn die armen Tiere,
die ihres Todes enden, wenn auch blind,
weil wir noch alle ungestorben sind.

— — — — — — — — — — — — — —

Denn dieses macht das Sterben fremd und schwer,
dass es nicht unser Tod ist; einer, der
uns endlich nimmt, nur weil wir keinen reifen:
drum geht ein Sturm, uns alle abzustreifen.

xi

RAINER MARIA RILKE to *Marianne von Goldschmidt-
Rothschild, on 5 December, 1914*

. . . mir hats zu denken gegeben neulich, wie die äus-
serste Kunst das Grausamste unschuldig macht. Sehen Sie
doch nur diesen Strom glücklichsten Lichts, der herein-
dringt, um die wahnsinnigste Gewalt an den hellsten Tag
zu reissen: wer einen Märtyrer so darstellte, der hätte den
erhabensten Geist auf seiner Seite—, aber hier geschieht
ein Verbrechen, und das Bild lehnt sich nicht dagegen auf,
das Bild umfasst es wie Natur und die seligen Farben hin-
ter dem unerhört schmerzvollen Fuss hören nicht auf,
selig zu sein.
     Was ist das? Gibt es im Leben ähnliches? Gibt es Herz-
verhältnisse, die das Grausamste einschliessen, um der
Vollzähligkeit willen, weil die Welt doch erst Welt ist,
wenn *Alles* darin geschieht, ich konnte mir Gott immer
nur als Den denken, der *alles* zulässt, dem fortwährend das
ganze unerschöpfliche Geschehn abgewandelt gegenüber-
steht. Wer das jetzt durchaus wüsste, wie müsste der un-
beirrt sein.

BIBLIOGRAPHY

AICHHORN, AUGUST (1925), *Wayward Youth*. New York: Viking Press, 1939, pp. xiii + 236.

ALEXANDER, FRANZ and FRENCH, THOMAS M. (1946), *Psychoanalytic Therapy*. New York: Ronald Press Co., pp. xiii + 353.

—— and STAUB, HUGO (1929), *The Criminal, the Judge and the Public*. New York: The Macmillan Co., 1931, pp. xx + 238.

ANTHONY, SYLVIA (1940), *The Child's Discovery of Death*. London: Kegan Paul, pp. xvi + 231.

AUGUSTINE, *Confessions*, quoted from the Translations by William Watts, Harvard University Press, and by F. J. Sheed, New York: Sheed & Ward.

BERGLER, EDMUND and RÓHEIM, GÉZA (1946), Psychology of Time Perception. *Psychoanalytic Quarterly, 15*:190-206.

BERNFELD, SIEGFRIED and FEITELBERG, SERGEI (1930), The Principle of Entropy and the Death Instinct. *International Journal of Psycho-Analysis, 12*:61-68, 1931.

BETTELHEIM, BRUNO (1943), Individual and Mass Behavior in Extreme Situations. *Journal of Abnormal and Social Psychology, 38*:417-452.

BIBRING, EDWARD (1936), The Development and Problems of the Theory of the Instincts. *International Journal of Psycho-Analysis, 22*:102-131, 1941.

—— (1943), The Conception of the Repetition Compulsion. *Psychoanalytic Quarterly, 12*:486-519.

BLOCH, OSCAR (n.d.), *Vom Tode*. Stuttgart: Junker Verlag, pp. 562.

BOAS, GEORGE (1950), The Acceptance of Time. *University of California Publications in Philosophy, 16*:249-270.

BONAPARTE, MARIE (1938), Time and the Unconscious. *International Journal of Psycho-Analysis, 21*:427-468, 1940.

BORING, LUCY D. and EDWIN G. (1917), Temporal Judgments After Sleep; pp. 255-279 in *Studies in Psychology*. Worcester, Mass.: Louis N. Wilson, pp. 337.

BORNSTEIN, BERTA (1948), Emotional Barriers in the Understanding and Treatment of Young Children. *American Journal of Orthopsychiatry, 28*:691-697.

BRADLEY, A. C. (1904), *Shakespearean Tragedy*. London: Macmillan, pp. xi + 498.

BROMBERG, WALTER and SCHILDER, PAUL (1936), The Attitude of Psychoneurotics towards Death. *Psychoanalytic Review, 23*:1-25.

BROOKS, CLEANTH (1947), *The Well Wrought Urn*. New York: Reynal & Hitchcock, pp. xi + 270.

BROWN, G. BALDWIN (1907), *Rembrandt*. London: Duckworth, 1907, pp. xi + 341.

BRUN, RUDOLF (1953), Über Freuds Hypothese vom Todestrieb. *Psyche, 7*:81-111.

BRUNSWIK, EGON (1929), Zur Entwicklung der Albedowahrnehmung. *Zeitschrift für Psychologie, 109*:40-115.

—— (1934), *Wahrnehmung und Gegenstandswelt*. Vienna: Deuticke, pp. xi + 244.

—— (1947), *Systematic and Representative Design of Psychological Experiments*. University of California Syllabus Series No. 304. Berkeley and Los Angeles: University of California Press, pp. vi + 60.

BRUSH, EDWARD N. (1930), Observations on the Temporal Judgment during Sleep. *American Journal of Psychology, 42*:408-411.

COLEMAN, ROSE W., KRIS, ERNST, and PROVENCE, SALLY (1953), The Study of Variations of Early Parental Attitudes. *The Psychoanalytic Study of the Child, 8*:20-47. New York: International Universities Press.

DAVIDSON, HENRY A. (1952), *Forensic Psychiatry*. New York: Ronald Press, pp. vii + 398.

DEUTSCH, FELIX (1936), Euthanasia: A Clinical Study. *Psychoanalytic Quarterly, 5*:347-368.

—— (1949), *Applied Psychoanalysis*. New York: Grune & Stratton, pp. 244.

DEUTSCH, HELENE (1930), The Significance of Masochism in the Mental Life of Women. *International Journal of Psycho-Analysis, 11*:48-60.

—— (1933), Homosexuality in Women. *International Journal of Psycho-Analysis, 14*:34-56.

DOFLEIN, FRANZ (1919), *Das Problem des Todes und der Unsterblichkeit bei den Pflanzen und Tieren*. Jena: Fischer, pp. 119.

EHRENBERG, RUDOLF (1923), *Theoretische Biologie*. Berlin: Springer, pp. 348.

—— (1946), *Der Lebensablauf*. Heidelberg: Lambert Schneider, pp. 274.

EURIPIDES, Alcestis. *The Complete Greek Drama,* Vol. I, translated by Richard Aldington. New York: Random House, 1938.

FEDERN, PAUL (1929), Selbstmordprophylaxe in der Analyse. *Zeitschrift für psychoanalytische Pädagogik, 3:*379-389.

—— (1930), The Reality of the Death Instinct Especially in Melancholia. *Psychoanalytic Review, 19:*129-151, 1932.

FENICHEL, OTTO (1939), The Counter-Phobic Attitude. *International Journal of Psycho-Analysis, 20:*263-274.

—— (1942), Neurotic Disturbances of Sleep. *International Journal of Psycho-Analysis, 23:*62-64.

FERENCZI, SANDOR (1924), *Thalassa: A Theory of Genitality.* New York: Psychoanalytic Quarterly, Inc., 1938, pp. 110.

FLIESS, ROBERT (1953), Countertransference and Counteridentification. *Journal of the American Psychoanalytic Association, 1:* 268-284.

FORD, CLELLAN S. and BEACH, FRANK A. (1951), *Patterns of Sexual Behavior.* New York: Harper, pp. viii + 307.

FREUD, ANNA (1936), *The Ego and the Mechanisms of Defense.* New York: International Universities Press, 1946, pp. x + 196.

—— (1950), On Sleeping Disturbances, paper read at Clark University, Worcester, Mass., on April 21, 1950.

FREUD, SIGMUND (1893), Some Points in a Comparative Study of Organic and Hysterical Paralysis. *Collected Papers, 1:*42-58. London: Hogarth Press, 1924.

—— (1900), The Interpretation of Dreams. *The Standard Edition of the Complete Psychological Works of Sigmund Freud, Vols. IV, V.* London: Hogarth Press, 1953.

—— (1905a), *Three Essays on the Theory of Sexuality.* London: Imago Publishing Co., pp. 133.

—— (1905b), Wit and Its Relation to the Unconscious, pp. 632-803 in *Basic Writings of Sigmund Freud.* New York: Modern Library, translated and edited by A. A. Brill, pp. vi + 1001.

—— (1909a), Notes Upon a Case of Obsessional Neurosis. *Collected Papers, 3:*293-383. London: Hogarth Press, 1925.

—— (1909b), Family Romances. *Collected Papers, 5:*74-78. London: Hogarth Press, 1950.

—— (1909c), General Remarks on Hysterical Attacks. *Collected Papers 2:*100-104. London: Hogarth Press, 1924.

—— (1912-1913), *Totem and Taboo.* New York: Norton, 1952, pp. x + 172.

—— (1913), The Theme of the Three Caskets. *Collected Papers*, 4:244-256. London: Hogarth Press, 1925.

—— (1914), On Narcissism: An Introduction. *Collected Papers*, 4:30-59. London: Hogarth Press, 1925.

—— (1915a), Thoughts for the Times on War and Death. *Collected Papers*, 4:288-317. London: Hogarth Press, 1925.

—— (1915b), Instincts and Their Vicissitudes. *Collected Papers*, 4: 60-83. London: Hogarth Press, 1925.

—— (1915c), Observations on Transference-Love. *Collected Papers*, 2:377-391. London: Hogarth Press, 1924.

—— (1917a), One of the Difficulties of Psycho-Analysis. *Collected Papers*, 4:347-356. London: Hogarth Press, 1925.

—— (1917b), A Childhood Recollection from *Dichtung und Wahrheit*. *Collected Papers*, 4:357-367. London: Hogarth Press, 1925.

—— (1917c), Mourning and Melancholia. *Collected Papers*, 4:152-170. London: Hogarth Press, 1925.

—— (1918), From the History of an Infantile Neurosis. *Collected Papers*, 3:473-605. London: Hogarth Press, 1925.

—— (1920a), *Beyond the Pleasure Principle*. London: Hogarth Press, 1948, pp. 90.

—— (1920b), The Psychogenesis of a Case of Homosexuality in a Woman. *Collected Papers*, 2:202-231. London: Hogarth Press, 1924.

—— (1921), *Group Psychology and the Analysis of the Ego*. New York: Liveright, 1949, pp. 134.

—— (1923), *The Ego and the Id*. London: Hogarth Press, 1949, pp. 88.

—— (1924a), The Passing of the Oedipus-Complex. *Collected Papers*, 2:269-276. London: Hogarth Press, 1924.

—— (1924b), The Economic Problem in Masochism. *Collected Papers*, 2:255-268. London: Hogarth Press, 1933.

—— (1930), *Civilisation and Its Discontent*. London: Hogarth Press, 1949, pp. 144.

—— (1932), *New Introductory Lectures on Psychoanalysis*. New York: Norton, 1933, pp. xi + 257.

—— (1937), Analysis Terminable and Interminable. *Collected Papers*, 5:358-371. London: Hogarth Press, 1950.

—— (1938), *An Outline of Psychoanalysis*. New York: Norton, 1949, pp. 127.

FRIEDLANDER, KATE (1940), On the "Longing to Die." *International Journal of Psycho-Analysis*, 21:416-426.

GILL, A. MORTON (1947), Pain and the Healing of Peptic Ulcers. *Lancet*, March 8, 1947, pp. 291-294.

GODDARD, HAROLD C. (1951), *The Meaning of Shakespeare*. Chicago: The University of Chicago Press, pp. xii + 691.

GOETTE, ALEXANDER (1883), *Über den Ursprung des Todes*. Hamburg and Leipzig: Leopold Voss, pp. 81.

GOETZ, BRUNO (1952), Erinnerungen an Sigmund Freud. *Neue Schweizer Rundschau, 20*:3-11.

GRABER, GUSTAV HANS (1930), *Zeugung, Geburt und Tod*. Baden-Baden: Merlin Verlag, pp. 180.

GROTJAHN, MARTIN (1942), The Process of Awakening. *Psychoanalytic Review, 29*:1-19.

GUTHRIE, W. K. C. (1935), *Orpheus and Greek Religion*. London: Methuen, pp. xix + 287.

GUTTMACHER, MANFRED S. and WEIHOFEN, HENRY (1952), *Psychiatry and the Law*. New York: Norton, pp. viii + 476.

HARTMANN, HEINZ (1939), Ich-Psychologie und Anpassungsproblem. *Internationale Zeitschrift für Psychoanalyse und Imago, 24*:62-135.

—— (1947), On Rational and Irrational Action. *Psychoanalysis and the Social Sciences, 1*:359-392. New York: International Universities Press.

—— (1948), Comments on the Psychoanalytic Theory of Instinctual Drives. *Psychoanalytic Quarterly, 17*:368-388.

—— (1950), Comments on the Psychoanalytic Theory of the Ego. *The Psychoanalytic Study of the Child, 5*:74-96. New York: International Universities Press.

—— (1953), Contribution to the Metapsychology of Schizophrenia. *The Psychoanalytic Study of the Child, 8*:177-198. New York: International Universities Press.

—— KRIS, ERNST and LOEWENSTEIN, RUDOLPH M. (1946), Comments on the Formation of Psychic Structure. *The Psychoanalytic Study of the Child, 2*:11-38. New York: International Universities Press.

HARTMANN, MAX (1906), *Tod und Fortpflanzung*. Munich: Ernst Reinhardt, pp. 37.

HEIDEGGER, MARTIN (1927), *Sein und Zeit*. Halle: Max Niemager, pp. xi + 438.

HEIM, KARL (1949), *Christian Faith and Natural Science*. New York: Harper, pp. 256.

324 BIBLIOGRAPHY

HOFSTEDE DE GROOT, C. (1906), Die Urkunden über Rembrandt. *Quellenstudien zur holländischen Kunstgeschichte,* Vol. 3. Haag: Martinus Nijhoff.

HUSSERL, EDMUND (1905-1910), *Vorlesungen zur Phänomenologie des inneren Zeitbewusstseins,* ed. by Martin Heidegger. Halle: Niemager, 1928, pp. v + 367-496.

—— (1913), Ideen zu einer reinen Phänomenologie und phänomenologischen Philosophie. *Allgemeine Einführung in die reine Phänomenologie,* Vol. I. Haag: Martinus Nijhoff, 1950, pp. xvi + 483.

JACOBSON, EDITH (1953), The Affects and Their Pleasure-Unpleasure Qualities in Relation to the Psychic Discharge Process, pp. 38-66 in *Drives, Affects, Behavior,* ed. by Rudolph M. Loewenstein. New York: International Universities Press, pp. 399.

JAHODA, ERNST (1948), *Sterben und Sterben Lassen.* Wien: Selbstverlag, pp. 39.

JANKÉLÉVITCH, S. (1910), La mort et l'immortalité d'après les données de la biologie. *Revue Philosophique, 69*:358-380.

JASPERS, KARL (1919), *Psychologie der Weltanschauungen.* Berlin: Springer, 1925, pp. xiii + 486.

JONES, ERNEST (1911), On "Dying Together." *Essays in Applied Psycho-Analysis, 1*:9-15. London: Hogarth Press, 1951.

—— (1912), An Unusual Case of Dying Together. *Essays in Applied Psycho-Analysis, 1*:16-21. London: Hogarth Press, 1951.

—— (1924), Mother-Right and the Sexual Ignorance of Savages. *Essays in Applied Psycho-Analysis, 2*:145-173. London: Hogarth Press, 1951.

—— (1927a), The Early Development of Female Sexuality, pp. 438-451 in *Papers on Psycho-Analysis.* Baltimore: Williams & Wilkins, 5th ed. 1948, pp. vii + 504.

—— (1927b), Discussion on Lay Analysis. *International Journal of Psycho-Analysis, 8*:174-198.

JUNG, C. G. (1910), Über Konflikte der kindlichen Seele. *Jahrbuch für psychoanalytische und psychopathologische Forschungen,* 2:33-58. For a revised version, see Psychic Conflicts in a Child, pp. 8-35 in *The Development of Personality.* New York: Pantheon Books, 1954, pp. viii + 235.

JUSTI, CARL (1888), *Diego Velasquez und sein Jahrhundert,* 2 Vols. Bonn: Max Cohen.

KAMMERER, PAUL (1923), *Tod und Unsterblichkeit.* Stuttgart: Moritz, pp. viii + 122.

KEISER, SYLVAN (1949), The Fear of Sexual Passivity in the Masochist. *International Journal of Psycho-Analysis, 80*:162-171.

KELLER, GOTTFRIED, Der Landvogt von Greifensee. *Züricher Novellen,* Vol. VI. Stuttgart, Berlin: I. G. Kottasch, 1912 (my own translation).

KELSEN, HANS (1943), *Society and Nature.* Chicago: University of Chicago Press, pp. viii + 391.

KRIS, ERNST (1939), On Inspiration, pp. 291-302 in *Psychoanalytic Explorations in Art.* New York: International Universities Press, 1952, pp. 358.

LESSING, GOTTHOLD EPHRAIM, Letter to Johann Joachim Eschenburg on December 31, 1777. *Lessings Werke, 1*:47. Selections, ed. by Julius Petersen et al. Berlin: Bong, n.d.

LIPSCHÜTZ, ALEXANDER (1915), *Allgemeine Physiologie des Todes.* Braunschweig: Vieweg, pp. viii + 184.

MANN, THOMAS (1949), *Die Entstehung des Doktor Faustus: Roman eines Romans.* Amsterdam: Bermann-Fischer, pp. 204.

MAUTHNER, FRITZ (1922-1924), *Der Atheismus und seine Geschichte im Abendlande,* 4 Vols. Stuttgart, Berlin: Deutsche Verlagsanstalt.

MEAD, GEORGE HERBERT (1932), *The Philosophy of the Present.* Chicago, London: Open Court Publishing Co., pp. xv + 199.

MENNINGER, KARL A. (1938), *Man Against Himself.* New York: Harcourt, Brace, pp. xii + 485.

MERLAN, PHILIP (1947), Time Consciousness in Husserl and Heidegger. *Philosophy and Phenomenological Research, 8*:23-54.

MONTGOMERY, THOS. H. (1906), On Reproduction, Animal Life Cycles and the Biographical Unit. *Transactions of the Texas Academy of Sciences, 9*:75-94.

MÜHLMANN, M. (1910), Das Altern und der physiologische Tod. *Sammlung anatomischer und physiologischer Vorträge und Aufsätze,* No. 11, ed. by E. Gaupp and W. Nagel. Jena: Fischer.

—— (1914), Beitrag zur Frage nach der Ursache des Todes. *Virchow's Archiv, 215*:1-77.

MÜLLER-FREIENFELS, RICHARD (1920), *Psychologie der Kunst,* Vol. 1. Leipzig: Teubner, 1922, pp. vii + 248.

MUIR, KENNETH (1952), Some Freudian Interpretations of Shakespeare. *Proceedings of the Leeds Philosophical Society (Literary and Historical Section), 7*:43-52.

NEEDLES, WILLIAM (1953), A Note on Orgastic Loss of Consciousness. *Psychoanalytic Quarterly, 22*:512-518.

NIETZSCHE, FRIEDRICH (1881/82), Die fröhliche Wissenschaft. *Nietzsches Werke*, Vol. VI. Leipzig: Kroener.

NOTHNAGEL, HERMANN (1900), *Das Sterben.* Vienna: Moritz Perles, pp. 55 (contains also the facsimile of the author's notes upon his physical state a few hours before his death.)

NUNBERG, HERMANN (1932), *Allgemeine Neurosenlehre auf psychoanalytischer Grundlage.* Bern: Huber.

OLDEN, CHRISTINE (1953), On Adult Empathy with Children. *The Psychoanalytic Study of the Child, 8*:111-126. New York: International Universities Press.

OPARIN, A. I. (1936), *The Origin of Life.* New York: Dover Publications, 1953, pp. xxv + 270.

PARK, ROSWELL (1912), Thanatology. *Journal of the American Medical Association, 58*:1243-1246.

PARROT, THOMAS MARC (1949), *Shakespearean Comedy.* New York: Oxford University Press, pp. xi + 417.

PERROUX, FRANÇOIS (1954), The Gift: Its Economic Meaning in Contemporary Capitalism. *Diogenes*, No. 6 (Spring), 1-21.

PFISTER, OSCAR (1930), Schockdenken und Schockphantasien bei höchster Todesgefahr. *Internationale Zeitschrift für Psychoanalyse, 16*:430-455.

PLATO, Apology. Phaedo. *The Dialogues of Plato,* translated by M. A. Jowett. New York: Random House, 1937.

POELCHAU, HAROLD (1949), *Die letzten Stunden.* Berlin: Volk und Welt, pp. 152.

PRESCOTT, WILLIAM H. (1843), *History of the Conquest of Mexico* and *History of the Conquest of Peru.* New York: Modern Library, n.d., pp. xxxvi + 1288.

PÜTTER, AUGUST (1911), *Vergleichende Physiologie.* Jena, Fischer, pp. vii + 72.

QUILLER-COUCH, SIR ARTHUR (1926), *Introduction to the Merchant of Venice.* London: Cambridge University Press, 1953, pp. xxxiii + 193.

RANK, OTTO (1911), Ein Beispiel von poetischer Verwertung des Versprechens. *Zentralblatt für Psychoanalyse, 1*:109-110.

REICH, ANNIE (1951), On Counter-Transference. *International Journal of Psycho-Analysis, 32*:25-31.

REICHENBACH, HANS (1951), *The Rise of Scientific Philosophy.* Berkeley, Los Angeles: University of California Press, pp. xi + 333.

RILKE, RAINER MARIA (1903/10), *The Notebooks of Malte Laurids Brigge,* translated by M. D. Herter Norton. New York: Norton, pp. 237.

—— (1903), Das Stunden-Buch. Drittes Buch: Das Buch von der Armut und dem Tode. *Gesammelte Werke,* Vol. II. Leipzig: Insel Verlag, 1930.

—— (1914), Letter to Marianne von Goldschmidt-Rothschild of 5 December, in *Briefe.* Wiesbaden: Insel Verlag, 1950.

—— (1925), Briefwechsel in Gedichten mit Erika Mitterer. *Aus Rainer Maria Rilkes Nachlass, 2. Folge.* Wiesbaden: Insel, 1950, pp. 63.

RIVERS, W. H. R. (1911), The Primitive Conception of Death, pp. 36-50 in *Psychology and Ethnology.* New York: Harcourt, Brace, pp. xxviii + 324.

ROSENZWEIG, FRANZ (1921), *Der Stern der Erlösung,* Frankfurt a.M.: J. Kauffmann, pp. 532.

—— (1953), *His Life and Thought,* presented by Nahum N. Glatzer. New York: A Schocken Book published with Farrar, Straus & Young, pp. xxxviii + 400.

SCHILDER, PAUL (1921), Über die kausale Bedeutung des durch Psychoanalyse gewonnenen Materials. *Wiener klinische Wochenschrift, 29:*355-356.

—— (1925), *Introduction to a Psychoanalytic Psychiatry.* New York: International Universities Press, 1951.

—— (1927), Theorie der Psychoanalyse, pp. 1-12 in *Bericht über den II. allgemeinen ärztlichen Kongress für Psychotherapie.* Leipzig: Hirzel.

—— (1935), *The Image and Appearance of the Human Body.* New York: International Universities Press, 1950, pp. 353.

SCHILLER, F. C. S. (1935), *Are* all Men Mortals. *Mind, 44:*204-210.

SCHORR, G. (1931), Die Thanatologie in ihrer Bedeutung für die Person, pp. 347-424, in *Die Biologie der Person,* Vol. 2, ed. by Th. Brugsch and F. H. Lewy. Vienna, Berlin: Urban & Schwarzenberg.

SILBERER, HERBERT (1911), Symbolik des Erwachens und Schwellensymbolik überhaupt. *Jahrbuch für psychoanalytische und psychopathologische Forschungen, 3:*621-660.

SIMMEL, ERNST (1926), The "Doctor Game," Illness and the Profession of Medicine. *International Journal of Psycho-Analysis, 7:*470-483.

SIMMEL, GEORG (1908), *Soziologische Untersuchungen über die Formen der Vergesellschaftung.* Leipzig: Duncker & Humblot, pp. 782.

—— (1910), Zur Metaphysik des Todes. *Logos, 1*:57-70.

—— (1918), Tod und Unsterblichkeit, pp. 99-153 in *Lebensanschauung: Vier Metaphysische Kapitel.* Munich, Leipzig: Duncker & Humblot, pp. 245.

SIMON, ERNST (1949), Religious Humanism, pp. 304-325 in *Goethe and the Modern Age,* ed. by Arnold Bergstraesser. Chicago: Henry Regnery Company, 1950, pp. xii + 402.

SMITH, GEORGE D., ed. (1949), *The Teaching of the Catholic Church,* 2 Vols. New York: Macmillan Co.

SPENGLER, OSWALD (1918), *The Decline of the West,* 2 Vols. New York: Knopf, 1926.

SPIELREIN, SABINE (1923), Die Zeit im unterschwelligen Seelenleben. *Imago, 9*:300-317.

STENGEL, ERWIN (1935), Zur Kenntnis der Triebstörungen und der Abwehrreaktionen des Ichs bei Hirnkranken. *Internationale Zeitschrift für Psychoanalyse, 21*:544-560.

STERBA, RICHARD (1932), The Cosmological Aspect of Freud's Theory of Instincts. *American Imago, 6*:157-161, 1949.

—— (1948), On Hallowe'en. *American Imago, 5*:213-224.

STONE, IRVING (1943), *They Also Ran: The Story of the Men Who Were Defeated for the Presidency.* New York: Doubleday, pp. xi + 389.

STONE, LEO (1951), Psychoanalysis and Brief Psychotherapy. *Psychoanalytic Quarterly, 20*:215-236.

SULLIVAN, J. W. N. (1927), *Beethoven, His Spiritual Development,* New York: Knopf, pp. 144.

SUSMAN, MARGARETE (1954), Goethes Verhältnis zum Tod, pp. 24-37 in *Gestalten und Kreise.* Stuttgart, Konstanz: Diana, pp. 366.

SZASZ, THOMAS S. (1952), On the Psychoanalytic Theory of Instincts. *Psychoanalytic Quarterly, 21*:25-48.

TANSLEY, SIR ARTHUR (1952), *Mind and Life.* London: George Allen, Unwin, pp. ix + 171.

TOWNSEND, H. G. (1946), On the History of Philosophy. *University of California Publications in Philosophy, 16*:159-178.

TROTTER, WILFRED (1919), *Instincts of the Herd in Peace and War.* New York: Macmillan, 1947, pp. 270.

TÜRCK, HERMANN (1899), *Die Bedeutung der Magie und Sorge in Goethes Faust.* Jena: Historisch-Philosophische Gesellschaft.

TURNER, W. J. (1938), *Mozart, the Man and His Works*. New York: Doubleday, 1954, pp. 392.

ULLMANN, HANS (1926), Die Lebensdauer des Menschen, pp. 859-1024 in *Die Biologie der Person*, Vol. 1, ed. by Th. Brugsch and F. H. Lewy. Vienna, Berlin: Urban & Schwarzenberg.

VARNHAGEN VON ENSE (1843), Tagebücher von K. A. Varnhagen von Ense. *Aus dem Nachlass Varnhagens von Ense*, Vol. 2. Leipzig: Brockhaus, 1861, pp. 423.

VON SAAZ, JOHANNES, Der Ackermann aus Böhmen des Johannes von Saaz, ed. Alois Bernt. *Altdeutsches Schrifttum aus Böhmen*, Vol. I. Heidelberg: Carl Winters Universitätsbuchhandlung, 1929.

VON SALIS, J. R. (1936), *Rainer Maria Rilkes Schweizer Jahre*. Frauenfeld, Leipzig: Huber, pp. 223.

VON UEXKÜLL, J. (1926), *Theoretical Biology*. New York: Harcourt, Brace, pp. xvi + 362.

WACH, JOACHIM (1934), *Das Problem des Todes in der Philosophie unserer Zeit*. Tübingen: J. C. B. Mohr, pp. 48.

WALKER, KENNETH (1942), *The Circle of Life*. London: Jonathan Cape, pp. 156.

WEININGER, OTTO (1904), *Über die letzten Dinge*. Vienna: Braumüller, 1912, pp. xxiii + 178.

WEISMANN, AUGUST (1884), *Über Leben und Tod*. Jena: Gustav Fischer, 1892, pp. 68.

WEISS, EDOARDO (1935), Todestrieb und Masochismus. *Imago*, 21:393-411.

WILDER, THORNTON (1937), *The Bridge of San Luis Rey*. New York: Grossett & Dunlap, pp. 235.

WORRINGER, WILHELM (1906), *Abstraction and Empathy*. New York: International Universities Press, 1953, pp. xv + 144.

ZILBOORG, GREGORY (1943a), *Mind, Medicine and Man*. New York: Harcourt, Brace, pp. vi + 344.

—— (1943b), Some Primitive Trends in Civilized Justice. *Journal of Criminal Psychopathology*, 4:599-604.

ZUCKERMAN, S. (1932), *The Social Life of Monkeys and Apes*. New York: Harcourt, Brace, pp. xii + 356.

Note: Translations, if not indicated otherwise, are by the author.

INDEX

Acting out, 230-236, 239-240
Action
  arrested vs. unbound, 16-21
  psychology of, 87, 90, 93-94
Activity-passivity, 66; see also
  Case Two
Adam, 309-310
Adler, A., 22
Admetus, 186-187
Aesthetics, 97, 306; see also Art
Aged (Aging), 47-48, 53
Aggression
  and belief in immortality, 295-297
  and death, see Death
  and ego formation, 83-85
  and ego functions, 36
  and frustration, 13, 35, 37, 83-84
  and martyrdom, 292
  and masses, 111-112
  as manifestation of death instinct,
    33, 46, 112, 255
  origins of, 12-14, 37, 46
Aichhorn, A., 248, 319
Alcestis, 186-187
Alexander, F., 65, 194, 319
All Souls' Day, 15
Altruism, 129, 163
Ambivalence
  and dying, 149-153
  and suicide, 65-67
  in development of mankind, 13-15
  in psychotherapy, 126, 238-240
  lack of, as therapeutic factor,
    146-148
Amenorrhea, 137
American civilization, and death,
  45-46, 293
American Jurisprudence, 235
Anabolism, 8
Animals, vulnerability of in sexual
  excitement, 76
Annihilation, fear of, 267-268
Anthony, S., 12, 319

Anxiety, concept of, 277-280; see
  also Death, fear of; and Terror
Apes, 61-62
Aphanisis, 78-79
Aristotle, 282
Art, representation of suffering in,
  95-99, 305-307
Arteriosclerotic patients, 40
Atomic bomb, 108
Atropos, 3, 21
Augustine, 265, 268-272, 319

Bauer, J., 136
Beach, F. A., 85, 321
Beethoven, L., 95-99, 113
  death mask of, 95-99
Bemächtigungstrieb, 12
Bergler, E., 271, 319
Bernfeld, S., 8, 36, 256, 319
Bettelheim, B., 92, 319
Bibring, E., 8, 30, 319
Biology, 6-8, 22, 31, 112; see also
  Death
Birth, and death, 44, 48, 51-52; see
  also Childbirth
Bloch, O., 39, 319
Boas, G., 281, 319
Body image, 216, 295; see also
  Death, and Ego
Bonaparte, M., 63, 319
Boring, E. G., 274, 319
Boring, L., 274, 319
Bornstein, B., 296, 319
Bradley, A. C., 19, 320
Bromberg, W., 320
Brooks, C., 76, 320
Brown, G. B., 320
Brun, R., 11, 34, 64, 69, 78, 320
Bruno, G., 107, 315
Brunswick, E., 270, 320
Brush, E. N., 274, 320

Cancer, 42, 58, 130-137, 156, 166-171;
  see also Death, and Malignancy

330

Capital Punishment, 42, 59, 117
Case One, 125, 128-153, 168
    diagnosis of physical pathology through dream, 134-138
    personal history, 128-134
    technical implications, 138-153
Case Two, 49, 53, 125, 131, 152, 154-197, 244, 246-248, 263
    personal history, 154-184
    technical procedures, 184-197
Case Three, 49, 53, 125, 131, 138, 144, 161, 168, 198-240
    forensic-psychiatric implications, 210-240
    personal history, 199-210
Cassandra, 109
Castration (complex),
    and death, 74-75, 78-80, 279, 304
    pathology of, 86
    pictorial representation of, 305-307
Catabolism, 8
Catatonia, 90
Catholic church, 54-55; see also Death, Priest, and Religion
Cells
    and destiny, 7, 32
    and organism, 31-32, 256-262
    see also Death, biology of; Growth; and Propagation
Character disorders, 27, 201; see also Case Three
Charlatan, 168-171
Child
    adults' empathy with, 296
    concept of life and death, 62
    concept of time, 185
    development of, 72; see also Ego, development of
    old father—young mother constellation, impact on development of, 177
    phobic symptom related to mother's repressed memory, 220-221
    role of loss of, to mother, 75, 246
    substituting for deceased child, 177
Childbirth, 48, 76-77; see also Birth
Childlessness, 75, 199-205
Chinese, 45
Christ, 96, 108-109
Christianity, 49, 73, 116-119, 296,

308-310; see also Death, Immortality, and Religion
Clotho, 21
Coleman, R. W., 140, 320
Compulsion, see Obsessional neurosis
Concentration camp, 92
Conception, 51-52
Counterparanoid attitude, 173-176
Counterphobic attitude, 173
Countertransference, 243-250
Creativity, 299-301
    and disease, 102-103, 113-115
Criminal, 121
Crucifixion, 91, 108-109

Davidson, H. A., 217, 320
Death
    and aggression, 13-15, 27-28, 42-46, 292, 295-297
    and ambivalence, 27-28, 65-67, 146-153
    and the masses, 108-112
    and the pleasure principle, 71-80, 283
    and time, 42, 265-283
    as an individually formed mental process, 251-254
    as a psychologically determined event, 104-107, 263-265
    as consummation of life, 41, 43, 106-107, 263-265, 276
    as crystallization point of culture, 44-45
    as precondition of life, 3-9, 23-24, 57
    attitudes to, 40-58, 71-73
    biology of, 6-9, 22, 39-40, 250-262
    Christian concept of, 44, 54, 73, 283, 308-310
    defenses against idea of, 15, 28, 42, 44, 267; see also Denial, and Reversal
    fear of, 10, 40, 43, 59-60, 93, 267, 277-280
    historical changes in concept of, 44-47; see also Thanatology
    instinct, see Death instinct
    knowledge of impending, 40, 48-50, 57-61, 143, 181-182, 245, 278; see also Case Two

Death *(Cont'd)*
  lack of representation in unconscious, 12, 28, 36, 60, 62-63
  libidinization of idea of, 183
  obstacles to its systematic investigation, 39-50, 251-252
  painless, 48, 245, 283
  place of, in humans, 59-70
  pre-mourning as a preparation for, 180-181
  problem of giving information about fatal disease, 49-51, 55, 57-60
  psychology of, 40-50; *see also* Time
  retrograde effect of on life, 52
  symbolic representation of, *see* Symbolism
  unconscious awareness of, 59-60, 113, 143
  wishes, 12, 40
  world without, 46-48
  see also Dying, Euthanasia, Orthothanasia, *and* Time
Death instinct, 8-9, 98
  and biology, 255-262
  and life instinct, 14, 31-33, 63-64, 153, 258
  and masses, 110-112
  history of theory of, 10-29
  manifestations of, 33-34, 255
  theory of, 30-34, 64-70, 78, 85-86, 279
  see also Aggression, and Instinct (ual Drives)
Defense
  against feminine masochism, 186-188
  against idea of death, *see* Death, Denial, *and* Reversal
  and joke, 12
Dehiscence, 308-309
Delilah, 306-307
Delinquency, 75, 121, 160, 194, 246-250
Denial, 91, 188, 246
  of death, 28, 44-45, 149, 244, 278-279, 293-294
Depression, 77, 145, 157, 178, 223; *see also* Melancholia
Der Ackermann aus Böhmen, 5

Destructiveness, *see* Aggression, Death instinct, *and* Sadism
Deutsch, F., 53-54, 140, 214, 245, 320
Deutsch, H., 48, 186, 320
Dickens, C., 129
Disease
  and creativity, 102-103, 113-115
  denial of, 130-131, 167-171
  effect of organic stimulation on psychic processes, 213-216
  informing patient about fatal nature of, 49-51, 55, 57-60; *see also* Case One and Two
  meaning of, 102-103
  see also Cancer, Death, Malignancy, *and* Psychosomatic Symptoms
Doflein, F., 258, 320
Donne, J., 76
Dream
  and physical needs, 213-214
  hypnopompic, 273-274
  leading to discovery of organic pathology, 131-132, 134-136
  time experience in, 270
Dying
  and ambivalence, 149-150
  and giving up of object cathexes, 180-182
  and killing, 42-43
  and release of aggression, 140-141
  psychotherapy with, *see* Psychotherapy
  together, 126, 248
  see also Death, *and* Suicide

Ego
  and biological functions, 73, 254
  and body, 271-272
  and death, 71-86
  and discharge of aggression, 36
  and extreme danger, 92, 181-182
  and id, 34
  and instinctual frustration, 83-84
  and irrationality, 151-152
  and mourning, 45, 180-182
  and organic disease, 214-216, 254-255
  and paranoid ideas, 173-176
  and sleep, 72-73, 272, 274
  and suicide, 65-70, 73
  and superego, 70

Ego (Cont'd)
  and unconscious, 221
  biological matrix of, 256-257
  changes before death, 53
  defect, 83; see also Case Three
  development, 81-86, 254, 272
  drives, 26-27; see also self-preservation
  pathology of functions, 40
Ehrenberg, R., 3, 6-8, 102, 320
Emotions
  and time experience, 265-283
  see also Anxiety, Death, Mourning, and Terror
Empedocles, 67
Epicurus, 60
Eros, see Libido, Life Instinct, and Sexual instincts
Eschenburg, J. J., 314
Ethics
  and euthanasia, 118-122
  in psychiatry, 159-161, 198-199, 229-240; see also Case Three
Euripides, A., 186, 321
Euthanasia, 116-122, 189, 283-295; see also Orthothanasia
Existentialism, 4-6, 8, 276, 279-280

Family romance, 286-289
Fantasy
  in persons suddenly facing extreme danger, 181-182
  of dying in process of giving birth, 183
Father, unique relation to son, 55-57
Faust, 264, 271
Federn, P., 67, 78, 145, 321
Feitelberg, S., 8, 36, 256, 319
Fenichel, O., 73, 75, 173, 320
Ferenczi, S., 76, 85, 320
Fliess, R., 249, 321
Folklore, 14, 308
Ford, C. S., 85, 321
Friedlander, K., 65, 322
French, T. M., 194, 319
French Revolution, 149
Freud, A., 54, 72, 129, 321
Freud, S., 3 et passim
  Beyond the Pleasure Principle, 8, 30
  bibliographical references, 321

  on aggression, 11-15, 112
  on ambivalence, 13-15
  on analyst's analysis, 221
  on animal's vulnerability in sexual excitement, 76
  on biology and psychology, 251
  on chief obstacle in analysis of males, 74-75
  on consciousness, 81-82
  on death instinct, 8-9, 30-38, 112, 255, 257, 260; see also Aggression, and Thanatology
  on dream mechanism, 213
  on impulse toward higher development, 85
  on libido and pain, 141
  on mourning, 45, 180
  on narcissistic cathexis, 149, 296
  on neurotics' ideas about their past, 287
  on oedipus complex, 253-254
  on optimism, 177
  on pleasure-unpleasure experience, 280-281
  on psychic etiology, 138
  on psychology of hero, 244
  on transference love, 227
  response to patient's poverty, 245
  revision of instinctual theory, 11, 24
  The Interpretation of Dreams, 213
  "The Theme of the Three Caskets," 14-29
  "Thoughts for the Times on War and Death," 24, 26-28
  Three Essays on the Theory of Sexuality, 12
  Totem and Taboo, 13-15, 62
  Wit and Its Relation to the Unconscious, 12, 22
Future
  and martyrdom, 290-293
  concrete representation in treatment of dying, 145-148; see also Case Histories
  concept of, 185, 268
  experience of, 265-280
  representation of, 76

Genius, 55-56, 114; see also Creativity, J. W. Goethe, and T. Mann

Gifts
    of patient to therapist, 219-235
    of therapist to patient, 126, 134,
    138, 144-148
Gill, A. M., 101, 323
Goddard, H. C., 16, 323
Goethe, J. C., 55-56
Goethe, J. W., 34, 51, 55-56, 67, 113,
    264, 271, 296, 300-302, 304
Goethe, J. W. T., 51
Goette, A., 257, 323
Goetz, B., 245, 323
Goldschmidt-Rothschild, M., 317
Graber, G. H., 48, 323
Grossman, F. G., 305
Grotjahn, M., 273, 323
Growth, and death, 256-265
Guthrie, W. K. C., 312, 323
Guttmacher, M. S., 217, 219-220, 323

Halloween, 15
Hamlet, 72
Hartmann, H., 36, 65, 81, 83, 151-
    152, 256, 323
Hartmann, M., 258-259, 323
Hatuey, 296
Heart Disease, 171
Hedonism, 45-46
Heidegger, M., 3-8, 32, 41, 264, 279,
    303, 323
Heim, K., 57, 323
Hitler, A., 175
Hofstede de Groot, C., 307, 324
Holy Communion, 54-55
Hostility, see Aggression, Death in-
    stinct, and Sadism
Housman, A. E., 301
Husemann, W., 291
Husserl, E., 265, 269, 272-274, 324
Hypnosis (Hypnotic state), 224, 230,
    272, 276
Hysteria, 216

Identification
    of patient with therapist, 246
    of therapist with patient, 248-250
Identity, feeling of, 87-94, 281; see
    also Reality, and Time
Illusions
    formation of, 287-288; see also
    Family romance, and Past
    incapacity to form, 158; see also
    Case Two

Immortality, belief in, 142-143, 268,
    286, 295-297, 310
Individuality
    and attitudes to death, 51-58
    and physiological functions, 297-
    305
Individualization, 53-55, 57, 298,
    301-302
Infante Philipp Prosper, 305
Inspiration, 300-301
Instinct(ual drives)
    and rational behavior, 108-112
    fusion and defusion of, 26, 33, 63,
    112
    neutralization of, 33
    see also Death instinct, Ego drives,
    Libido, Life Instinct, Self-pres-
    ervation, and Sexual instincts

Jacobson, E., 280, 324
Jahoda, E., 116-117, 324
Jankélévitch, S., 258, 324
Jaspers, K., 4, 312, 324
Jokes, 12
Jones, E., 78-79, 126, 136-137, 287,
    324
Jung, C. G., 22, 62, 324
Justi, C., 305, 324

Kammerer, P., 258, 324
Keiser, S., 76, 325
Keller, G., 120, 315-316, 325
Kelsen, H., 267, 325
Killing, see Murder
King Lear, 15-24
Kris,, E., 83, 140, 301, 320, 323, 325

Lachesis, 21
Latency period, 54
Lazarus, 40-41
Lessing, G. E., 60-61, 314, 325
Libido
    absence of, 96-97
    as propulsive evolutionary force,
    85
    sublimated, 139-142
    see also Life instinct, Mourning,
    Sexual instinct, and Transfer-
    ence
Life
    effect of prolongation of, 47
    instinct, 8-9, 14, 31-33, 63-64, 153,

Life *(Cont'd)*
 258; *see also* Libido, Self-preservation, *and* Sexual instincts
 origin of, 32
 prolongation of, 255-257
Lincoln, A., 253
Lipschütz, A., 256, 325
Literature, 14
 psychoanalytic interpretations of,
  22-23
 see also Goethe, Keller, Mann,
  Rilke, *and* Shakespeare
Loewenstein, R. M., 83, 323
Love, and hate, *see* Ambivalence
Love object
 loss of, 40, 90-91, 93; *see also*
  Child, loss of
 withdrawal of cathexis from, *see*
  mourning
Lying, 288

Malignancy, psychosomatic theory
 of, 167-170; *see also* Cancer,
 Death, *and* Disease
Mann, T., 103, 113-114, 325
Marriage, 299
Martyrdom, 96, 150, 290-293, 308
Masochism, 48, 69, 97, 178, 186-188,
 200, 216
 and denial of disease, 130-131
Masses, and death, 108-112, 149
Maturation, 81
Mauthner, F., 44, 325
Mead, G. H., 52, 288, 325
Medicine
 and creativity, 113-115
 and death, 39-43, 46-47, 63
 man, 101
 modern vs. primordial, 101-102
Melancholia, 68, 77-78, 163; *see also*
 Depression
Memory, *see* Past
Menninger, K. A., 37, 325
Merlan, P., 265, 269, 273, 325
Metazoon, 259
Ministry, 119, 127, 146, 247; *see also*
 Christianity, *and* Religion
Money, *see* Property
Monkeys, 61-62
Montgomery, T. H., 256, 325
Mother-child relationship, and psy-
 chotherapy, 140

Mourning, 45, 148-149, 180-182
Mozart, L., 98
Mozart, W. A., 98-99, 113
Mühlmann, M., 256, 258, 325
Muir, K., 22, 325
Müller-Freienfels, R., 249, 325
Murder, and fear of death, 42-43
Myth, of fall of man, 309-310
Mythology
 Christian, 308
 Greek, 109-110

Narcissism, 74-75, 287, 290, 296
Needles, W., 76, 325
Neurosis
 and sexual drives, 27
 effect of interruptions in treat-
  ment of, 194-195
Neurotic symptoms, function of, 91
Nietzsche, F., 30-31, 288-289, 314,
 316, 326
Nothnagel, H., 258, 265, 326
Nunberg, H., 34, 326

Obscenity, 12
Obsessional (compulsive) neurosis,
 90, 108
Oedipus complex, 15, 253-255
 and knowledge of death, 62
 and personality structure, 52
 as barrier against instinctual gratification, 64
Olden, C., 296, 326
Oparin, A. I., 32, 326
Optimism, 177
Orgasm
 and death, 76
 and time experience, 271-272
Orthothanasia, 283-295, 301-302, 305-
 312

Pain
 and libidinal distribution, 140-141
 fear of, 48
 representation of in art, 95-99
 see also Euthanasia, *and* Pleasure
Parcae, 3, 21
Park, R., 250, 326
Parrot, T. M., 18, 326
Passivity, and activity, 66; *see also*
 Case Two

Past
  experience of, 265-272, 287-289, 296
  identity of, 92
  neurotics' illusions about, 287-288
  national illusions about, 287-288
Penis envy, and child-bearing envy, 192-193
Peptic ulcer, 101-102
Perception, and time, 269-274
Perroux, F., 126, 326
Personality structure
  changes of, 52-54
  creation of new, in face of danger, 181-182
Perversion, 69, 79
Pfister, O., 11, 181-182, 278, 326
Phobia, 220-221
Phylogenesis, and ontogenesis, 253-254
Plato, 282, 326
Pleasure
  and unpleasure experience, 280-281; see also Pain
  principle, 46, 71-80; see also Death
  role of, in ego formation, 84-85
Poelchau, H., 49, 107, 291, 315, 316, 326
Poetry, 34, 300-304
Pregenitality, 15
Prescott, W. H., 296, 326
Present
  concept of, 52, 92, 185
  experience of, 268-272
Priest, 119, 127, 146, 247; see also Ministry, and Religion
Primal horde, 61-62
Procreation, 287
Projection, 91, 237, 287
Prometheus, 310
Propagation, 63, 257-260
Property
  meaning of, 91
  role of in psychiatric treatment, 212-213, 218-240; see also Case Three
Protoplasm, 261-262
Protozoon, 259-262
Provence, S., 140, 320
Psychiatry
  forensic problems, 216-240

therapeutic problems, see Psychotherapy
Psychic determinism, 104-105
Psychic processes, aiding physical diagnosis, 135-138; see also Dream
Psychoanalysis
  applied, 12, 22
  technique of, see Psychoanalytic treatment
  theory of, 8-9, 30-38; see also Death instinct
Psychoanalytic treatment
  and honesty, 160-161
  and testament, 230-235
  compared with psychotherapy, 213, 226, 230-233
  effect of interruptions of, 194-195
  see also Delinquency, and Schizophrenia
Psychosis, 36, 80
  postoperative, 58
  see also Schizophrenia, and Senile dementia
Psychosomatic symptoms, 201, 204, 207
  and organic disease, 214-217; see also Disease
Psychosurgery, 121
Psychotherapist
  and belief in immortality, 142-144, 151
  attitude toward death, 150-153, 243-250
  dangers to, in dealing with dying, 125, 198; see also Case Three
  effect of absence of, 194-197
  effect of medical training on, 251-253
  expressing sublimated love, 139-142, 151
  honesty of statements of, to patient, 159-161, 170-171
  mobilization of contradictory attitudes in, 142-144, 150-153
  problem of informing patient about fatal disease, 49-51, 55, 57-60; see also Case Three
  therapeutic ambition of, 238-240
  unconscious utilization of transference, 220-229

Psychotherapist (Cont'd)
see also Countertransference, and Psychotherapy

Psychotherapy
and alleviation of ambivalence, 146-153
and economic status of patient, 212-213
and fees, 138-139, 144-145
and "gift situation," 112, 134, 138, 144-148
and hopeless reality situations, 244-245
and patient's belief in therapist's omnipotence, 209-210
and somatic disease, 125, 167-171, 207
changing patient's environment, 125, 164
dependent on patient's co-operation, 170-171
effect of therapist's absence, 194-197
gift situation in, see Gifts
of rich patients, 212-213
role of transference in, 224-240
with the dying patient, 119-240

Puberty, 52, 54, 255
Pütter, A., 256, 326

Quiller-Couch, A., 16, 18, 326

Rank, O., 18, 326
Reality
and feeling of identity, 87-94
and instinctual drives, 83-84
experience of, 87-94
principle, 46, 77-78, 287
Regression, 54, 112, 140, 278
Reich, A., 249, 326
Reichenbach, H., 266, 326
Religion, 44, 91, 119
and belief in immortality of soul, 145-146, 268, 295-297
see also Christianity, Ministry, and Priest
Rembrandt, R., 305-307
Repetition
compulsion, 30-31
of events, 289-290
Repression, and body ego, 213-216
Reversal, into opposite, 15

Rilke, R. M., 34, 300-305, 307-308, 317, 327
Rittmeister, J., 107
Rivers, W. H. R., 79, 327
Róheim, G., 271, 319
Rosenzweig, F., 10-11, 254-255, 313, 327

Sadism, 12, 26, 46; see also Aggression, and Death instinct
St. Paul, 310
Samson, 305-306
Satire, 12
Schilder, P., 66, 85, 263, 295, 320, 327
Schiller, F. C. S., 71, 327
Schizophrenia, 68-69, 121, 160, 194, 246
Schorr, G., 39-40, 327
Science, and denial of death, 44-45
Self-destruction, see Suicide
Self-preservation, 93-94
and death, 93-94, 100-104
instinct of, 26-27, 31, 65
Selzer, C., 196
Senile dementia, 40, 59-60, 63, 268
Sexual instincts, 12-14, 27; see also Instinct(ual Drives), Libido, and Life instinct
Shakespeare, W., 15-24, 313
Shock treatment, 121
Sickness, see Cancer, Disease, and Malignancy
Silberer, H., 273, 327
Simmel, E., 101, 327
Simmel, G., 4, 23-24, 44, 56, 82-83, 185, 279, 298-299, 313-315, 328
Simon, E., 302, 328
Sleep, 69, 72-73, 76, 272-275, 285; see also Dream
Smith, G., 310, 328
Social institution, effect of changes of on individual, 100-104, 255
Socrates, 58, 71-72, 284-286
Spengler, O., 282, 328
Spielrein, S., 268, 328
Staub, H., 65, 319
Stengel, E., 135-136, 328
Sterba, R., 8, 15, 42, 328
Stone, I., 111, 328
Stone, L., 224, 328
Structurization, 6-7, 254

Suggestion, 170, 220
Suicide, 37, 64-70, 80, 96, 104, 165-166, 178-179, 186-194, 222; see also Aggression
Sullivan, J. W. N., 98, 328
Superego
  and aggression, 36, 112
  and melancholia, 68
  and past, 288
  and suicide, 65, 70
Superstition, connected with death, 41, 44, 108
Susman, M., 302, 328
Symbolism, of death, 14-29, 69, 73, 97, 109-110, 304
Szasz, T. S., 34, 257, 258, 328

Tansley, A., 255, 328
Terror, 277-278
Testament, see Will
Thanatology
  biological concept and aspects, 22, 250-262, 609
  Freud's, 8-15, 30-38, 112
  history of Freud's, 10-29
  metaphysical concept, 3-9
  obstacles to its formation, 39-50
  problems in Freud's, 35-38
  psychological concept; see Death instinct, and Freud
The Merchant of Venice, 15-24
Time
  and death, 42, 265-283
  psychological vs. physical, 185
  psychology of, 265-283
  see also Future, Past and Present
Tolstoy, L., 39, 114
Townsend, H. G., 282, 328
Transference
  and acting out, 230-235
  and alleviation of pain, 119
  and childhood fantasy, 140
  and reality, 197
  and structural changes, 53
  avoidance of negative, in treatment of dying, 126, 152
  interpretation of, 224-226
  unconscious utilization of, 220-229

undue influence on, by therapist, 219-229
  see also Psychoanalytic treatment, Psychotherapist, and Psychotherapy
Trauma, effect of, 91-92, 215
Trotter, W., 111-112, 328
Türck, H., 264, 328
Turner, W. J., 99, 329

Ullman, H., 257, 329
Unconscious, vs. conscious motives, 221-229
Unconsciousness, 274-275
Undue influence, 217, 219-229

Varnhagen von Ense, 296, 329
Velasquez, D., 305
Von Saaz, J., 46, 329
Von Salis, J. R., 300, 302, 329
Von Uexküll, J., 84, 329

Wach, J., 9, 44, 329
Walker, K., 39, 329
War, 10-11, 24-28, 109-110
Wealth, see Property
Weihofen, H., 217, 219-220, 323
Weininger, O., 288, 329
Weismann, A., 257-258, 329
Weiss, E., 78, 329
Werther, 67, 113
Wilder, T., 107, 329
Will, 208-211, 217-240
  problem of testamentary competency, 208-211, 217-219
  undue influence, 217, 219-229; see also Psychotherapist, and Transference
Wish fulfillment, and psychotherapy, 140, 145-148; see also Gifts, and Transference
Worringer, W., 249, 329

Young, E., 309

Zilboorg, G., 252, 291, 329
Zuckerman, S., 61, 329